DOUBLE
FEATURES

SELECTED AND EDITED BY
Nancy Carr, Michael J. Elsey, Louise Galpine, Josh Sniegowski, and Mary Williams

CONTRIBUTORS
Elizabeth Friedman
Mary Klein
Summer McDonald
Bill Siegel

Cover and section divider design: Anne Jordan and Mitch Goldstein

Interior design: THINK Book Works

Published by the Great Books Foundation in partnership with
Harrison Middleton University.

DOUBLE
FEATURES

BIG IDEAS IN FILM

THE GREAT BOOKS FOUNDATION
A nonprofit educational organization

Published and distributed by

THE GREAT BOOKS FOUNDATION

A nonprofit educational organization

233 N. Michigan Avenue, Suite 420
Chicago, IL 60601
www.greatbooks.org

Printed in the United States of America
First printing
9 8 7 6 5 4 3 2 1

Library of Congress Cataloging-in-Publication Data has been applied for.

Notes by the author are not bracketed; notes by the Great Books Foundation, an editor, or a translator are [bracketed].

About the Great Books Foundation

The Great Books Foundation is an independent, nonprofit educational organization that creates reading and discussion opportunities for all. We believe that literacy and critical thinking encourage reflective and well-informed citizens and that discussion of powerful and enduring ideas promotes empathy, community, and democratic participation.

Founded in 1947, the Great Books Foundation was established to promote liberal education for the general public. In 1962, the Foundation extended its mission to children with the introduction of Junior Great Books®. Since its inception, the Foundation has helped thousands of people throughout the United States and in other countries begin their own discussion groups in schools, libraries, and community centers. Today, Foundation instructors conduct hundreds of workshops each year, in which educators and parents learn to lead Shared Inquiry™ discussion.

About Harrison Middleton University

Harrison Middleton University is a great ideas, great works, great conversations, distance learning university that offers graduate education in the humanities with concentrations in imaginative literature, natural science, philosophy and religion, and social science. Harrison Middleton University promotes student-faculty scholarship through research, discussion, and the development of collaborative publications.

Contents

Introduction

While cinema has been constantly evolving as an art form since its earliest days, one of its central aspects has remained constant: the power of movies to fill audiences with a passion that can be difficult to comprehend.

The love of film takes many forms. Some people appear to be born with sprocket holes instead of veins and with silver-nitrate fluid running through their bodies instead of blood; they may need to see a new film every day in order to feel sane. Other aficionados have an insatiable appetite to explore every imaginable genre. For those whose love of cinema is more casual, movies serve as a welcome respite from the everyday. And then there are those of us whose love for moving images has led to intense study of the craft of filmmaking. For us, it is exciting to discover firsthand just how powerful the cinematic medium can be.

Many people remember their first cinematic experience with great clarity, for in that moment, childhood excitement and the desire to see something new and foreign likely outweighed whatever merits the film itself possessed. In March 1985, when I was four and a half years old, my parents took me to see Bill L. Norton's Disney/Touchstone adventure *Baby: The Secret of the Lost Legend*. The impression it made on me cannot be overstated. I cried inconsolably when the animatronic father dinosaur was killed by evil poachers, and again when the mother dinosaur was separated from her baby. My parents had to take me out to the lobby for a calming-down session, but soon enough I was ready to get back into that auditorium, and I recall my tears turning to joy when the human heroes saved the day and the dinosaurs were reunited.

Such is the power of the movies. Even as a child, you can project yourself into the world onscreen, imagine yourself as part of the action, and feel devastated one moment and jubilant the next. That first film changed my life forever, and although it has neither the greatest production values nor the most logical plot, it holds a special place in my heart. Cinema has an ability to connect with audience members regardless of their ages or expectations, in ways that are often unanticipated.

Over the years, I've become intrigued, perplexed, frustrated, and enamored of movies, and my appreciation for the form has grown in a deeply personal way. I remember a particular family outing to see French director Jean-Jacques Annaud's magisterial film *The Bear* and being moved beyond comprehension, as an eight-year-old, by its natural imagery and themes of family and love. And I'll never forget the first R-rated film I saw in the theater, when my father took me to see the wildly vulgar and hilarious baseball comedy *Major League*. The yearly late-August "back to school" movie outings with my mother and sister, when we'd smuggle a picnic lunch or Roy Rogers takeout into the theater, were always highlights. We'd check out films like Amy Heckerling's Austen-adaptation comedy, *Clueless*, and Chris Noonan and George Miller's transcendent talking-pig opus, *Babe*.

As an adolescent, my experience of movies, and my appreciation for them, continued to widen. A film that scared and thrilled me in equal measure was *Terminator 2: Judgment Day*. Director James Cameron showed audiences something genuinely new, and the bold widescreen images in that film, from the visions of nuclear holocaust to the warm embrace of a mother and son, remain etched in my mind. A very different movie, *The Rocketeer*, introduced me to the power of retro-cool style. The posters alone hooked me, and seeing how director Joe Johnston and his collaborators combined the conventions of television serials with big-screen special effects filled me with wonder. And while much of Oliver Stone's *JFK* sailed over my head, experiencing it in the theater was an astonishing experience. I'd never seen editing or cinematography handled in such a fashion (who had?), and it deepened my understanding of how images could be shaped by filmmakers and received by audiences.

The year 1994 marked a true turning point for me as a film buff, with the one-two punch of *Pulp Fiction* and *Natural Born Killers*. Quentin Tarantino's unbridled passion and clear-cut talent as a writer and director tore a massive hole in the fabric of the movie industry; he essentially created his own genre (one that drew legions of imitators). Those two films seismically altered the way the studio and independent film worlds coexisted, as Tarantino showed how edgy, provocative material enacted by major movie stars could comment on society and filmmaking itself. Tarantino's unexpected juxtapositions led me to recognize how other directors also shook things up. The action pyrotechnics and

European flavor of Luc Besson's *Léon* challenged what I thought about morally flexible protagonists, while the blend of formal daring and narrative classicism from Robert Zemeckis in *Forrest Gump* still awes me. Alongside retrospective theatrical screenings of films like *Close Encounters of the Third Kind*, *The Searchers*, *Blade Runner*, *The Leopard*, and *Taxi Driver*, my father showed me *The Godfather*, *The Godfather: Part II*, and *Goodfellas*, which is my favorite movie of all time. Seeing Martin Scorsese's Vegas crime saga *Casino* and Michael Mann's existential crime epic *Heat* cemented it for me: I was a goner forever. I'll carry these filmgoing memories with me always, looking ahead to the time when it will be right for me to continue the cycle and go to the movies with my own son.

The collective agreement to gather with a group of strangers in a darkened theater to watch moving images on a screen is one of the most unusual human behaviors of recent times. We will sit together and, in relative silence, watch a story unfold; ideally, we will grow as a result of this shared experience. This practice has gone on for over one hundred years, and I hope it will never be abandoned. The experience of seeing movies in the theater has changed in recent years, but certain elements remain the same because people love to be entertained en masse. What could replace the communal, electric charge when the audience in a sold-out auditorium watches a film like *Saving Private Ryan* or *No Country for Old Men* with rapt attention? As a viewer, I find this feeling nearly indescribable.

Filmmakers have been changing the cinematic art form through style, technique, and content since the format was invented. From silent films in black and white to the "talkies" and color, from Academy ratio to the birth of Cinemascope and anamorphic widescreen, and then into more technologically advanced realms such as 3-D and IMAX, motion pictures have always had something bold to offer. Even as the filmmaking landscape has seen a conversion from the days of Kodak-Eastman to the digital realm, the stories that movies tell continue to break new ground, with more variety than ever. There is a film out there for everyone; it's just a matter of being open to new possibilities. Having now watched thousands of movies over three decades, I can't imagine a life without the sense of wonder that cinema has instilled in me.

This book celebrates thoughtful, passionate writing about films and filmmakers from the last seventy years. The selections have been chosen to inspire discussion and encourage readers to examine the art of motion pictures from many angles. The writers here will lead you to revisit favorite works, discover new ones, and consider multiple interpretations. How do filmmakers speak to you as a person, and how does their work inform your daily life? In what ways do the films you watch change your perception of the world? It's questions like these that make exploring this complex art form a constantly new and enlightening experience.

—Nick Clement

Nick Clement is a freelance writer and movie lover who has contributed to Variety *magazine, We Are Cult, Taste of Cinema, Back to the Movies, and MovieViral. He is the cofounder of Podcasting Them Softly, and lives in Connecticut with his family.*

DOUBLE
FEATURES

CREATING

CREATING

How do filmmakers engage with different ideas and concerns, and what do their films bring to public discourse? When directors, producers, editors, and screenwriters collaborate to create a movie, how does their work affect the way we think, see, and interact with our world?

In "Yossarian is Alive and Well in the Mexican Desert" (1969) by **Nora Ephron**, the journalist travels to the film set of *Catch-22* to witness the dynamics between cast and director as they recreate a war in an isolated stretch of desert.

David Mamet, in his essay "Countercultural Architecture and Dramatic Structure" (1991), argues for a particular method of direction and posits his own rules for filmmakers.

Christine Vachon, in the selection from her memoir *Shooting to Kill* (1998), presents a more fluid approach to filmmaking, and her record of the conflicting elements of independent cinema raises complex questions about rebellion and subversion.

In "Laugh, Cry, Believe: Spielbergization and Its Discontents" (2007), **J. Hoberman** assesses the impact of director Steven Spielberg's oeuvre and how our sense of childhood and family has been informed by movies.

Walter Murch, in a selection from *In the Blink of an Eye* (2001), illustrates the effects of technical innovations on the creative act and shows how visual understanding is central to the editor's work.

Richard Hutson's essay "One Hang, We All Hang: *High Plains Drifter*" (2007) explores the ramifications of violence onscreen in our offscreen world, and questions the tie between director and film.

Chris Rodley interviews auteur **David Lynch** in a selection from *Lynch on Lynch* (1997), in which Lynch seemingly declines to offer us an insight into his directorial thought process.

Yossarian Is Alive and Well in the Mexican Desert

Nora Ephron

G uaymas, Mexico. It is a moment of intense concentration. Mike Nichols, the director of the film, is sitting in a blue director's chair, his face contorted, his hands clenched, his eyes squeezed shut. He finally opens his mouth to speak. "Bladder," he says. "Whimsy. Dailies. Rumble. Barren. Crystal. Pastry."

"No," says Tony Perkins, who is seated next to him. "Not pastry."

"Strudel," says Nichols triumphantly. "Strudel. Pepsi. Cancer. Stopwatch . . ."

A film is being shot here. Not at the moment, of course. At the moment, the director of the film is playing a memory game with one of the actors while the crew figures out how to work a broken water machine that is holding up the shooting. The name of the film is *Catch-22*. It is budgeted at $11 million, is on location in the Mexican desert, and is based on Joseph Heller's best-selling World War II novel. "I've tried, as they say, to preserve the integrity of the novel," says screenwriter Buck Henry. "Don't print that unless you put after it: 'He said this with a glint in his eye and a twitch in his cheek and a kick in the groin.' Because if that line so much as looks as if I said it seriously I'll kill you." Among the graffiti scrawled on the wall of the portable men's room on the set is one that reads, "Help Save Joe Heller."

A film is being shot here—between memory games, word games, repartee, kibitzing, and general good cheer. *Catch-22*, the story of Capt. John Yossarian and his ultimate refusal to fly any more bombing missions. The movie of the year. A-film actors signed up for before they knew what parts they were playing or how much money they would get for their work. With Alan Arkin starring as Yossarian, and Orson Welles (General Dreedle), Martin Balsam (Colonel Cathcart), Dick Benjamin (Major Danby), Norman Fell (Sergeant Towser), Jack Gilford (Doc Daneeka), Tony Perkins (Chaplain Tappman), and Paula Prentiss (Nurse Duckett). Art Garfunkel, of Simon & Garfunkel, will make his acting debut as Lieutenant Nately. "What I feel like here," said Seth Allen, a young actor in the film, "is a near great."

Whether *Catch-22* will be a masterpiece, merely a very funny film, or the first failure for Mike Nichols after two smash hit movies (*The Graduate* and *Who's Afraid of Virginia Woolf?*) and seven hit plays (among them *The Odd Couple, Luv,* and *Plaza Suite*) is at this point almost an irrelevant question for the actors in it. What matters is that the film is a chance to work with Nichols, who, at thirty-seven, is the most successful director in America and probably the most popular actors' director in the world. Says Orson Welles: "Nobody's in his league with actors." What's more, he is the first American director since Welles made *Citizen Kane* in 1941 to have complete creative control over his final product—including the contractual right of final cut and the option of not showing his rushes to studio executives.

Nichols is too modest and far too intelligent not to realize the absurdity of being in this position after making two films and directing for only six years. "Every time you get too much for what you've put in," he says, "you know it's going to come out of you later." But for now, he is going about his business—wandering about the set, in stylish fatigue jacket and slender corduroy pants; offering Oreos and Oh Henrys to the crew; bringing his low-key techniques to his actors' assistance; and somehow managing to keep his macroproduction company happy and on schedule. *Catch-22* is to shoot in Mexico until early April, move to Los Angeles for four weeks of airplane interior shots, and then on to Rome until mid-June. After ten months of editing, it will be ready for release in late 1970.

It has taken eight years to bring Heller's book to the shooting stage. In the interim, the novel, after a slow beginning and mixed reviews, has become a modern classic, with a Modern Library edition and two million paperback copies in print. The film property has passed from

Columbia to Paramount/Filmways, from Richard Brooks (who did little or nothing with it for three years) to Mike Nichols, from Jack Lemmon (who originally wanted to play Yossarian) to Arkin, and from one unsuccessful treatment by Richard Quine to four drafts by Buck Henry (whose previous film credits include *The Graduate* and *Candy*). It took Nichols, producer John Calley, and designer Richard Sylbert over a year just to find the ideal spot to build the island of Pianosa and its air base—largely because the logical locations in Italy, Sicily, Sardinia, and Corsica no longer look like the Italy, Sicily, Sardinia, and Corsica of 1944.

Casting began, with Nichols selecting a group of actors, all of whom look like ordinary people, to play fighter pilots, and with Frank Tallman, the stunt pilot, rounding up a group of authentic fighter pilots, all of whom look like movie stars, to fly the planes. Tallman also set to work locating and assembling a squadron of B-25s—eighteen of them, each purchased, repaired, and made skyworthy at an average cost of $10,000. (One of the planes, a wedding present from heiress Barbara Hutton to playboy Porfirio Rubirosa, came complete with reclining seats, bed, and leather-paneled toilet.)

Sylbert and Calley finally found the location last summer on the northwest coast of Mexico, twenty miles from the town of Guaymas, Sonora, the home of Guaymas shrimp and little else. The location was a flawless one photographically—with ocean flanking it on one side and mountains set just two miles behind—but it was reachable only by boat. It cost $180,000 to build the five-mile highway to the spot, and $250,000 more for the 6,000-foot runway. Both construction jobs were undertaken, ecstatically, by the mayor of Guaymas, who just happens to own a contracting company. Seventy-five *peones* working with machetes cleared the one-mile-square site of cactus, brush, and rattlesnakes, leaving only mesquite trees, which resemble the small olive trees native to Italy.

And Pianosa rose from the sand, with its tents, corrugated tin huts, mess hall, control tower, lister bag setups, and piles of bombs stacked like supermarket oranges along the runway. War-beaten stone buildings were designed with collapsible walls, in preparation for the moment in *Catch-22* when Milo Minderbinder (played by newcomer Jon Voight) leads the men in a bombing raid on their own base.

The most critical problem Nichols and Henry faced in translating the book into cinematic terms was finding a style for Heller's macabre comedy. "The book and, as a result, the film, have to be somewhat dreamlike, not quite real—either something remembered, or a nightmare," said Nichols. "That's very hard to do with living actors, with pores and noses, because they're so definitely there. If you're making a film in which an officer says, 'You mean the enlisted men pray to the same God that we do?' and in which the men bomb their own base, you have to find a style that makes it clear, from the beginning, that such things can happen."

The solution was to make the story arise from a fever Yossarian develops after being stabbed in the side by Nately's whore; the film leaps back and forth from vaguely remembered horror to farce to better remembered horror. "The picture will be cut as if Yossarian's delirium were cutting it," Henry explained. The style has been further carried out in the set—which has a ghostly quality—and in Nichols's decision to send home two hundred extras after the first week of shooting, leaving only Yossarian and his friends to fill out the huge air base. In addition, David Watkin, the English cinematographer who shot Richard Lester's Beatles films, has lit *Catch-22* so that all the actors are in shadow and the background is burned out; the effect is of a subliminal limbo.

Like the novel, the film hangs on the notion of Catch-22, a masterpiece of muddled military logic. "Let me get this straight," says Yossarian to Doc Daneeka in the script. "In order to be grounded I have to be crazy. And I must be crazy to keep flying. But if I ask to be grounded—that means I'm not crazy any more and I have to keep flying."

"You got it," says Doc Daneeka. "That's Catch-22."

As a multitude of reporters and critics have observed since the book was published in October 1961, *Catch-22* has almost become a primer for the thinking that has seemed to be guiding the war in Vietnam. At the same time, the predicament of Yossarian has become more relevant in the context of the antiwar movement in this country. "The interesting thing about the book," says Henry, who despite his disclaimer has been quite faithful to the novel, "is the enormous power of prophecy Heller had. He was writing about a man who had finally decided to opt out and who in the end ends up in Sweden. That was a total absurdity when he wrote it, a really far-out kind of insanity. Well, it's come true."

"I don't think of this as a film about World War II," adds Nichols. "I think of it as a picture about dying and a picture about when you get off and at what point you take control over your own life and say, 'No, I won't. *I* decide. *I* draw the line.'"

That *Catch-22* is being made in an atmosphere of such good feeling is as much a part of Nichols's approach as any of the directing techniques he utilizes. "If you're on the set, shooting," Nichols explained, "and you say, 'Let's do it again,' and there's one guy who rolls his eyes or turns away or groans, it sours it for everybody. John and Buck and I said, 'Let's see if for once we can have nobody like that—just people who like each other.' And it worked." Many of the cast members are old friends and about half have worked with Nichols before. They have been laughing ever since a chartered jet brought them from Los Angeles to Mexico on January 2 and landed them smack in the middle of the utterly barren, desolate desert. "Look at this," Bob Newhart said, as he stepped out of the plane. Everyone looked around at what looked like the end of the world. "Ten years ago I could have bought land here," said Newhart, "and look at it now."

When the film is between takes, the cast sits around and roars with laughter as Newhart spins out a routine on nightlife in Guaymas (there is none) or as Buck Henry and Tony Perkins improvise on the subject of free falling and parachute jumping.

Perkins: "What about all this we hear about the free fall mass?"

Henry: "There are two free fall masses."

Perkins: "The eleven o'clock and the seven o'clock?"

Henry: "No. In the fall of 1965 a town of 1,300 people in Nevada went up and made a fall."

Perkins: "I was speaking of the free fall mass, not the mass free fall."

Henry: "The free fall mass is where the falling priest throws the wafer and the parishioners jump out of the plane and dive for it. It's called diving for the wafer. That's where the expression comes from. Dive for the wafer, dig for the wine."

Perkins: "What about this lady who jumped with her cats?"

Henry: "Well, actually, that story was not reported accurately. There was a lady, but she jumped with her lawyer, whose name was Katz."

9

When the film is shooting, the director and crew stand behind the camera, biting their lips and gritting their teeth to keep from exploding with laughter during the take. Nichols's snorts of appreciation affect the actors in about the same way the bowl of food did Pavlov's dogs. "I'm so overjoyed when he laughs," said Paula Prentiss, "that I don't even care that half the time I don't know what he's laughing at."

"You never get hung up if Mike is directing you," said Miss Prentiss's husband, Dick Benjamin. "If you're doing a scene you're not comfortable with, he senses it, and before it can get to be a problem for you, he gives you two or three specific things to do—like a piece of business or a new line or something. And you think, 'Oh, I get to do *that*.' Like a kid who's been given a birthday present. Everything else sort of falls into place and you get your little goodies. And Mike talks in terms of that. He'll say, 'I've really got a present for so-and-so when he gets to Rome.' And he means he's got some wonderful shot, something to do, some way the actor will look that is just sensational. And you really take it as a present."

Sometimes Nichols will give an actor a short suggestion or line reading that will suddenly clarify the role. To Benjamin, who was playing a scene in which he was supposed to be terrified of Orson Welles's General Dreedle, Nichols—who was himself terrified of Orson Welles—said simply, "Watch me."

To Austin Pendleton, who was confused as to how to play Welles's son-in-law, Colonel Moodus, Nichols gave a line reading that, said Pendleton, "gave me the key to the whole thing. I realized he wanted me to play the kind of person who says the most insulting things as if he's being terribly friendly." To Norman Fell, Nichols suggested playing Sergeant Towser as a military mammy; as a result, Fell delivers the most bloodcurdling lines with a funny little smile on his face, as if he were talking about chicken and gravy and wonderful biscuits.

Occasionally, Nichols will add an especially intimate gift to the proceedings. One morning, he was shooting a closeup of Buck Henry (who also appears in the film, as Lieutenant Colonel Korn). Henry was to lean over and whisper to Balsam: "He's talking to you." Balsam was to pop to attention and deliver an answer. Nichols shot two takes of the scene and then called Henry over for a conference. "Let's do another," he said. Henry returned to position and the scene began again. "He's talking to you!" hissed Henry, and he leaned over and goosed Balsam. Balsam jumped, his eyes bugged out of his head, and he managed to deliver his line before losing his composure. The crew broke up. "Nichols Directs," said Henry, "A Monograph of the Unusual Techniques of a Young American Director: 'Use three fingers,' he said to me."

On another occasion, Nichols was shooting a love scene between Arkin and Miss Prentiss, who plays Nurse Duckett. The footage—of Yossarian's hand sliding up Duckett's leg—was fine, but Nichols had not been able to get the right vocal reaction from the actress. He called a take for sound only. And as Arkin began to slip his hand up Miss Prentiss's skirt, Nichols grabbed her from behind and plunked his hands onto her breasts. "I let out this great hoot," said Miss Prentiss, "which Mike was very happy with. Then I was so overcome with emotion I had to go into a corner and be alone. Whenever someone touches me I'm in love with him for about eight hours."

"It's perfectly possible," Nichols concedes, "that we can have this great time now, making the film, and then have it not be a good picture. The two have nothing to do with each other. But then, none of us knows whether the picture is any good even long after it's finished, so you might as well be happy while it's going on. And when the actors break up and the crew is stuffing handkerchiefs into their mouths trying not to laugh at Dick Benjamin—or whoever it is—I love it. I love it now. Afterward, it's up for grabs anyway."

For the actors, at least, making an Air Force film has turned out to be very much like being in the Air Force. Not when they are working; when they work, making *Catch-22* is like being at a party, a festival, a love-in. But because so many of the actors have small parts, they have a great deal of time to kill in a town where there is almost nothing to do. As a result, many of them spend their empty days discussing how many days of shooting each has to go. When they tire of kicking that subject around, they move on to other tried-and-true service talk. "I'll tell you what we do around here in our free time," said Alan Arkin. "We sit in the barracks out at the set with our muddy boots on and talk about women. That's what you do in the Army, isn't it? Sit around in your muddy boots and talk about women? I don't know why we do it. Almost everyone here is with his wife or his girlfriend. But that's what we do."

They complain about the food in the mess hall—that is, the mess hall on the set, which doubles as a lunch commissary complete with regulation Army trays. They complain about the living accommodations at the Playa de Cortés, Guaymas's somewhat unsatisfactory attempt at a luxury hotel. They complain about their isolation from the outside world. And they complain about the incredible difficulty of obtaining newspapers and placing long-distance calls. "We make bets on who's going to go insane," says Newhart, "or has already gone insane. In fact, maybe we've all gone insane and we're all together and we don't know it and we'll go home and my wife will call Paramount and say, 'Listen, my husband is insane.' We have no norm here. We have no way of judging."

That everyone in this squadron of professed lunatics is good-natured, noncompetitive, and thoroughly professional is small consolation. By February, several of the cast members had begun to complain that the company was *too* nice. "If only there were a lemon here," said Perkins. "It would give us something to talk about."

Any location—outside of London, Paris, and Rome—is bound to breed complaint; but the actors, who seem to be playing a private game of Kvetch-22, have hardly been on a dull movie. Within the first two weeks of shooting, a case of hepatitis broke out, requiring that the entire company be inoculated. A B-25, caught in prop wash, nearly crashed into the control tower while shooting was going on. Susanne Benton, a starlet who plays General Dreedle's WAC, complete with seven pairs of falsies and a rubber behind by Frederick's of Hollywood, was accidentally clobbered by a camera during a take and passed out cold. Two actors, mistakenly released for a short trip to New York, were headed off on the way to the airport by a hastily dispatched helicopter, which landed, à la James Bond, ahead of them on the highway. There was even an unexpected, action-packed visit from John Wayne—though reports differ as to exactly what happened during it.

According to general consensus, Wayne, on his way to make a Western in Durango, radioed the field for permission to land his plane. Permission was granted. When Wayne arrived, producer Calley met him and asked if he would like to see the shooting, which was going on in a tent some distance away. No, Wayne said, he wanted to drive to a part of the location to see some land he was thinking of buying. But some time later he showed up at the set. He stood around, apparently waiting for a welcoming party; but none of the actors knew him, and Nichols and Henry did not emerge to greet him. Wayne went to the Playa de Cortés and spent the evening in the bar, drinking, smashing glassware, and complaining that he had been snubbed—possibly for political reasons. Ultimately, he fell and broke a couple of ribs.

"We didn't snub him at all," Henry said later. "We were in the tent, and for some undiscernible dumb reason, no one said, 'Come on out and meet the big guy.' We're trying to make up for it by getting a print of *The Green Berets* and showing it to the crew. In the meantime, we've just been sitting around here, watching the days go by, and waiting for him to come back and bomb us."

The arrival of Orson Welles, for two weeks of shooting in February, was just the therapy the company needed: at the very least, it gave everyone something to talk about. The situation was almost melodramatically ironic: Welles, the great American director now unable to obtain big-money backing for his films, was being directed by thirty-seven-year-old Nichols; Welles, who had tried, unsuccessfully, to buy *Catch-22* for himself in 1962, was appearing in it to pay for his new film, *Dead Reckoning*. The cast spent days preparing for his arrival. *Touch of Evil* was flown in and microscopically reviewed. *Citizen Kane* was discussed over dinner. Tony Perkins, who had appeared in Welles's film *The Trial*, was repeatedly asked What Orson Welles Was Really Like. Bob Balaban, a young actor who plays Orr in the film, laid plans to retrieve one of Welles's cigar butts for an admiring friend. And Nichols began to combat his panic by imagining what it would be like to direct a man of Welles's stature.

"Before he came," said Nichols, "I had two fantasies. The first was that he would say his first line, and I would say, 'NO, NO, NO, Orson!'" He laughed. "Then I thought, perhaps not. The second was that he would arrive on the set and I would say, 'Mr. Welles, now if you'd be so kind as to move over here . . .' And he'd look at me and raise an eyebrow and say, 'Over there?' And I'd say, 'What? Oh, uh, where do you think it should be?'"

Welles landed in Guaymas with an entourage that included a cook and experimental filmmaker Peter Bogdanovich, who was interviewing him for a Truffaut-Hitchcock-type memoir. For the eight days it took to shoot his two scenes, he dominated the set. He stood on the runway, his huge wet Havana cigar tilting just below his squinting eyes and sagging eye pouches, addressing Nichols and the assembled cast and crew. Day after day, he told fascinating stories of dubbing in Bavaria, looping in Italy, and shooting in Yugoslavia. He also told Nichols how to direct the film, the crew how to move the camera, film editor Sam O'Steen how to cut a scene, and most of the actors how to deliver their lines. Welles even lectured Martin Balsam for three minutes on how to deliver the line "Yes, sir."

A few of the actors did not mind at all. Austin Pendleton got along with Welles simply by talking back to him.

"Are you sure you wouldn't like to say that line more slowly?" Welles asked Pendleton one day.

"Yes," Pendleton replied slowly. "I am sure."

But after a few days of shooting, many of the other actors were barely concealing their hostility toward Welles—particularly because of his tendency to blow his lines during takes. By the last day of shooting, when Welles used his own procedure, a lengthy and painstaking one, to shoot a series of close-ups, most of the people on the set had tuned out on the big, booming raconteur.

But Mike Nichols managed to glide through the two-week siege without showing a trace of irritation with Welles. And whenever the famous Welles eyebrow rose after one of Nichols's camera decisions, Nichols would turn to him and smile and say, "No good, huh? Where should it go?"

"Mike controlled the Welles thing simply by respecting Welles," said Pendleton. "After all, if there's any one person who has the right to say where a cut should be made, it's Orson. Mike respected that. And Orson knew it."

At the same time, Nichols carefully smoothed the ruffled feathers among his company. And he got a magnificent performance, from Welles as well as from the rest of the cast. "The Welles situation, which brought a lot of people down, was almost identical to the tension that was written in the script," said Peter Bonerz, a young West Coast actor who plays McWatt in the film. "We were all under the thumb of this huge, cigar-smoking general, as written, and at the same time, we were under the thumb of this huge, cigar-smoking director. The discomfort that we were feeling was real, and I'm sure it looks grand on film."

One day shortly after Welles had left (taking with him his general's uniform, which he wore around Guaymas for two days until a costume man was able to retrieve it), Nichols sat in his trailer on the set. Outside, it was hot, dusty, and windy. But the trailer was air-conditioned, with an icebox full of brownies imported from Greenberg's bakery in New York, and Nichols sat eating one and talking about himself, his success, and the Welles episode.

"What I wanted to say to Welles was this—I wanted to say, 'I know you're Orson Welles, and I know I'm me. I never *said* I was Mike Nichols. Those *other* people said that.' What I mean by that is that he's a great man. I know he's a great man. I never said I was. And of course, you can't say such things.

"We were talking about [Jean] Renoir one day on the set, and Orson said, very touchingly, that Renoir was a great man but that, unfortunately, Renoir didn't like his pictures. And then he said, 'Of course, if I were Renoir, I wouldn't like my pictures either.' And I wanted to say to him, 'If I were Orson Welles, I wouldn't like *my* pictures either, and it's OK, and I agree with you, and what can I do?'

"I never said all that stuff about me. I'm not happy about this thing that's building up about me, because it has nothing to do with me. I mean, the things I've done are neither as good as the people who carry on say they are, nor are they as bad as the reaction to the reaction says they are. They're just sort of in-between. I'm not flagellating myself and saying I've turned out only junk, because I'm not ashamed of it and some of it I like very much. But Orson said to somebody that he didn't just want to be a festival director." Nichols paused. "Well, I guess if you have the festivals and *Cahiers* and Pauline Kael and Andrew Sarris you want to make pictures that break box-office records. And it also works the other way around.

"I was very moved by Welles. I knew what it felt like to be him in that situation, to come into a company in the middle, to have a tremendous reputation not to like acting, to be used to being in control—and I was sorry when people didn't see what that felt like. Where the camera is and what it does is so much a part of his life—how is he suddenly supposed to ignore it? Take somebody like Elizabeth Taylor—when she is acting, she knows where the light is and how close the shot is. Orson knows whether he's in focus or not. Literally. If you know that much, what are you supposed to do with it? You can't throw it out. And I know that if I were acting in a movie, it would be very hard for me not to say, 'I wonder if you would be kind enough to consider putting the camera a little more there so that when I do this . . .' How do you kill that knowledge?"

Nichols stopped, lit a Parliament from a stack of cigarette packs on the trailer table, and began to talk about what the Beatles used to call The Fall. "I almost can't wait for it to come," he said. "Because I'm somewhat upset by the Midas thing and also by the reaction to the Midas thing. I don't like a critic to tell me that I set out to make a success, because it's not true. There's enough worry in thinking that you set out to do the very best you could and came out with only a success—that's depressing about oneself. You know, none of the great movies has been a popular success. I can't think of any exceptions. But you accept that there's a great difference between yourself and the artists who make films. It's like when you're fourteen years old and you realize that Tchaikovsky would have liked to be Mozart—he just didn't have a choice. And I'm not even making a comparison there. But you have to go on as yourself. I'd like to be better, but I can't."

From outside the trailer came a knock, and a voice said, "Mr. Nichols, we're ready for you now." The water machine was working. The actors were on the set. And Nichols hopped out of the air-conditioned vehicle into the heat and began to walk over to the stone building where the cameras were set up. A few feet away, Buck Henry was having difficulty with a crossword puzzle. "Are there any Hindus here?" he was shouting. "One of your festivals is bothering me." A film is being shot here.

Countercultural Architecture and Dramatic Structure

David Mamet

was a student in the turbulent sixties in Vermont at a countercultural college. In that time and place, there flourished something called a school of Countercultural Architecture. Some people back then thought that traditional architecture had been too stifling, and so they designed and built a lot of counterculture buildings. These buildings proved unlivable. Their design didn't begin with the idea of the building's purpose; it began with the idea of how the architect "felt."

As those architects looked at their countercultural buildings over the years, they may have reflected that there's a reason for traditional design. There's a reason that doors are placed a certain way, there's a reason that sills are made a certain way.

All those countercultural buildings may have expressed the intention of the architect, but they didn't serve the purpose of the inhabitants. They all either fell down or are falling down or should be torn down. They're a blot on the landscape and they don't age gracefully and every passing year underscores the jejune folly of those countercultural architects.

I live in a house that is two hundred years old. It was built with an axe, by hand, and without nails. Barring some sort of man-made catastrophe, it will be standing in another two hundred years. It was built with an understanding of, and a respect for, wood, weather, and human domestic requirements.

It's very difficult to shore up something that has been done badly. You'd better do your planning up front, when you have the time. It's like working with glue. When it sets, you've used up your time. When it's almost set, you then have to make quick decisions under pressure. If you design a chair correctly, you can put all the time into designing it correctly and assemble it at your leisure. In fact, the ancient chairmakers—which is to say chairmakers up until about the turn of the century—used to make their chairs without glue because they correctly understood not only the nature of joints but the nature of woods. They knew which woods would shrink and which would expand with age, so that these woods, when correctly combined, would make the chair stronger over time.

I recognized two things in finishing up my second movie. When you're doing the movie, after you finish with the shot list but before you start shooting it, you have a period called "preproduction." In preproduction, you say, "You know what would be a good idea? To really make the audience understand that we're in a garage, what about a sign that says 'garage.'" So you meet with your art department and you talk a lot about signs and you make up a lot of signs. I made two movies and I made up a lot of signs. You never see the signs in a movie—never. You just never see them. They are after-the-fact attempts to shore up that which was not correctly designed. Another handy but useless "reminder" tool is the process of looping, or ADR (automatic dialogue reading—dialogue recorded and inserted after the movie has been shot), to communicate to the audience information the film lacks. For example, dubbing words into somebody's mouth when we see his back on the screen. To wit: "Oh, look, here we go down that staircase that we're trying to get to the bottom of." That never works either. Why? Because all that the audience cares about is *what is the thrust of the scene*—what does the hero want? More precisely, what is the essential aspect of the shot? They aren't there to look at signs, and they won't look at them. You can't force them to look at them. It is the nature of human perception to go to the most interesting thing; and just as we know in terms of the dirty joke, the most interesting thing is *what happens next* in the story that you promised the audience you were going to tell them. You can't make them stop and look at the sign. They don't care to indulge you by listening to your looping, so you'd better do your work beforehand.

That work is done in understanding the nature of the materials and using that understanding in the design of the film. That's basically what a film is; it's a design. You know, all these personally felt statements of people who try to put a lot of garbage into the shot and pan around a bunch to show how moved they are by their chosen subject: these are just like countercultural architecture. They may be a personal statement, but they don't serve the turn of the inhabitants or, in this case, the turn of the viewers who would like to know *what happens next*. You tax the audience every time you don't move on to the next essential step of the progression as quickly as possible. You're taxing their good nature. They may indulge you for political reasons—which is what most of modern art is about. Political reasons being "Dammit, I *like* those kinds of bad movies" or "I *like* that kind of countercultural statement. I am one of that group, and I endorse the other members of this group who appreciate the sort of things that fellow is trying to say." The audience can endorse the triviality of modern art, but they can't like it. I suggest you think about the difference between the way people talk about any performance artist and the way they talk about Cary Grant. And to you lovely enthusiasts who will aver that the purpose of modern art is not to be liked, I respond, "Oh, grow up."

The job of the film director is *to tell the story through the juxtaposition of uninflected images*—because that is the essential nature of the medium. It operates best through that juxtaposition, because that's the nature of human perception: to perceive two events, determine a progression, and want to know what happens next.

"Performance art" works, as it's the nature of human perception to order random images in favor of an overriding preconception. Another example of this is neurosis. Neurosis is the ordering of unrelated events or ideas or images in favor of an overriding preconception.

"I am," for example, "an unsightly person": that's the overriding preconception. Then, given any two unrelated events, I can order them to make them mean *that*. "Oh, yes, I understand. This woman came out of the hall and did not seem to notice me and rushed into the elevator and quickly pushed the button and the elevator closed because I am an unattractive person." That's what neurosis is. It is the attempt of a disordered mind to apply the principle of cause and effect. This same attempt takes place subconsciously in the viewer of a drama.

If the lights go out and the curtain goes up, the overriding idea is "a play is taking place"; "someone is telling me a story."

The human brain, understanding that, will take all of the events in the play and form them into a story just as it forms perception into neurosis. It is the nature of human perception to connect unrelated images into a story, because we need to make the world make sense.

If the overriding idea is that *a play is taking place*, then we will form the images that we see between the time the curtain goes up and the time the curtain comes down *into* a play whether or not they have been structured as one. Just so with the movie, which is why bad filmmaking can "succeed." It is our nature to want to make sense of these events—we can't help it. The human mind would make sense of them even if they were a random juxtaposition.

This being the nature of human perception, the smart dramatist will use it to his or her advantage and say, "Well, if the human mind is going to do all that anyway, why don't *I* do it first? Then I will be going with the flow rather than battling against the tide."

If you aren't telling a story, moving from one image to another, the images have to be more and more "interesting" per se. If you *are* telling a story, then the human mind, as it's working along with you, is perceiving your thrust, both consciously and, more important, subconsciously. The audience members are going to go along with that story and will require neither inducement, in the form of visual extravagance, nor explanation, in the form of narration.

They want to see what's happening next. Is the guy going to get killed? Is the girl going to kiss him? Will they find the money buried in the old mine?

When the film is correctly designed, the subconscious and the conscious are in alignment, and we *need* to hear what happens next. The audience is ordering the events just as the author did, so we are in touch with both his conscious and his unconscious mind. We have become involved in the story.

If we don't care what happens next, if the film is *not* correctly designed, we may, unconsciously, create our own story in the same way that a neurotic creates his own cause-and-effect rendition of the world around him, but we're no longer interested in the story that we're being told. "Yes, I saw that the girl put the kettle on the fire and then a cat ran out on stage," we might say of "performance art." "Yes, I saw, but I don't quite know where it's going. I'm following it, but I am certainly not going to risk my unconscious well-being by becoming involved."

That's when it stops being interesting. So that's where the bad author, like the countercultural architect, has to take up the slack by making each subsequent event *more* diverting than the last; to trick the audience into paying attention.

The end of this is obscenity. Let's really see their genitals, let's really endanger the actor through stunts, let's really set the building on fire. Over the course of a movie, it forces the filmmaker to get more and more bizarre. Over the course of a career, it forces a filmmaker to get more and more outré; over the course of a culture, it forces the culture to degenerate into depravity, which is what we have now.

Interest in a film comes from this: the desire to find out what happens next. The less reality conforms to the neurotic's view, the more bizarre his explanation must become, the end of which development is psychosis—"performance art" or "modern theater" or "modern filmmaking."

The structure of any dramatic form should be a syllogism—which is a logical construct of this form: If A, then B. A play or movie proceeds from a statement: "*if A*" (in which a condition of unrest is created or posited), to a conclusion: "*then B*" (at which time entropy will once again rear its corrective head, and a condition of rest will have been once again achieved).

For example, as we've seen, if a student *needs a retraction*, he will pursue a series of actions that will lead him to the retraction or to an irrevocable denial of the retraction. And then he will be at rest; a condition of entropy will have been achieved.

This *entropy* is one of the most interesting aspects of our life as a whole. We are born, certain things happen, and we die. The sexual act is a perfectly good example. Things are called into motion that did not heretofore exist and that demand some form of resolution. Something is called into existence that did not heretofore exist, and then the unrest that this new thing creates has to be resolved, and when it's resolved, the life, the sexual act, the play, is done. That's how you know when it's time to go home.

The guy solved his problem at the whorehouse. The guy lost all his money at the racetrack. The couple was reunited. The bad king died.

How do we know this is the end of the story? Because *the rise to power of the bad king* was the problem that we came to see solved. How do we know that *when they kiss* it's the end of the movie? Because it's a movie about the boy not getting the girl. The solution of the problem posited at the beginning of the experience is the end of the story. That's also how we know the scene is over, isn't it?

We said that the scene is the correct unit of study. If you understand the scene, you understand the play or movie. When the problem posited by the scene is over, the scene is over. A lot of times in movies you want to get out of the scene *before* the problem is over and have it answered in the *next* scene, as a matter of fact. Why? So that the audience will follow you. They, you will remember, want to know what happens next.

To get into the scene late and to get out early is to demonstrate respect for your audience. It's very easy to manipulate an audience—to be "better" than the audience—because you've got all the cards. "I don't have to tell you *anything*; I can change the story in midstream! I can be whatever I want. Go to hell!" But listen to the difference between the way people talk about films by Werner Herzog and the way they talk about films by Frank Capra, for example. One of them may or may not understand something or other, but the other understands what it is to tell a story, and he *wants* to tell a story, which is the nature of the dramatic art—to tell a story. That's all it's good for. People have tried for centuries to use drama to change people's lives, to influence, to comment, to express themselves. It doesn't work. It might be nice if it worked for those things, but it doesn't. The only thing the dramatic form is good for is telling a story.

If you want to tell a story, it might be a good idea to understand a little bit about the nature of human perception. Just as, if you want to know how to build a roof, it might be a good idea to understand a little bit about the effects of gravity and the effects of precipitation.

If you go up into Vermont and you build a roof with a peak, the snow will fall off. You build a flat roof, the roof will fall down from the weight of the snow—which is what happened to a lot of the counter-cultural architecture of the 1960s. "There may be a reason people have wanted to hear stories for ten million years," the performance artist says, "but I really don't *care*, because *I have something to say.*"

The film business is caught in a spiral of degeneracy because it's run by people who have no compass. And the only thing *you* can do in the face of this downward force is tell the truth. Anytime anyone tells the truth, that's a counterforce.

You cannot hide your objective. No one can hide your objective. No one can hide. Contemporary American films are almost universally sloppy, trivial, and obscene. If your objective is to succeed in the "industry," your work, and your soul, will be exposed to these destructive influences. If you desperately crave acceptance by that industry, you will likely become those things.

The actor cannot hide his or her objective, neither can the playwright, neither can the film director. If a person's objective is truly—and you don't have to do it humbly, because you'll get humble soon enough—to *understand the nature of the medium*, that objective will be communicated to the audience. How? Magically. I don't know how. Because it will. It just can't be hidden. In addition to what you will or will not learn about the medium through your desire to understand it, that desire *itself* will be manifested.

I carve wood sometimes. It's magical how the wooden object creates itself. One becomes enthralled by and very observant of the grain of the wood, and the piece tells you how to carve it.

Sometimes the piece is fighting back against you. If you're honest in making a movie, you'll find that it's often fighting back against you too. It's telling you how to write it. Just as we found in the "got a retraction" movie.

It's very, very difficult to do these very, very simple problems. They're fighting back against you, these problems, but the mastery of them is the beginning of the mastery of the art of film.

Shooting to Kill

(selection)

Christine Vachon

A DAY IN THE LIFE

On the way to my office in Manhattan today, I passed a movie shoot on the street and was hailed by the second assistant director, a hearty girl from the Bronx I used to work with. "It's this nightmare low-budget movie," she explained, and then started the litany: "I mean, it's eight o'clock, and crew call's in twenty minutes, and there isn't any coffee, and everyone is late, and the grip truck went to the wrong location, and the APOC just quit, the sides aren't here, and the DP wants a light we didn't order . . ."

"STOP!" I said. "I can't hear this!" Low-budget filmmaking is like childbirth. You have to repress the horror or you'll never do it again. I bid her goodbye and continued on my way, past the $800,000 movie set where the crew looked like a bunch of thirteen-year-olds with tool belts and baseball caps. A lone production assistant desperately tried to keep an eye on two open vehicles while homeless people milled around, attentive. The craft service table—the mandated food and drink station—was especially grim: a jar of iced tea mix, a black banana, a handful of broken chips, some used paper cups. That sums it up, I thought: a pathetic table in the middle of nowhere with nothing on it you'd eat in a million years.

This is the romantic world of low-budget filmmaking. It's the world in which I've toiled for fifteen wearisome, exhilarating years, working for little money on the kinds of movies that seldom end up at the local multiplex. And unless someone gives me $40 million to make a picture about bisexual rockers, or a sympathetic pedophile, or a woman who wakes up one day and realizes that modern society is slowly poisoning her to death, it's the world in which I'll stay. That I'm forever "independent" makes me a little sad—until I arrive at my office and see the posters for the films I've produced, provocative and risky films on which I've felt like an intimate collaborator: *Poison, Swoon, Kids, Safe, I Shot Andy Warhol, Go Fish, Velvet Goldmine.* Hollywood producers often have to eat worse than black bananas.

The office of my company, Killer Films, is packed with assistants and interns and is woefully short on working air conditioners. My desk is a mess, strewn with papers relating to ten or more projects, some in development, some in pre- and postproduction, and some on the verge of release. All they have in common is my name as a producer.

The job of producer is one of the great mysteries of the moviemaking process. When I'm asked what producers do, I say, "What *don't* they do?" I develop scripts; I raise money; I put together budgets; I negotiate with stars willing to work for said (generally meager) budgets; I match directors with cinematographers, cinematographers with production designers, production designers with location managers; I make sure that a shoot is on schedule, on budget, on track; I hold hands; I stroke egos. I once had to bail an actor out of jail (for gay bashing, no less). I give interviews explaining what producers do, especially producers of independent, low-budget movies by directors who struggle to put their singular visions on the screen, however much of a challenge those visions might pose for the so-called mass audience. I sit here at my desk with the phone ringing, the fax machine clicking, the assistants and interns running in and out, getting a buzz from the power.

And sometimes I sit here stunned at my powerlessness. Basically, a low-budget movie is a crisis waiting to happen. You stretch every one of your resources to its limit, and then you constantly push that limit. You have to be creative on your feet, because if something goes wrong (and something always goes wrong), you can't just throw money at it. You have to take scary leaps off high buildings, knowing that the landing might be hard.

I'm fortunate to have had a miraculously easy landing with the first feature I produced, a movie written and directed by Todd Haynes called

Poison. The theme was transgression, and the approach was the opposite of straight. The film consisted of three different stories woven together, each shot in a different style: a black and white horror film, a mock documentary, and a lush, homosexual prison romance. In script form, it was just tough to read. Half its funding came from Todd's extended family and their Los Angeles friends (among them, amazingly enough, Sherwood Schwartz, the creator of *Gilligan's Island* and *The Brady Bunch*), the other half from foundations and arts agencies, including (and most notoriously) the National Endowment for the Arts. What nearly brought the endowment down would help us make our names.

The movie had won a prize at the 1991 US (Sundance) Film Festival in Park City, Utah, and had been picked up by a small distributor, Zeitgeist. We were anticipating a tiny arthouse release. Then, an amazing thing happened: Two weeks before the scheduled release, the Reverend Donald Wildmon, an antipornography activist and head of the American Family Association, saw a favorable review in *Variety* that mentioned the film's homoeroticism and also cited its partial NEA funding. So he sent letters to every member of the Senate and the House, saying, in effect, "Are you aware that this film, which was made with your tax dollars, is filthy, pornographic, and homosexual?"

The upshot was chaos. Our phones literally did not stop ringing. We made all the papers. We made *Entertainment Tonight.* Previously, performance artists like Karen Finley had come under fire for using taxpayers' money to do naughty things with yams and chocolate syrup, but movies capture the public and media's interest in a way that "minority" arts don't. This was the first time the wrath of the Religious Right was being directed at something that more than a handful of people at a time could actually see—something that could actually show up *in your hometown.* The head of the NEA, John Frohnmayer—that poor fellow, banished shortly thereafter—came out in support of *Poison.* He organized a screening in Washington, DC, after which a member of the Far Right was quoted in the *Washington Post* as saying that the movie was so filthy she wanted to take a bath in Clorox.

The bottom line was a $50,000 opening weekend at the Angelika Film Center in New York City—a record that wasn't broken for years.

Poison is a good example of how it's easiest to make a movie when you don't know what you're doing. Ignorance makes you fearless. I didn't know how risky limited partnerships were. I didn't know that we shouldn't have gone into production without all the money in hand that we needed to finish the film. I didn't know that a thousand dollars for production design was a bad joke, and that the costume designer would be spending nights in my apartment sewing prison uniforms. If I knew then what I know now, I never would have made the movie. That's the paradox of low-low-budget filmmaking. You have to expect the worst, plan for the worst, and repress all thoughts about the worst.

All first independent features are done with sleight of hand. They're built on contradictions, and their driving force has to be passion for the project. That's the exhortation under every how-to in this book.

I've been passionate about movies all my life. My parents took me to *Patton* when I was seven years old: they liked it, they thought I ought to see it. In Manhattan, where I grew up, there were theaters nearby—the Thalia and the Metro—that showed movies in repertory such as *The Rules of the Game* and *The 400 Blows*. The mid-seventies was the tail of the last great era in American filmmaking, the time of *The Conversation*, *Mean Streets*, and *Nashville*, when mainstream directors and writers could still wrestle with difficult truths and pose questions for which they had no easy answers. Video hadn't arrived yet: if you loved a movie and wanted to watch a scene again, you had to go back and sit through the whole thing. I sat through *The Poseidon Adventure* five times.

As an undergraduate at Brown, I could study film only through the semiotics department, which meant an immersion in theory. I spent a year in Paris studying with Julia Kristeva and Christian Metz and going to lectures by Michel Foucault, then returned to Brown to make the requisite impenetrable student movie. Did all that semiotics and structuralism have an impact on my producing? I don't know, but I did see some interesting stuff: Straub, Robbe-Grillet, Rivette's *Céline and Julie Go Boating*—films that might be hard to sit through now but that deepened my understanding of the medium. I've gotten into trouble with colleagues for saying that the aesthetic of some young directors seems closer to *Three's Company* and *Full House* than to Renoir or Truffaut, but I can't retract my underlying conviction that the more you know about the history of film, the better you can imagine its possibilities.

I didn't go to film school. I know, lots of people learn the basics there. The problem is that everyone who comes out says, "I want to be a director." *Somebody* has to make the coffee.

When I came back to New York in the summer of '83, I made a lot of coffee. Thus began a series of jobs that I hoped would teach me all I needed to know to make independent films. I wanted to understand the structure of a movie crew. (I was, after all, a structuralist.) As a gofer, I'd go-fer drinks, props, equipment, and, at the behest of one notorious producer, cocaine. On an independent movie, you can usually get a job without having any prior experience as long as you're willing to work for free. (I paid the rent by working all night as a freelance copyeditor for high-priced law firms. In the eighties, you could make twenty-five bucks an hour just for sitting around and waiting for some jittery associate to drop a brief on your desk at three in the morning.)

I had a lot of jobs: assistant editor, location scout on music videos, second-unit coordinator, second assistant director. One of the most useful in terms of my future producing was script supervisor. That's the person who sits with a fat, annotated copy of the shooting script and a Polaroid, making sure there's continuity from one shot or sequence to the next and that you're getting all the coverage you need. I was stationed by the camera all the time, so I learned how a low-budget film gets "covered"—how you can shoot a scene with a minimum number of takes and angles. Bare-bones movies tend to skimp on coverage, because film stock is often the greatest expense. On a studio picture, it's the opposite—film is the least expensive thing in the budget, a fraction of a big star's salary.

The movie I remember most from those early years is *Parting Glances*, a superb-looking gay drama made for a few hundred thousand and released in 1986. I did a lot of jobs on that one, including acting as an extra in the party scene. They needed someone to synchronize the sound on what they'd shot every day, so the director, Bill Sherwood, would come back from filming at one in the morning and watch dailies with me.

Hard as it is to believe, there weren't many models at the time for a microbudget movie with a gay theme shot with money the director had raised himself. (Bill would stop shooting when he ran out of funds and start again months later.) Some of the financing came from gay men— five thousand dollars here, ten there—who wanted to see their lives depicted onscreen for the first time. (Some investors got parts in the movie in exchange for their money.) And some of it came from Bill's parents, who cherished him, and who I figured were well-to-do. They weren't especially—which I learned when I went to Battle Creek, Michigan, for his funeral in 1990, after his death from AIDS. He couldn't get another movie made, but his legacy is indelible. He said, "Okay, I've got an apartment, I've got friends who can act," and he made a movie on his own terms. The tremendous, pitch-in attitude he inspired is still, for me, the essence of the independent scene—even though it isn't present as much nowadays, with so many low-budget films being shot and so much competition for talent.

For a long time I didn't quite realize that I wanted to be where the money was. I thought I'd be an assistant director, the person who schedules the movie and runs the set, reprimands people and yells, "Quiet!" and "Roll sound!" and directs all the extras and makes the stunts happen. It's a terrible job, but it's also kind of fun, because you're the center of it all. On the other hand, you end up being a lightning rod for anxiety on the set, which is exhausting.

Everything changed when, in 1987, a college friend, Barry Ellsworth, found a generous private donor and asked if I wanted to form a production company with him and another Brown alumnus, Todd Haynes. I had known Todd vaguely at Brown, but apparently he had been kind of scared of me. I had worked in the school cafeteria as a short-order cook. I made the omelets. No one else wanted to do that because it was really high pressure—*twoeggsovereasysixpancakesthreeomelets*—but I found it exciting, a rehearsal for being a producer. I was a mean short-order cook, though. You had to step up and say what you wanted and move on, and if you didn't obey my rules you had to go to the back of the line.

Whatever Todd's fears about my nature, he wasn't about to pass up a (small) salary and a chance to produce and direct provocative, experimental shorts that would be a step up from the primitive, just-me-and-my-camera work that characterized the New York avant-garde of that era. Actually, there were two camps in the New York independent scene. People were making either super-experimental films, which were often like watching paint dry for two hours, or slick calling-card movies that were essentially mini-Hollywood pictures. There was little in between. We wanted to make films that were both avant-garde and entertaining—such as *Blue Velvet*, which had just come out and seemed to signal a new direction. One of the strongest mandates of the company was to change people's perception that "experimental" was synonymous with "excruciating." Still, we were semiotics majors, concerned with the "means of production," so we called ourselves "Apparatus." We wrote an incredibly pretentious statement of purpose, which I'd quote from if I hadn't burned it.

The project that Todd was finishing up when we started Apparatus was a forty-three-minute stop-action film (co-written with Cynthia Schneider) he'd made over a summer in a graduate program at Bard College. It was called *Superstar: The Karen Carpenter Story*, starred a bunch of Barbie dolls, and charted the rise of the pop group the Carpenters as the lead singer wasted away from anorexia nervosa. The night he first screened it changed my life. It was astonishing on so many levels. It was incredibly entertaining, and when you watch a lot of movies in semiotics class, you start to worry that maybe that's not the point. It was also brilliant and searching, a meditation on identity and the destructive pressures of environment. When it began, there were gasps and laughs from the audience, because it was so funny and perfect to have Karen Carpenter played by a Barbie doll. But at the end, when the doll turned around and half her face was gone, carved away by weight loss, it wasn't so funny anymore, and some people actually burst into tears. Watching *Superstar*, I thought, "This is the kind of filmmaking I want to be involved in." Todd remembers that I said to him: "I want to produce your next film."

Superstar was triumphantly received at Sundance and other film festivals, but we could never screen it commercially because Richard Carpenter and his lawyers served Todd with an order to cease and desist distribution. They wouldn't give permission to use the original music that served as the devastatingly ironic soundtrack. This, of course, has helped to cement the picture's status as a cult item, something that shows up now and then in bootleg on the black market or under the counters at hipper video stores. It also planted Todd—and, hence, Apparatus—in the consciousness of critics and members of the alternative media. In the next three years, leading up to *Poison*, we cut our teeth on a series of risky shorts that played regularly at small venues all over New York City (places such as the Collective for Living

Cinema, most of which, alas, no longer exist). People would submit their scripts to us as if applying for a grant, and we'd produce the ones we liked for twenty to thirty thousand dollars. We made a couple of really bad films. But we also made some that were very, very good.

Apparatus set the tone for what I'm doing now. When I started working in independent films, I thought that the way that you had to run a production was in a state of crisis. That's what I was taught. The offices where I worked were hysterical places: the producer screamed at the line producer, who screamed at the coordinator, who screamed at the office production assistant, who screamed at the intern. There was a lot of finger-pointing: "*This* didn't get done! It's your fault, your fault, *your* fault!" You were constantly darting out of the line of fire; you'd leave at night shaken, sick to your stomach, needing a drink. Many people think that if you're not in a state of crisis on a movie, you're not really working.

I learned from Todd that it didn't have to be that way. When we started making movies together, he said, "Don't yell at me and I won't yell at you. Let's just not be like that." I was amazed. In part it's simply a matter of respecting other human beings. But it's also good business: the amount of time spent trying to blame somebody else is simply not worth it. The bottom line is *you cannot be a producer unless you understand that it's all your fault.* Nobody wants to feel culpable for something gone wrong, but if you're the boss, you have to be the boss all the way. You take a deep breath and accept responsibility for every stupid little thing. And once people stop fearing that they're going to be targeted for blame, they start thinking for themselves, and they're no longer paralyzed by the thought that they're going to screw up and someone's going to scream at them.

That said, I yell at people all the time.

In this book, I'm going to tell you what producers do and how you can do it, too. But first I'm going to tell you what this producer does—what I did today, in fact—to give you a sense of the range.

9 a.m.

Velvet Goldmine, Todd Haynes's musical about the birth of "glam" rock in the early seventies, is being edited elsewhere in Manhattan. We're breathing a little easier because a rough video assembly was shown to financiers a few days ago, it looked sensational, and—here's the really important part—they released our salaries, which had been held as insurance against the movie's completion.

In a couple weeks, *Kiss Me, Guido*, a comedy about a pair of unlikely roommates (one gay, one working-class macho Italian) will open; many days there are reports on my desk of media screenings in New York and Los Angeles. The superimportant critics usually won't disclose what they think, but editors and feature writers will often stop to chat with the publicist, and you can get a sense of how the movie will ultimately be received. ("It's very charming and funny," says one writer in today's report. "Overall, I thought it was weak," says another.)

Another picture that's done and waiting to go is the directorial debut of the photographer Cindy Sherman, a low-budget horror film called *Office Killer*. On my desk sits a series of hilarious exploitation-movie posters that feature a strangled model in secretarial garb and catch phrases such as "While You Were Out . . ." and "Working Here Can Be Murder."

My partner, Pam Koffler, and I have a number of scripts in development. One is true-life account of the murder of a young Nebraska woman who pretended to be a man (to be called *Take It Like a Man*). Then there are biographies of the designer Halston and Bettie Page, the S&M centerfold of yore. *The Michael Alig Story* is a true-life black comedy about the murder of a Puerto Rican club kid. We've also optioned a tumultuous Hollywood novel, Bruce Wagner's *I'm Losing You*, which we're going to shoot in LA with Bruce as director. Most visibly, we're gearing up for shooting what is now titled *Todd Solondz Untitled*, an amazing ensemble drama on the theme of erotic fixation from the writer-director of *Welcome to the Dollhouse*.

The distributor, October Films, had told us that we'd get a medium-range budget to make *Todd Solondz Untitled*, and that the sum would not be cast-contingent. But when Patricia Arquette dropped out (because of an illness in her family), October got cold feet. Now they say they'll only give us the agreed-upon sum if we sign one of their "approved" stars to play Bill, the psychiatrist who, in the course of the film, drugs a pair of little boys and has (off-camera) sex with them. The list of actors they provided featured some odd names (Tom Cruise?). Todd Solondz chose three; none could decline fast enough. Big-name actors often lament that they don't take enough risks, but no star is breaking down our door to play a child molester. (On the other hand, young actresses are flying themselves in from the West Coast to audition for the character of Joy, the seeming ditz who reveals unexpected layers of obsessiveness and vulnerability.) Without a star to play Bill, October's offer drops by a couple of million, take it or leave it.

10:03 a.m.

Todd Solondz says take it, take it. He didn't have stars in *Welcome to the Dollhouse*. He doesn't need the added pressure. He sits at my desk while Pam and I explain what it means to do the film with around two-thirds of what was already a minuscule budget. It might mean fewer shooting days— No, he says, let's cut something else. Okay: it might mean that the sequence set in a Florida retirement community will have to be reconceived, or else moved to the Catskills or New Jersey. He's not sure about that one, either. Well, then: goodbye to separate offices for the production—we'll have to cram everyone into this one.

More significantly, it might mean that Todd Solondz will have to reconceive the film and that we'll all have to take salary cuts. It turns out, however, that for Todd, this is the least important obstacle. "If the movie does well, then give me a part of that because I'll feel I've earned it; I've done my job," he says, in his oddly passionate drone. "This is such a risky movie." After *Welcome to the Dollhouse*, a lot of companies pursued him; he could have made a relatively big-budget picture with real stars. But he wrote a nonjudgmental film about a pedophile. He's my kind of filmmaker.

10:40 a.m.

Todd leaves to audition more actors in a local church basement while Pam makes phone calls to nail down a designer, a director of photography, and a location manager. One big agency has aggressively advised their clients that participating in this sordid film (in any capacity, even technical) will do grave damage to their careers. I hit the roof and call one of the offending agents, who says, "Hey, that's what I do." When a script arrives from the same agency, I have my assistant fire off a letter that says we're no longer accepting their submissions. Hey, that's what I do.

11:20 a.m.

Todd Haynes has returned from England (where he spent six months shooting *Velvet Goldmine*) to discover that his Brooklyn apartment had been overrun by rats. On Friday, the biggest rat he ever saw got caught in a glue trap in his bathroom. Day and night it screams. Meanwhile, he has been peeing in a bottle and dumping the contents into the kitchen sink. I offer to send an intern to dispose of the vermin, which is the least I can do, given that Todd has yet to participate in the editing of the movie and his physical and mental health are paramount. Then Jim, Todd's ex-boyfriend (and the editor of *Velvet Goldmine*) comes over, carries the agonized rodent downstairs in a bag, and—with great regret—bludgeons it to death with a bottle. Still shaken, Jim goes upstairs and finds another rat, bigger than the first, in another glue trap. This he beats to death with less hesitation. I follow all this avidly. When a movie is in process, you can't be too involved in the lives of your principal players.

11:45 a.m.

Music rights are one of my biggest headaches today. In *Velvet Goldmine*, there's a scene in which Ewan McGregor and Jonathan Rhys Meyers lip-sync to Lou Reed's "Satellite of Love." It turns out that the number might cost as much as $50,000. This means we'll need to squeeze more money from our backers, or we won't get the song. The executive producers are starting to get edgy: I'm getting faxes filled with veiled threats. Meanwhile, *Kiss Me, Guido* has turned into a licensing nightmare. In one of the film's funnier scenes, the mismatched roommates watch *The Sound of Music* on TV. It turns out that to feature the clip, we not only need permission of the studio, but of all the actors who appear. And not just Julie Andrews—every little von Trapp child. I don't know what we'll do if one of them got religion in the last thirty-two years and doesn't want to be seen in a movie that embraces the homosexual lifestyle. My co-producer, Ira Deutchman, and I get our lawyer, John Sloss, on it, pronto.

1 p.m.

Today we do something out of the ordinary. Pam and I have lunch with a real Hollywood movie star: Shirley MacLaine, who wants to make her directorial debut on a slight but compelling script about an alienated young boy who likes to dress up as a girl. John Hart, the producer who works across the hall, has invited Pam and me to join him on the project. My hopes are not high, so I'm not broken up when Shirley and I don't connect. She doesn't seem to get what Killer Films—or most independent films—are about. She thinks a "little movie" costs $10 million. (Try a tenth of that.) Later, Pam gently suggests that I didn't do a great job of hiding what I was feeling, which was insulted. That's probably why Pam and I make a good team—she's good at letting someone know she likes them and even better at not letting them know she doesn't. Actually, although I wouldn't want to produce for Shirley MacLaine, I wasn't immune to her aura. When we traded stories about our childhoods and she referred, in passing, to her kid brother, Warren, I was starstruck: Warren . . . Warren Beatty! She grew up with Warren Beatty!

3:30 p.m.

Good news when I come back from lunch. *The Sound of Music* kids are all represented by one lawyer, which will mean a lot fewer hours spent tracking them down and waiting for letters of release to be signed.

3:42 p.m.

My relief is interrupted by a summons: I'm being sued by DuArt, a leading New York lab. It's their screwup, but it's one more thing I have to call my lawyer back about. This all began with Kim Peirce, who shot a short student film we're now developing into *Take It Like a Man*. Kim had it processed at DuArt but didn't have enough money to get it out—a typical student scenario. DuArt holds a lot of student negatives prisoner, which is their right. So I called the company and proposed paying half of the $4,000 Kim owed in return for the work print, which we could then edit into a trailer to show to potential investors. DuArt would keep the negative. The company agreed, but somehow that agreement got lost in the system, and now they're suing me for the other two thousand. What a waste of time.

4 p.m.

There is outside interest in *Take It Like a Man*, of a sort. Pam and I go out for coffee with a guy who'd called us up out of nowhere—a representative for what one lawyer referred to as "high-net-worth individuals." The man wants to invest in the movie, which at this point has a budget of under a million dollars. Limited partnerships, as I'll discuss later, are not so common these days, partly because the tax incentives are gone and partly because would-be investors have learned that they have a good chance of losing their children's college tuitions. But this guy grew up in Nebraska, where the incident on which the film is based took place; he'd seen *I Shot Andy Warhol* at Sundance and liked it; and he wanted an entrée into the biz. Pam and I politely ignore his casting suggestions: limited partners make no creative decisions, and can be a pain if they have ambitions in that area. In fact, we say nothing at all to encourage him. But he's so convinced that this will make a great film, and so determined to break into movies, that he does all the selling. We sit and listen as he talks himself into investing.

5 p.m.

Back in the office, I call Lindsay Law, head of Fox Searchlight, to sound him out on what he thinks of the second draft of *Simply Halston* that Dan Minahan (who co-wrote *I Shot Andy Warhol*) has just delivered. I think Dan nailed Halston on this draft—he got under the designer's prickly behavior and found the human being who created the persona. He made Halston sympathetic, and the writing became a lot livelier. Lindsay and I talk for a long time; I tell him that I think the middle's soft, but that the last act has a hundred times more tension. Lindsay agrees. My sense is that, pending rewrites, he could be poised to give us a go-ahead. I call Dan and tell him Lindsay liked it, and Dan feels better. He can go to work on that soft middle.

Development of *Simply Halston* has been intense, because there are a couple of other seventies, Studio 54–type projects out there that we're competing with. No, that's not true, we're not really competing with them—they aren't all the same. But studios and the media will lump them together, the way that *I Shot Andy Warhol* got lumped together with *Basquiat*. Rather than argue with a distributor about why the comparison doesn't make sense, you have to deal with it—because if you don't, you're apt to get the plug pulled on your picture. Dan was supposed to deliver his second draft two weeks earlier, but he was late, and Lindsay was livid because those two other projects had a jump on us. He had gambled on Dan's script, and he was feeling as if he'd lost the gamble. Usually I protect a writer from that kind of pressure, but I let Dan know because we were all up against it. After he got over the shock he went to work. Now the mood is upbeat. We have a shot at "competing" again. As dumb as that sounds.

5:30 p.m.

A messenger arrives bearing tidings of great joy. It's the deal memo from October Films: the green light on *Todd Solondz Untitled*! When

Todd returns from auditioning actors, we present him with our prize. "Now it's real," he says, awed. "Now it's scary. Now I'm really gonna do it."

This was a good day, overall. No matter how many lawsuits, pointless meetings, budget crises, and stray bits of nonsense this office has had to endure, we got a green light on a feature motion picture—which is only the thirteenth time we've had that happen. We're no longer in that gray limbo where we have to convince agents and actors and creative personnel that the deal is done. We can begin the job of building a team. We can go for it, secure in the knowledge that we haven't made one aesthetic decision as a result of being umbilically attached to a marketing department.

I don't want to sound snotty about the marketing aspect of movies. While it's true that, in the best of all possible worlds, independent films are genuinely alternative, genuinely original visions, there's no such thing as an absolutely independent film. There's still an economy at work: the movie has to go into the marketplace, and people have to want to see it. Much of the money I get comes from Hollywood sources, and not because they want to underwrite my brilliant career. To do what I do, I have to believe that the films I produce will be so vital that they will find an audience—or else will create one of their own.

There's a joke about an art professor who begins his first lecture by saying: "You might not know much about art, but you know what you like. Well, after taking this course you still won't know much about art—but you'll know what *I* like." Actually, knowing what a decent professor likes is about as much as you can hope for when the subject isn't math or science. And because making movies is such a peculiar activity, in which art and commerce and psychology get all mixed up, the most useful instruction I can offer is by way of illustration, not prescription.

In other words, when you read this book, you'll learn about producing by learning what *I* like. You'll read about my experiences in the areas of development, budgeting, casting, shooting, editing, releasing, and of course, fighting those battles with artistic personnel and studio executives, with names occasionally omitted—not to protect the cretinous, but to ensure that after writing a book about producing I can continue to produce. You'll find heavily annotated budgets and contracts, along with my own production diaries written in the heat of such tumultuous shoots as *I Shot Andy Warhol* and *Velvet Goldmine*. You'll get a sense of what it's like in the trenches, which is the best preparation for being there I know of.

There's a mystique about the movies. You walk down the street and see a film shooting—as I did this morning—and there's a phalanx of people there to keep you away. You can sort of glimpse the actors, and there's a crane, and the crew, and everyone's doing their thing. You think, "Wow, there's a movie." This book will demystify the process without, I hope, demystifying it too much. Not just anyone can make low-budget movies that matter—it takes incredible nerves, and passion, and, oh yes, talent. It takes knowing everything, but not knowing so much that you're not prepared to take the leap off that high building—the leap of faith. The director, at times, has the luxury of despairing, but the producer does not, or else the whole thing will spiral out of control.

The one thing that all great producers have in common is the courage of their convictions. A part of me loves reading articles about alleged monster producers, like the guy who has a special button on his phone that means: MORE STRING CHEESE NOW! Making movies is an immoderate activity. You have to stay sane and also embrace the madness if you want to shoot to kill.

THE NEXT MOVIE

In the early eighties, following the commercial success of such films as *Parting Glances*, *Stranger Than Paradise*, and *My Beautiful Laundrette*, people began to rhapsodize about a new kind of moviemaking—a genuine alternative to the studio-processed schlock that had become even more flagrant with the rise of entertainment conglomerates. Here were movies that didn't need to gross fifty or a hundred million dollars to justify the leading actor's salary or the studio's massive overhead. Here were movies that could find a small sliver of an audience and still manage to earn their money back, launch careers, and—oh yes—enrich the culture.

A lot of the distributors that profited from those films developed grand designs, began to produce their own features for less-than-frugal sums, and went belly-up. The press pronounced the independent movement dead, or, at least, drained of blood; government money grew scarce; and many important exhibitors closed up shop, fatally weakened by the one-two punch of funding cuts and the rise of home video.

Then came *Pulp Fiction*, *Shine*, *Sling Blade*, *Welcome to the Dollhouse*, and *The English Patient*, and the movement was reborn—although it was different in important ways from what had preceded it. Suddenly, independent distributors were selling themselves to major studios, content to serve as arthouse divisions and, in some cases, to abandon the kinds of movies that had made them successful in the first place. (In the wake of *Pulp Fiction*, there were scores of dreadful Tarantino imitations, basically formulaic but cultivating an outlaw status, and most of them flopped.)

I'm waiting for the independent-film movement to be pronounced dead again—terminally co-opted. But we've been down this road before. Pretty soon, a movie will come along for an audience that no studio had previously perceived; it will sell for lots of money at a festival, and kick off new careers and new genres; and, again, that phoenix will rise from those ashes. Once-marginal places like Sundance that have now become less marginal, even mainstream, will be replaced by others more marginal. (The Slamdance Festival already exists, and so does Slumdance.) As one underground becomes absorbed, another will form to take its place.

Meanwhile, I'll continue to make the same sort of films I always have—some with studio money, others with independent financing. I try not to concern myself with what the press says the new trend is or whether I'm in or out of fashion. Mostly, what I think about is the next movie, helping the director to figure out how to translate his or her vision from the page to the screen, and finding the exact right cinematographer, actors, and crew with whom to collaborate. I feel so *lucky* to be able to produce films for artists like Todd Haynes, Tom Kalin, Todd Solondz, Mary Harron, Rose Troche, Bruce Wagner, Dan Minahan, and all the rest.

Todd Haynes and I wanted the experience of seeing *Velvet Goldmine* to be like that of seeing the great movies of the sixties and seventies, such as *Bonnie and Clyde, Midnight Cowboy, 2001*, and *Nashville*. Those films began and you didn't know where they were going—you had no idea what you'd see before you saw it and yet you felt happy in your disorientation, because you trusted the people who made them not to lead you astray. You were a participant, allowed to form your own judgments about the characters and their situations.

I still feel that way from time to time, at films such as *Sweetie, Welcome to the Dollhouse, Boogie Nights*, and the one of mine I'm proudest of—*Safe*.

As I wrote in the first chapter, I don't want you to think that everyone can make a great independent movie, especially people whose chief motivation is to become rich and famous. (That can, of course, be a subsidiary motivation.)

Accessibility cuts both ways. For real artists to have the power to put their visions on film, the floodgates have to be opened to everyone, whatever their reasons for making a film. The net must be cast wide, which is why my office still reads unsolicited manuscripts. And if my work—and this book—can inspire that one little dispirited person in the middle of nowhere to go out and make a great movie, then it's worth all the other movies that flow through those same portals.

As Bruce Wagner, the director of *I'm Losing You*, puts it, independent film is "a whole new arena of hope." And what I want most passionately is for aspiring producers, directors, and writers to treat it with something like reverence. H. L. Mencken notwithstanding, *a lot* of people have gone broke underestimating the public's intelligence. Whereas I truly believe that if you fashion a great work, it will—ultimately—be seen. I have to believe that, or I wouldn't be doing what I'm doing.

Laugh, Cry, Believe: Spielbergization and Its Discontents

J. Hoberman

L et no one say the American movie industry has not taken seriously its social mission.

Nearly a lifetime ago and in the midst of another war, several hundred Hollywood creators gathered on the University of California's Los Angeles campus. The mood was excited, resolute, and militant. The stakes were high. Their conclave was taking place, as one participant put it, barely "a cannon shot" from the studios where they worked.

Hollywood in the crosshairs: held over the first weekend of October 1943, organized by the Hollywood Writers' Mobilization, officially greeted by President Franklin Roosevelt and Vice President Henry Wallace (and the fraternal Writers and Artists of the Soviet Union), the Writers' Congress was dedicated to the proposition that (as its chairman, Warner Brothers screenwriter Robert Rossen, declared) movies had the power to influence human behavior, help defeat the Axis, and positively shape the postwar world.

Congress participants were mainly screenwriters. Some were Communists, but not everyone. Darryl F. Zanuck—who addressed a Saturday morning panel on the "responsibility of the industry"—was the top production executive at Twentieth Century Fox. "We must play our part in the solutions of the problems that torture the world," he maintained. "We must begin to deal realistically in film with the causes of wars and panics, with social upheavals and depression, with starvation and want and injustice and barbarism under whatever guise."

This urgently self-important, change-the-world sense of responsibility did not end with civilization's victory over fascism. Four years later, Zanuck was again in the vanguard, producing *The Iron Curtain* (Hollywood's first exposé of Communist espionage) and, soon after, celebrating an early Cold War success (flying over the Soviet blockade to resupply West Berlin) in *The Big Lift.* By then, some of the Congress's most prominent figures—Rossen, John Howard Lawson, Edward Dmytryk—had been blacklisted, even jailed, for the indiscretion of their Communist beliefs.

There were real consequences for dream-factory politics: Hollywood exercised its responsibility and maintained a public role through the Cold War. The studios produced anti-Communist film noirs, cooperated with the Pentagon to make Korean War dramas or celebrate new air force technology, and ministered to the nation's sense of spiritual destiny with spectacular tales from ancient Rome or the Old Testament. Less obviously, the industry supported the status quo by manufacturing consensus, adaptation, and reassurance as part of the process that French philosopher Jacques Ellul would call "sociological propaganda."

During the Kennedy era's duck-and-cover days, Hollywood operated as though prepared to go to war, albeit uncertain which branch of the government—Pentagon or president—to obey. In 1963, the Department of Defense [DOD] declined to assist Paramount in filming the military coup in *Seven Days in May,* though according to star-producer Kirk Douglas, the project was supported by JFK himself. The DOD also refused to help Columbia with the nuclear disaster movie *Fail-Safe.* The makers of the rival atomic doomsday scenario *Dr. Strangelove*—a rare example of an unambiguously critical Hollywood movie—knew better than to ask. Meanwhile, armed with the knowledge that two films on accidental nuclear warfare were in preparation, General Curtis LeMay encouraged Universal to make the 1963 *A Gathering of Eagles,* dedicated to the Strategic Air Command.

Around 1960, actors began to supplant studios as the industry's motor and an inevitable element of narcissism entered the process. John Wayne was only the first Hollywood freedom fighter to leverage the power of stardom as means for political pamphleteering or, if you prefer, public service. ("Could art be useful?" the underground film-maker Jack Smith wondered, by way of proposing Hollywood movies that might feature "Tony Curtis and Janet Leigh busily making yogurt; Humphrey Bogart struggling to introduce a basic civil-law course into public schools, [or] infants being given to the old in homes for the aged by Ginger Rogers.")

As second-tier star Ronald Reagan began his ascent into the show business stratosphere, Wayne's lead was followed by young dissidents like Warren Beatty, Robert Redford, and Jane Fonda. Their movies might be construed as oppositional, but then theirs was a turbulent epoch when, for the first time since the Great Depression, the movie industry faced insolvency, and even that most American of genres, the Western, became, in its final stages, a vehicle of protest. By the time Reagan assumed the role of president, the nature of star politics had been long since normalized.

The current star-pol paradigms include Mel Gibson (on the right), George Clooney (on the left), and Governor Arnold Schwarzenegger (front and center). But one need only have watched last March's Oscar telecast [in 2006]—five socially conscious movies competing for best picture, a self-congratulatory clip montage evoking vintage "problem films" of Hollywood past—to realize how integral to the movie industry's self-image Zanuck's long-ago call to his fellow filmmakers remains.

Certain directors—the practiced self-promoters Oliver Stone and Spike Lee come to mind—see themselves as political commentators. Recently, they have been joined by a few producers, on both the secular left (eBay founder Jeff Skoll) and the Christian right (Bush fundraiser Philip Anschutz). But the embodiment of responsible, socially aware moviemaking is that repository of the industry's institutional memory known as Steven Spielberg.

No one since Reagan has so demonstrated a belief in the redemptive nature of Hollywood entertainment. Such faith is not without a material basis. Spielberg's status as a moneymaker peaked a dozen years ago, when his two greatest hits, *E.T.* and *Jurassic Park,* were first and third on the list of all-time Hollywood box office attractions, with *Jaws* and

Raiders of the Lost Ark still inhabiting the top ten. But even today, Spielberg is credited with nine of Hollywood's hundred highest-grossing movies—more than those directed by his nearest rivals, George Lucas and Peter Jackson, combined.

As a manipulator of the medium, Spielberg ranks with the greatest—king of cute Walt Disney and master of suspense Alfred Hitchcock. In a sense, Spielberg synthesizes Disney and Hitchcock. Astoundingly attuned to mass-audience psychology, he is at once ruthlessly sadistic and cloyingly saccharine, a filmmaker who opened his first blockbuster by implicating the audience in an aquatic sex-murder committed by a giant serial-killer shark, and the only filmmaker since Disney who might sincerely employ "When You Wish Upon a Star" (the original closing music for *Close Encounters of the Third Kind*). Naturally privileging sentiment above reason, Spielberg's movies are shamelessly dependent on such cues. But music is hardly his only means of persuasion. *Jaws* amply demonstrated Spielberg's willingness to inflict pain upon the spectator.

Different as Disney's *Snow White* or Hitchcock's *Psycho* might be, each film exhibits a rage for control readily attributable to its maker. And yet, one doubts Disney ever questioned the purity of his intentions or Hitchcock lost sleep pondering the psychological implications of his films; as the world's preeminent maker of entertainments for children, the former was a priori virtuous, while as the professionally ghoulish virtuoso of onscreen murder, the latter had no need to demonstrate his moral virtue. Spielberg, however, is the representative of the aging "movie generation"—and thus acutely self-conscious, if not downright anxious to do the right thing.

There is a sense in which Spielberg's oeuvre is divided against itself, characterized by the Good Steven's feel-good movies and the more hostile entertainments devised by his evil twin. Bad Steven surfaced first to make his bones with *Jaws*—a phenomenal success and still an unsurpassed thrill mechanism, enriched by a post-Watergate political subtext concerning deceptive, mendacious public officials. Bad Steven lives to terrorize audiences in the name of fun, making movies like the egregious *Indiana Jones and the Temple of Doom,* the amusingly self-reflexive *Jurassic Park,* and last summer's intermittently effective remake of *War of the Worlds.*

Good Steven is epitomized by the reverent sci-fi suburbia of *Close Encounters of the Third Kind* and *E.T. the Extra-Terrestrial,* movies that, in constructing the audience of kids of all ages, effectively out-Disneyed Disney. Beginning with his 1985 adaptation of *The Color Purple,* however, Good Steven assumed a sense of adult responsibility with a series of serious movies—not unlike the then fifty-year-old cinema-of-quality associated with MGM producer Irving Thalberg, a secular saint of Hollywood's golden age. The multiple-Oscar-winner *Schindler's List* is the most significant of these—the list also includes the slave-ship drama *Amistad* and Spielberg's second Oscar picture, *Saving Private Ryan.* The latter, like *Schindler's List,* has aspects of Bad Steven. The extended D-Day sequence that ushers in the movie's restaging of World War II is a terrifying assault on the audience that goes well beyond the mutilation, dismemberment, and carnage of *Jaws.* It's also a virtuoso piece of filmmaking, perhaps the strongest single passage in the entire Spielberg oeuvre.

Badness works—and yet, essentially middlebrow, Spielberg has never made a movie as daringly outré as Martin Scorsese's *Taxi Driver* or Brian De Palma's *Carrie* or David Lynch's *Blue Velvet* or anything by David Cronenberg. None of Spielberg's movies has projected the epic sweep and historical perspective of Francis Coppola's first two *Godfather* films. If *Hook,* Spielberg's bizarrely confessional gloss on *Peter Pan,* was a fiasco, he is far too sensible to indulge a *grande folle* as convulsive as Coppola's *Apocalypse Now.* But as other directors of his generation fade from relevance, the awesomely productive Spielberg seems ever more central.

Something less than *artist,* Spielberg is also something more. He is the institution personified—the genius of the system, the whole Oscar Night shebang in one bearded, baseball-hat-wearing package. Spielberg is Hollywood's most successful director and most powerful producer, as well as a nouveau mogul, cofounder of the DreamWorks studio (recently sold to Paramount). He is a presidential friend and the Hollywood equivalent of a public intellectual, called upon, in the afterglow of *Schindler's List,* to furnish a Congressional investigating committee with expert testimony on the nature of hate crimes.

Spielberg's gifts as a filmmaker can be wildly overstated. But there's no denying his brilliance as a pop culture player—witness the coy strategy that, when it came time to release *Munich* last December, landed him once more on the cover of *Time* magazine and thus positioned his latest movie as a public event, "Spielberg's Secret Masterpiece."

As an ongoing business concern, Hollywood has a hegemonic duty—more pragmatic than ideological—to be, or at least attempt to be, all things to all people. In this Spielberg has been a faithful barometer.

Opening less than a year after Jimmy Carter's inspirational long-shot campaign (which, among other then-eccentricities, stressed the candidate's belief in the existence of UFOs), *Close Encounters of the Third Kind* rewrote the '50s alien-invasion script—and, in a sense, the Cold War—in terms of born-again optimism. Together with his commercial ally and fellow infantilizer George Lucas, Spielberg produced the quintessential entertainments for Ronald Reagan's Morning in America. While Lucas handled the military vision with *Star Wars* and its sequels, Spielberg provided the Indiana Jones foreign adventures and the suburban childhood romance.

The late '80s were a relatively rough patch for Spielberg. But the early '90s brought the apotheosis of the filmmaker's career—complete with his public identification with Bill Clinton, and vice versa. According to Spielberg biographer John Baxter, it was Warner Brothers executive Steve Ross—Spielberg's model for the character of Oskar Schindler—who converted the filmmaker to fervid Clinton supporter. After the 1992 election, Spielberg hosted the new president on several trips to Los Angeles; the world premiere of Spielberg's *Jurassic Park* (1993) was held in Washington, DC, as a benefit for Hillary Clinton's favorite charity, the Children's Defense Fund.

Reagan had laughingly plugged *Rambo*; Clinton tearfully endorsed *Schindler's List*. Who is to say that the movie did not provide him with a useful model, at least during his Balkan intervention? (Mrs. Clinton suggested as much on a 1999 trip to a Kosovar refugee camp.) In early 1994, the president joined the *Hollywood Reporter* in celebrating Spielberg's career: "From *Jaws* to *E.T.* to *Schindler's List,* his prolific work has made us laugh, cry, and believe in all the wonders of our imaginations. I join in honoring him for his unparalleled creativity and vision." Six months later, Spielberg spent the night at the White House—as part of a state dinner for Russian president Boris Yeltsin—and the next morning decided, along with two fellow guests, David Geffen and Jeffrey Katzenberg, to create a new studio, DreamWorks.

Thanks in part to Clinton's publicized friendships with Spielberg and other entertainment notables, the film industry proved a major source of Democratic fundraising. For the first time since the late 1940s, Hollywood even emerged as a political issue, most prominently for Senator Bob Dole's unsuccessful presidential campaign. Three of the Democrats' four leading contributors were movie studios or their parent companies, including DreamWorks (which ultimately would help raise $15 million during Clinton's term of office). Spielberg and his partners expressed a degree of post-Clinton donor fatigue during the 2000 campaign, but Spielberg's influence remained.

Soon after attaining the presidency, George W. Bush, not previously known for his interest in movies (or, indeed, any form of culture), cited *Saving Private Ryan* as his favorite motion picture—as well he might. One of the key Hollywood movies of the 1990s, notable for reviving the defunct genre of the "serious" combat film and proposing the army as a source of moral value, *Saving Private Ryan* expressed a potent new retro patriotism. Would American history have been changed if *Saving Private Ryan* had opened during the summer of 1996, with a genuine World War II hero running for president? (Perhaps it would only have been film history: Senator Dole had to be retired from politics—and pitching Viagra on TV—before the fantasy could fully be enjoyed.)

More than a tribute to the Greatest Generation, *Saving Private Ryan* was also a Hollywood movie's most ambitious attempt to wrest control of the national memory since Oliver Stone's *JFK*. With the Cold War over, Spielberg proposed a new raison d'être for American foreign policy. Not the liberation of Europe but rather saving a single enlisted man was, as one character put it, "the one decent thing we were able to pull out of this whole stinking mess" to "earn the right to go home." The movie thus articulated a tautology that Vietnam introduced into American political discourse—the purpose of the war is to support those troops that are already there.

Saving Private Ryan was an enormous commercial success, grossing well over $200 million. But as Bush's endorsement suggests, this World War II vision achieved canonical stature on his watch. Barely three years after the movie captured the nation's multiplexes, D-Day came home.

The histories of film and of what Jean-Luc Godard terms the "film of history" are parallel narratives. On September 11, 2001, the two intersected. For Americans, 9/11 was not only a national trauma and a political watershed but also an entertainment event—something viewed more or less simultaneously (and then repeatedly) by millions of people, something that would become as incantatory as the most persistent pop song.

Hollywood blockbusters are what bring us together as a nation—if not a planet—and spectacular mayhem is the mode's lingua franca. Thus, as a professional movie reviewer living six blocks north of the World Trade Center, my first impulse was to describe a disaster film, "the déjà vu of crowds fleeing Godzilla through Lower Manhattan canyons, the wondrously exploding skyscrapers and bellicose rhetoric of *Independence Day,* the romantic pathos of *Titanic,* the wounded innocence of *Pearl Harbor,* the cosmic insanity of *Deep Impact,* the sense of a world directed by Roland Emmerich for the benefit of Rupert Murdoch."

As an event, the only equivalent to 9/11 in American history is the four-day weekend of the Kennedy assassination. That too left its mark on Hollywood. Within days of the president's murder, newspapers published speculation that, with its brainwashed assassin, the 1962 movie *The Manchurian Candidate* might be implicated in the tragedy; visual references to the shooting that took place in Dallas would turn up in Hollywood movies less than two years later. The director Arthur Penn was responsible for several.

Awesomely telegenic as the terror attack on America was, and as amply anticipated as it had been by the catastrophic blockbusters of the fin-de-siècle, Hollywood took 9/11 very, very personally. The image had again remade the world. Hardly had the Trades fallen when the studios eagerly reported an FBI warning that they might well be the terrorists' next targets. On September 21, rumors of an impending attack swept Los Angeles. In the days following the disaster, the *Los Angeles Times* reported entertainment industry concern that "the public appetite for plots involving disasters and terrorism has vanished." What then would movies be about? Feeling guilty, industry leaders promised to produce a new form of socially responsible, positive filmmaking. One prominent producer of TV movies and miniseries hastily assured the *New York Times* that entertainment, post-9/11, would be "much more wholesome" and that "we are definitely moving into a kinder, gentler time." (Was that time, as his invocation of Bush I's nomination acceptance speech suggested, meant to be 1988?)

DreamWorks producer Walter Parkes explained that the present atmosphere precluded his studio from bankrolling any more movies like *The Peacemaker* and *Deep Impact*: "We make the movies that reflect, in one way or another, the experiences we all have. There are just some movies that you can't make from here on in." But wait... wasn't disaster something that we had just all experienced? Not everyone was as blunt or solipsistic as Robert Altman, who saw the terrorists as intellectual pirates, telling the Associated Press that the hijackers had copied Hollywood: "Nobody would have thought to commit an atrocity like that unless they'd seen it in a movie.... We created this atmosphere and taught them how to do it."

Hollywood expected to be punished. Instead, it was drafted. Soon after the attacks, the Pentagon-funded Institute for Creative Technologies at the University of Southern California, another "cannon shot" away from the studios, convened several meetings with screenwriters and directors. The proceedings were chaired by Brigadier General Kenneth Bergquist; the idea was for the industry talent to "brainstorm" terrorist scenarios and then offer solutions. (Elsewhere at the Pentagon, senior special operations officers were studying the urban guerrilla warfare depicted in *The Battle of Algiers*.)

In Congress, Representative Henry Hyde requested Hollywood's input into hearings on how the United States might successfully address the "hearts and minds" of the Arab world—a subject which would be satirized four years later by Albert Brooks's failed *Looking for Comedy in the Muslim World*. How could the movie industry resist the tacit invocation of World War II? Jerry Bruckheimer's *Pearl Harbor* had grossed $200 million in the spring and summer of 2001, but what truly seemed prophetic the day after September 11 was the movie's blend of blockbuster mega-disaster and historical war epic. *Black Hawk Down*, an artier Bruckheimer production, was rushed into theaters in late December and subsequently furnished on video to US military bases.

Throughout the winter of 2002, this visceral spectacle of US soldiers pinned down under Somali fire functioned as an exercise in virtual combat. Vice President Dick Cheney left his undisclosed location to join Secretary of Defense Donald Rumsfeld at the movie's gala Washington premiere. Rumsfeld even took a measure of credit: thanks to his personal intervention, *Black Hawk Down* was the first movie for which US troops were dispatched to a foreign country to aid in its production.

Black Hawk Down inspired patriotic sentiment, precipitated European ridicule, and invited antiwar protest, even as it stood in for the American debacle in Afghanistan that never quite happened. Nor was it the lone beneficiary of the new bellicosity. Upcoming war and action films were seized upon by the administration as useful metaphors as the administration waged war in Afghanistan and prepared to invade Iraq. Mel Gibson's Vietnam film *We Were Soldiers* and the Tom Clancy adaptation *The Sum of All Fears,* in which terrorists detonate a nuclear bomb in Baltimore, were treated as official art.

As *The Sum of All Fears* captured its second weekend, US Customs officials called a news conference to demonstrate their bomb-detection capability. The following Monday, Attorney General John Ashcroft issued his proud announcement that the currently beleaguered FBI and CIA had successfully collaborated on the arrest of one Abdullah al-Muhajir, born José Padilla in Brooklyn. Already detained for a month, Padilla was being held as a military prisoner and suspected of abetting an al Qaeda plot to produce the very scenario *The Sum of All Fears* so vividly illustrated.

All of these movies predated 9/11. Their inspiration came not from the attacks on New York and Washington or Team Bush's war on terror but the strong showing of *Saving Private Ryan,* which grossed $216 million and topped the box office for a month during the Lewinsky summer of '98, when Bill Clinton, too, was striving to show he was not just a lover but a fighter. If the universe loves coincidences, as Carl Jung maintained in his work on synchronicity, the dream life does so even more.

Having been announced on the eve of the millennium, as the Y2K panic was reaching its peak, Spielberg's science fiction policier *Minority Report* went into production in the spring of 2001 and wrapped that July. Fittingly, Spielberg's first post-9/11 release, premiering in June

2002, was a tale of precognitive police work that, as many reviewers pointed out, uncannily anticipated the attorney general's notions of preventative detention. This unexpectedly topical premise, taken from a 1956 story by Philip K. Dick, posits a future in which mutant "precogs" dream of murders before they occur, thus allowing the police to arrest killers in advance of their crimes.

"The guilty are arrested before the law is broken," per the movie's sell line. Thus, Spielberg expressed his own support for the extra-legality of Bush's war on terror.

Once the original shock and awe had worn off, Hollywood filmmakers naturally felt obliged to address the catastrophe. Given his role as the industry personified, how could Spielberg not find himself in the vanguard?

The aerial-conman comedy *Catch Me If You Can*—announced while *Minority Report* was shooting and put into production in February 2002 for Christmas release—had a certain post-9/11 resonance, harking back to the prehijacking days when air travel was innocent, sexy fun. But it was *The Terminal,* which opened in June 2004 and was the first Spielberg feature to have been entirely conceptualized during wartime, that inaugurated the director's post-9/11 trilogy of terror.

Based on the true story of an Iranian national stranded for years in a Paris airport, *The Terminal* directly—if squeamishly—addressed the new hell of air travel and America's corresponding fear of the foreign or Muslim-looking. The outlander, in this case, was Tom Hanks, winner of consecutive Oscars for playing the mentally challenged Forrest Gump and the AIDS-afflicted hero of *Philadelphia,* who need hardly have stretched his persona to portray one of Spielberg's benign, if not lovable, "others"—particularly as his previous role for the director was as the martyred leader and embodiment of American decency in *Saving Private Ryan.*

Part genius and part idiot, at once the hero and victim of globalism, Hanks's Viktor Navorski is an inadvertent refugee from an imaginary Balkan country who is unable to clear customs (and thus leave JFK) because of a midflight coup that has occurred back home in Krakozia. *The Terminal*'s press book quoted Spielberg's boilerplate assertion of his "immediate affinity" for Viktor's situation; it would be fascinating to know just what the filmmaker meant—was he feeling trapped, stateless, alien? Did he deem the new xenophobia and the profiling of foreigners justified?

"The country's detaining so many people there's no goddamn room anywhere," *The Terminal*'s mildly villainous airport manager complains—writing a check that the movie would never cash. Making Viktor a Middle Eastern, South Asian, or even Bosnian tourist might have given this unfunny comedy a political edge, as well as a measure of human pathos. But, according to Spielberg (or his publicist), "after *Catch Me If You Can*," the filmmaker "wanted to do another movie that could make you laugh and cry and feel good about the world."

In other words, *The Terminal* was designed as supremely comforting sociological propaganda. Angst is evoked to be dismissed. Our resourceful Viktor soon bonds with a multiethnic band of buddies. Hardly the terrifying jungle of the post-9/11 non-American world, *The Terminal*'s JFK is a petting zoo of multicultural cuteness. The melting pot has not melted away. Foreigners love us and we love them because Foreigners R Us. What's more, America Rools: it turns out that Viktor's reason for coming to America had nothing to do with politics or even economic opportunity. His old Krakozian daddy is the world's most devoted jazz fan, and Viktor wanted to secure a particular musician's autograph.

It may also be that Spielberg elected to spin *The Terminal*'s insipid absurdism as feel-good uplift because, by the time his new Patriot Act scenario opened, America had been at war in Iraq for more than a year. Indeed, the Pentagon even produced its own wildly (if only briefly) successful Spielberg scenario, attempting to personalize the war in the operation that would be known as *Saving Private Lynch*. A few weeks later, the president alighted on an aircraft carrier deck to proclaim our "mission accomplished." If that carefully choreographed performance was intended as the opening shot in Bush's upcoming presidential campaign, it was followed in September by Lionel Chetwynd's made-for-TV movie *DC 9/11: Time of Crisis*. Most of the principals were impersonated by look-alike actors—including Timothy Bottoms, who had previously played the president in the short-lived comedy series *That's My Bush!*

Even before 9/11 we were living an alternate national narrative. The purloined 2000 election—that other great, history-changing trauma—was buried in the rubble at Ground Zero. But as 9/11 rendered George W. Bush's dubious mandate divine, so Chetwynd's docudrama served as a legitimizing allegory. The Republican equivalent of *Fahrenheit 9/11, DC 9/11* appeared ten months earlier than Michael Moore's documentary, launching Bush's campaign with a preemptive fictionalizing strike. Tested by adversity, fictional Bush assumes control of the situation—putting a befuddled old Dick Cheney in his place and educating eager young Condoleezza Rice, while laying out American foreign policy for the next eighteen months. (The transformation of the nation's then-unelected leader into an action hero was paralleled by the most compelling Hollywood spectacle of the summer and fall— namely, the unprecedented blitzkrieg gubernatorial campaign waged by action hero Arnold Schwarzenegger.)

Hollywood's several liberal interventions into the 2004 presidential race largely avoided 9/11 and downplayed the war in Iraq. The disaster film *The Day After Tomorrow* blamed catastrophic climate changes on an American administration run by a bellicose anti-ecological vice president; Jonathan Demme's remade *Manchurian Candidate* advanced a sense of oil-fueled corporate conspiracy. As usual, Republicans far surpassed Democrats with their capacity to construct scenarios in life, rather than on theater screens. To reiterate only the most successful of these, volunteer Vietnam veteran John Kerry was effectively recast as a coward or worse, while the combat-averse Bush and Cheney were portrayed as resolute wartime leaders.

Although Spielberg consulted on one of Kerry's campaign films, he made no election-year statement per se. (In a sense, the extraordinary pageant of the Reagan funeral—subsuming all political conflict in a simplified, sentimental, personality-driven narrative—was the year's preeminent example of Spielbergization.) During the summer of 2004, the entertainment press reported Spielberg at work on a serious thriller—dealing with the 1972 massacre of Israeli athletes at the Munich Olympics and the clandestine Mossad campaign against the responsible Palestinian terrorists. Then, reportedly because the director feared this project itself might become a target for Islamic terrorists, the movie was postponed. In its place, Spielberg would remake the science fiction chestnut *War of the Worlds,* which went into production immediately after Bush's election.

No more lovable aliens. No less ambitious than the Republican candidate, Spielberg sought to invoke the trauma that was said to have precipitated America's current war and, not coincidentally, scare the bejesus out of the American public. "The whole thing is very experiential," Spielberg told reporters during the course of an on-set press conference. *War of the Worlds* would also be universal. Everyone on earth, Spielberg confidently predicted, could "relate to the [movie's] point of view, because it's about a family trying to survive and stay together... surrounded by the most epically horrendous events you could possibly imagine."

War of the Worlds was released in late June 2005 amid a surge of urban terror and fratricidal violence—*in Iraq,* where the number of civilian casualties in the two years since Bush's "Mission Accomplished" announcement now approached 25,000. As his particular mission, Spielberg promised something more than entertainment: dealing with the specter of interplanetary combat, *War of the Worlds* would not be *Starship Troopers* and "certainly not" the belligerent unofficial Wells remake, *Independence Day*: "We take it much more seriously than that," he said. *War of the Worlds* was "ultra-realistic, as ultra-realistic as I've ever attempted to make a movie, in terms of its documentary style."

What did Spielberg mean? While suitably fantastic in its representation of cosmic jihad, *War of the Worlds* was striking for staging the initial Martian attack on an actual New Jersey working-class city just across the Hudson from lower Manhattan. "Is it the terrorists!?!?!?!" child star Dakota Fanning cried in the first of many piercing shrieks. Nor was hers the lone "documentary" allusion to America's worst day. The movie's references to Martian "sleeper cells," not to mention its mise-en-scène of bewildered, dust-coated survivors and homemade "missing" posters, struck some reviewers as an outrageously tasteless trivialization.

And yet, as effectively Bad Steven as the movie's opening scenes certainly were, *War of the Worlds* ultimately resolved the horrible events it represented. The narrative trajectory was informed by a particular political logic. In tracking the emotional development of the frightened child's father (Tom Cruise) from callow, immature hotshot to responsible mensch, *War of the Worlds* provided an allegory, if not a defense, of George W. Bush's crisis-inspired growth into leadership—or at least the audience's willingness to grant him that growth. Screenwriter David Koepp's alternate reading, which followed Wells's own, suggested that *War of the Worlds* showed "how US military interventionism abroad is doomed by insurgency." But to see that movie—in which Martian vampire slugs stood in for American combat units, with Cruise as a surrogate Shiite paterfamilias—one would need to fight an internal revolution against years of Hollywood-inculcated narrative expectations.

War of the World's specific, "documentary" mise-en-scène left no room for ambiguity. Even Bill O'Reilly got the point: "Influenced by the death and destruction visited upon us by the Islamic killers…this isn't the usual Hollywood cheap-shot leftist propaganda. *War of the Worlds* actually reflects the view of everyday Americans rather than a few Beverly Hills pinheads." America took the hit and even the least likely among us rose to the occasion. *War of the Worlds* proved to be Spielberg's highest-grossing success since his 1997 sequel to *Jurassic Park*.

Munich began shooting the day *War of the Worlds* opened—it is in many respects that earlier movie's reiteration—and wrapped in early fall. Announcing itself as tragedy with the bombastic fanfare of a faux Jewish lament, *Munich* shows a gang of Palestinian terrorists scaling the wall of the Olympic Village to storm the Israeli compound, shooting some athletes and holding the rest hostage. The games continue, even as the whole world watches the debacle on TV. Spielberg compresses the gist of the 1999 Oscar-winning documentary *One Day in September* into a superbly edited McLuhanite frenzy; as with *Saving Private Ryan*, nothing else in the movie can match its opening.

This catastrophe is followed not by panicky flight, as in *War of the Worlds,* but, like *Saving Private Ryan,* with methodical vengeance. In the first of many unlikely but metaphorically charged scenes, Golda Meir personally organizes a Mossad hit squad, to be led by her favorite bodyguard, code-named Avner (Eric Bana). The team is given eleven targets; their mission takes them from Rome to Paris to Cyprus to Beirut to Athens to London. The source for this narrative, coyly denied by Spielberg until the moment of the movie's release, was George Jonas's 1984 *Vengeance*—an oft-disputed and essentially unverifiable account of the operation, told to the author by the pseudonymous Avner.

As in *Vengeance* and its 1986 HBO adaptation, *Sword of Gideon*, *Munich*'s commandos are both supercompetent and morally confused. Perhaps even *more* perplexed, as they are essentially functioning in the world of 2005. The terrifying introduction, with a band of Palestinian terrorists storming the Israeli compound in the Olympic Village, is the most powerful scene in the movie in part because it conjures up the hitherto only imagined hijacking of four American airliners on September 11. And like *Saving Private Ryan*'s D-Day, it whets a frightened audience's desire for revenge.

On one hand, and in what Spielberg might characterize as an example of "ultra-realism," the terrorists of that other Black September are typically evoked in terms that blatantly anticipate al Qaeda. On the other, in a more fantastic mode, *Munich* doggedly seeks to humanize these Palestinian others. Neither the lovable outlanders of *The Terminal* nor the terrifying aliens of *War of the Worlds*, the movie's semidifferentiated Palestinians represent a new dialectic, united with their Israeli enemy in common victimhood.

Much of the blame for this "moral equivalence" was assigned to screenwriter Tony Kushner, an outspoken critic of Israeli policy and, in a sense, heir to the left-wing screenwriters of the 1940s. Replying to his own critics, Spielberg made the suggestive gaffe of defending himself against "the sin of moral equivocation." And *Munich*'s least convincing, most utopian scene is pure Spielberg in its search for common ground... in America. Thanks to the mysterious French anarchist family who furnishes Avner's team with their information (don't ask), the Mossadniks are tricked into sharing an Athens safe house with a group of equally unwitting PLO operatives. The result is an Oslo summit that dare not speak its name: "You don't know what it is not to have a home," one Palestinian tells Avner, as Al Green croons his 1972 hit "Let's Stay Together" obtrusively in the background. This pop anthem addresses us all.

Although strongly criticized by American neoconservatives, *Munich* has relatively little to do with Israel per se—except insofar as it expresses the ambivalence felt by many American Jews regarding the Jewish state. "You are what we prayed for," Avner's mother (Israeli icon Gila Almagor) reassures the haunted hero, thus suggesting that in his brute application of justice he is a successor to the Golem of Prague. But not even she wants to know just what her guilt-ridden son did.

In Spielberg's dramatization, the Mossad mission prophesies Bush's—but without promising any resolution. "Every man we kill is replaced by worse," the unhappy Avner warns. "There is no peace at the end of this."

Munich has been praised as the most downbeat, and thus least Hollywood, movie Spielberg's ever made. However harrowing in parts, *Schindler's List* and *Saving Private Ryan* both contrived (as the filmmaker would say of *The Terminal*) to make you laugh, cry, and feel good about the world. No such consolation exists here: on the eve of the Oscars, Spielberg spun *Munich* as "a prayer for peace." But rather, it seems the filmmaker's cri de coeur, an unhappy justification for the war against terrorism.

Largely uncommented on, in the substantial op-ed midrash that has attached itself to the film's text, is *Munich's* implicit suggestion that there is an Israeli connection to Bush's war and that this connection is intrinsic. *Syriana,* last year's other serious movie about terror and the Middle East, solves this problem by leaving Israel out of the equation altogether. *Munich,* however, makes it clear that we defend Israel because *we could be next*—and, as the final shot of the lower Manhattan skyline makes abundantly clear, we were! In a unique spin on Old Testament foreshadowing, the war on terror that the movie shows to have been initiated by the Israelis is now ours to complete.

Like *The Terminal* and no less than *War of the Worlds, Munich* seeks to express support for an American foreign policy doctrine. The difference, in *Munich's* case, is that this policy is a policy that it (or Spielberg) cannot support. Small wonder that the movie is so depressed. How does one dramatize opposition to the war? Has even one prominent Democratic politician provided a clue? More to the point, how does one make the rational intervention Spielberg dreamed of making without sacrificing the emotional manipulation that is the filmmaker's stock-in-trade? Let's stay together, indeed.

Back in 1943, Darryl Zanuck had called for propaganda dressed in "the glittering robes of entertainment." But that star-spangled cloak brings its own ideological imperative. Entertainment—as Spielberg would naturally understand it—is permission to escape, as it were, into an improved reality. Thus, for much of the Bush administration, TV's

The West Wing functioned as a virtual liberal presidency. (And, per-haps in time for the 2008 election, Spielberg has begun to contemplate the nature of a good-war presidency. Among his upcoming projects is a biography of Abraham Lincoln, starring Liam "Schindler" Neeson.) As one Hollywood wag cracked on the occasion of the last Oscar presen-tations, the Academy of Motion Picture Arts and Sciences is the only branch of government the Democrats still control.

Searching for improved reality, *Munich* can address the Bush wars only indirectly and by first providing a tragic justification for those wars. The fantasy of contrition serves as an ending. The movies may alter history in its representation—or provide an alternative history. But the only world they really change is their own.

In the Blink of an Eye

(selection)

Walter Murch

CUTS AND SHADOW CUTS

t is frequently at the edges of things that we learn most about the middle: ice and steam can reveal more about the nature of water than water alone ever could. While it is true that any film worth making is going to be unique, and the conditions under which films are made are so variable that it is misleading to speak about what is "normal," *Apocalypse Now*, by almost any criteria—schedule, budget, artistic ambition, technical innovation—qualifies as the cinematic equivalent of ice and steam. Just considering the length of time it took to complete the film (I was editing picture for one year and spent another year preparing and mixing the sound), it turned out to be the longest post-production of any picture I have worked on, but that may consequently spill some light on what "normal" is, or might be.*

One of the reasons for that length was simply the amount of film that had been printed: 1,250,000 feet, which works out to be just over 230 hours. Since the finished film runs just under two hours and twenty-five minutes in length, that gives a ratio of ninety-five to one.

---

* And I had come on relatively late in the process. Richie Marks and Jerry Greenberg had already been editing for nine months when I joined them in August 1977, a few months after the end of shooting, and the three of us worked together until Jerry left in the spring of 1978. Richie and I then continued together, joined by Lisa Fruchtman, until I began to work on the soundtrack.

That is to say, ninety-five "unseen" minutes for every minute that found its way into the finished product. By comparison, the average ratio for theatrical features is around twenty to one.

Traveling across that ninety-five-to-one landscape was a little like forging through a thick forest, bursting upon open grassland for a while, then plunging into a forest again because there were areas, such as the helicopter sequences, where the coverage was extremely high, and other scenes where the coverage was correspondingly low. I think the Colonel Kilgore scenes alone were over 220,000 feet—and since that represents twenty-five minutes of film in the finished product, the ratio there was around one hundred to one. But many of the connecting scenes had only a master shot: Francis had used so much film and time on the big events that he compensated with minimal coverage on some of these linking scenes.

Take one of the big scenes as an example: the helicopter attack on Charlie's Point, where Wagner's "Ride of the Valkyries" is played, was staged as an actual event and consequently filmed as a documentary rather than a series of specially composed shots. It was choreography on a vast scale of men, machines, cameras, and landscape—like some kind of diabolical toy that you could wind up and then let go. Once Francis said "Action," the filming resembled actual combat: eight cameras turning simultaneously (some on the ground and some in helicopters), each loaded with a thousand-foot (eleven-minute) roll of film.

At the end of one of those shots, unless there had been an obvious problem, the camera positions were changed and the whole thing was repeated. Then repeated again, and then again. They kept on going until, I guess, they felt that they had enough material, each take generating something like eight thousand feet (an hour and a half). No single take was the same as any other—very much like documentary coverage.

Anyway, at the end of it all, when the film was safely in theaters, I sat down and figured out the total number of days that we (the editors) had worked, divided that number by the number of cuts that were in the finished product, and came up with the rate of cuts per editor per day—which turned out to be . . . 1.47!

Meaning that, if we had somehow known *exactly* where we were going at the beginning, we would have arrived there in the same number of months if each of us had made just under one-and-a-half splices per day. In other words, if I had sat down at my bench in the morning, made one cut, thought about the next cut, and gone home, then come in the next day, made the cut I thought about the day before, made another cut, and gone home, it would have taken me the same year it actually took to edit my sections of the film.

Since it takes under ten seconds to make one-and-a-half splices, the admittedly special case of *Apocalypse Now* serves to throw into exaggerated relief the fact that editing—even on a "normal" film*—is not so much a *putting together* as it is a *discovery of a path*, and that the overwhelming majority of an editor's time is not spent actually splicing film. The more film there is to work with, of course, the greater the number of pathways that can be considered, and the possibilities compound upon each other and consequently demand more time for evaluation. This is true for any film with a high shooting ratio, but in the particular case of *Apocalypse* the effect was magnified by a sensitive subject matter and a daring and unusual structure, technical innovations at every level, and the obligation felt by all concerned to do the very best work they were capable of. And perhaps most of all by the fact that this was, for Francis, a personal film, despite the large budget and the vast canvas of the subject. Regrettably few films combine such qualities and aspirations.

For every splice in the finished film there were probably fifteen "shadow" splices—splices made, considered, and then undone or lifted from the film. But even allowing for that, the remaining eleven hours and fifty-eight minutes of each working day were spent in activities that, in their various ways, served to clear and illuminate the path ahead of us: screenings, discussions, rewinding, rescreenings, meetings, scheduling, filing trims, note-taking, bookkeeping, and lots of plain deliberative thought. A vast amount of preparation, really, to arrive at the innocuously brief moment of decisive action: the cut— the moment of transition from one shot to the next—something that, appropriately enough, should look almost self-evidently simple and effortless, if it is even noticed at all.

---

* By comparison, an average theatrical feature might have a cuts-per-day figure of eight.

WHY DO CUTS WORK?

Well, the fact is that *Apocalypse Now*, as well as every other theatrical film (except perhaps Hitchcock's *Rope**), is made up of many different pieces of film joined together into a mosaic of images. The mysterious part of it, though, is that the joining of those pieces—the "cut" in American terminology†—actually does seem to work, even though it represents a total and instantaneous displacement of one field of vision with another, a displacement that sometimes also entails a jump forward or backward in time as well as space.

It works; but it could easily have been otherwise, since nothing in our day-to-day experience seems to prepare us for such a thing. Instead, from the moment we get up in the morning until we close our eyes at night, the visual reality we perceive is a continuous stream of linked images: in fact, for millions of years—tens, hundreds of millions of years—life on earth has experienced the world this way. Then suddenly, at the beginning of the twentieth century, human beings were confronted with something else—edited film.

Under these circumstances, it wouldn't have been at all surprising to find that our brains had been "wired" by evolution and experience to reject film editing. If that had been the case, then the single-shot movies of the Lumière brothers—or films like Hitchcock's *Rope*—would have become the standard. For a number of practical (as well as artistic) reasons, it is good that it did not.

The truth of the matter is that film is actually being "cut" twenty-four times a second. Each frame is a displacement from the previous one—it is just that in a continuous shot, the space/time displacement from frame to frame is small enough (twenty milliseconds) for the audience to see it as *motion within a context* rather than as twenty-four different contexts a second. On the other hand, when the visual displacement is great enough (as at the moment of the cut), we are forced

---

* A film composed of only ten shots, each ten minutes long, invisibly joined together, so that the impression is of a complete lack of editing.

† I was aware, talking to an Australian audience, of the bias inherent in our respective languages. In the States, film is "cut," which puts the emphasis on *separation*. In Australia (and in Great Britain), film is "joined," with the emphasis on *bringing together*.

to reevaluate the new image as a *different context*: miraculously, most of the time we have no problem in doing this.

What we *do* seem to have difficulty accepting are the kind of displacements that are neither subtle nor total: cutting from a full-figure master shot, for instance, to a slightly tighter shot that frames the actors from the ankles up. The new shot in this case is different enough to signal that *something* has changed, but not different enough to make us reevaluate its context: the displacement of the image is neither motion nor change of context, and the collision of these two ideas produces a mental jarring—a jump—that is comparatively disturbing.*

At any rate, the discovery early in this century that certain kinds of cutting "worked" led almost immediately to the discovery that films could be shot discontinuously, which was the cinematic equivalent of the discovery of flight: in a practical sense, films were no longer "earthbound" in time and space. If we could make films only by assembling all the elements simultaneously, as in the theater, the range of possible subjects would be comparatively narrow. Instead, Discontinuity is King: it is the central fact during the production phase of filmmaking, and almost all decisions are directly related to it in one way or another—how to overcome its difficulties and/or how to best take advantage of its strengths.†

The other consideration is that even if everything *were* available simultaneously, it is just very difficult to shoot long, continuous takes and have all the contributing elements work each time. European filmmakers tend to shoot more complex master shots than the Americans, but even if you are Ingmar Bergman, there's a limit to what you can handle: right at the end, some special effect might not work or someone

---

* A beehive can apparently be moved two inches each night without disorienting the bees the next morning. Surprisingly, if it is moved two *miles*, the bees also have no problem: they are forced by the total displacement of their environment to reorient their sense of direction, which they can do easily enough. But if the hive is moved two *yards*, the bees will become fatally confused. The environment does not seem different to them, so they do not reorient themselves, and as a result, they will not recognize their own hive when they return from foraging, hovering instead in the empty space where the hive used to be, while the hive itself sits just two yards away.

† When Stanley Kubrick was directing *The Shining*, he wanted to shoot the film in continuity and to have all sets and actors available all the time. He took over almost the entire studio at Elstree (London), built all the sets simultaneously, and they sat there, prelit, for however long it took him to shoot the film. But *The Shining* remains a special exception to the general rule of discontinuity.

might forget their lines or some lamp might blow a fuse, and now the whole thing has to be done again. The longer the take, of course, the greater the chances of a mistake.

So there is a considerable logistical problem of getting everything together at the same time, and then just as serious a problem in getting it all to "work" every time. The result is that, for practical reasons alone, we don't follow the pattern of the Lumière brothers or of *Rope*.

On the other hand, apart from matters of convenience, discontinuity also allows us to choose the best camera angle for each emotion and story point, which we can edit together for a cumulatively greater impact. If we were limited to a continuous stream of images, this would be difficult, and films would not be as sharp and to the point as they are.*

And yet, beyond even these considerations, cutting is more than just the convenient means by which discontinuity is rendered continuous. It is in *and for itself*—by the very force of its paradoxical suddenness—a positive influence in the creation of a film. We would want to cut even if discontinuity were not of such great practical value.

So the central fact of all this is that cuts *do work*. But the question still remains: *Why?* It is kind of like the bumblebee, which should not be able to fly, but does.

DRAGNET

If it is true that our rates and rhythms of blinking refer directly to the rhythm and sequence of our inner emotions and thoughts, then those rates and rhythms are insights into our inner selves and, therefore, as

---

* Visual discontinuity—although not in the temporal sense—is the most striking feature of ancient Egyptian painting. Each part of the human body was represented by its most characteristic and revealing angle: head in profile, shoulders frontal, arms and legs in profile, torso frontal—and then all these different angles were combined in one figure. To us today, with our preference for the unifying laws of perspective, this gives an almost comic "twisted" look to the people of ancient Egypt—but it may be that in some remote future, our films, with their combination of many different angles (each being the most "revealing" for its particular subject), will look just as comic and twisted.

characteristic of each of us as our signatures. So if an actor is success-ful at projecting himself into the emotions and thoughts of a character, his blinks will *naturally and spontaneously* occur at the point that the character's blinks would have occurred in real life.*

I believe this is what I was finding with Hackman's performance in *The Conversation*—he had assumed the character of Harry Caul, was thinking a series of Harry's thoughts the way Harry would think them, and, therefore, was blinking in rhythm with those thoughts. And since I was absorbing the rhythms he was giving me and trying to think sim-ilar thoughts myself, my cut points were naturally aligning themselves with his "blink points." In a sense, I had rerouted my neural circuitry so that the semi-involuntary command to blink caused me instead to hit the stop button on the editing machine.

To that same end, one of the disciplines I follow is to choose the "out point" of a shot by marking it in real time. If I can't do this—if I can't hit the same frame repeatedly at twenty-four frames per second—I know there is something wrong in my approach to the shot, and I adjust my thinking until I find a frame I *can* hit. I never permit myself to select the "out point" by inching back and forth, comparing one frame with another to get the best match. That method—for me, at any rate—is guaranteed to produce a rhythmic "tone deafness" in the film.

Anyway, another one of your tasks as an editor is this "sensitizing" of yourself to the rhythms that the (good) actor gives you, and then finding ways to extend these rhythms into territory not covered by the actor himself, so that the pacing of the film as a whole is an elabora-tion of those patterns of thinking and feeling. And one of the many ways you assume those rhythms is by noticing—consciously or uncon-sciously—where the actor blinks.

There is a way of editing that ignores all of these questions, what I would call the *Dragnet* system, from the 1950s TV series of the same name.

---

* One of the things about unsuccessful acting is that the actor's blinks seem to come at the "wrong" times. Although you may not notice this consciously, the rhythm of the actor's blinks don't match the rhythm of thoughts you would expect from the character he is playing. In fact, a bad actor is probably not thinking anything like what the character would be thinking. Instead: "I wonder what the director thinks of me, I wonder if I look okay," or "What's my next line?"

The policy of the show seemed to be to keep every word of dialogue onscreen. When someone had finished speaking, there was a brief pause and then a cut to the person who was now about to talk, and when he in turn finished speaking there was a cut back to the first person, who nodded his head or said something, and then when *that* person was finished, they cut back again, etc. It extended to single words. "Have you been downtown yet?" *Cut.* "No." *Cut.* "When are you going downtown?" *Cut.* "Tomorrow." *Cut.* "Have you seen your son?" *Cut.* "No, he didn't come home last night." *Cut.* "What time does he usually come home?" *Cut.* "Two o'clock." At the time, when it first came out, this technique created a sensation for its apparently hard-boiled, police-blotter realism.

The *Dragnet* system is a simple way to edit, but it is a shallow simplicity that doesn't reflect the grammar of complex exchanges that go on all the time in even the most ordinary conversations. If you're observing a dialogue between two people, you will not focus your attention solely on the person who is speaking. Instead, *while that person is still talking*, you will turn to look at the listener to find out what he thinks of what is being said. The question is, "When exactly do you turn?"

There are places in conversation where it seems we almost physically *cannot* blink or turn our heads (since we are still receiving important information), and there are other places where we *must* blink or turn away in order to make better sense of what we have received. And I would suggest that there are similar points in every scene where the cut *cannot* or *must* occur, and for the same reasons. Every shot has potential "cut points" the way a tree branches, and once you have identified them, you will choose different points depending on what the audience has been thinking up to that moment and what you want them to think next.

For instance, by cutting away from a certain character *before* he finishes speaking, I might encourage the audience to think only about the face value of what he said. On the other hand, if I linger on the character *after* he finishes speaking, I allow the audience to see, from the expression in his eyes, that he is probably not telling the truth, and they will think differently about him and what he said. But since it takes a *certain amount of time* to make that observation, I cannot cut away from the character too early: either I cut away while he is speaking (branch number one) or I hold until the audience realizes he is lying (branch number two), but *I cannot cut in between those two branches*—to do so would either seem too long or not long enough. The branch points are fixed organically by the rhythm of the shot itself and by what the audience has been thinking up to that moment in the film,* but I am free to select one or the other of them (or yet another one further on) depending on what realization I want the audience to make.

In this way, you should be able to cut from the speaker to the listener and vice versa in psychologically interesting, complex, and "correct" patterns that reflect the kinds of shifts of attention and realization that go on in real life: in this way, you establish a rhythm that counterpoints and underscores the ideas being expressed or considered. And one of the tools to identify exactly where these cut points, these "branches," may be is to compare them to our patterns of blinking, which have been underscoring the rhythm of our thoughts for tens of thousands, perhaps millions, of years of human history. Where you feel comfortable blinking—if you are really listening to what is being said—is where the cut will feel right.

So there are really three problems wrapped up together:

1. identifying a series of potential cut points (and comparisons with the blink can help you do this),
2. determining what effect each cut point will have on the audience, and
3. choosing which of those effects is the correct one for the film.

I believe the sequence of thoughts—that is to say, the rhythm and rate of cutting—should be appropriate to whatever the audience is watching at the moment. The average "real-world" rate of blinking is somewhere between the extremes of four and forty blinks per minute. If you are in an actual fight, you will be blinking dozens of times a minute because you are thinking dozens of conflicting thoughts a minute—and so when you are watching a fight in a film, there should be dozens of cuts per minute.† In fact, statistically the two rates—of

---

* One way to shift the actual branch points themselves is to place the shot in a different context, where the audience will be thinking (and noticing) different things.

† This would make the audience participate emotionally in the fight itself. If, on the other hand, you wanted to create an objective distance—to have the audience observe the fight as a phenomenon in itself—then you would reduce the number of cuts considerably.

real-life blinking and of film cutting—are close enough for comparison: depending on how it is staged, a convincing action sequence might have around twenty-five cuts a minute, whereas a dialogue scene would still feel "normal" (in an American film) averaging six cuts per minute or less.

You should be right with the blinks, perhaps leading them ever so slightly. I certainly don't expect the audience to blink at every cut—the cut point should be a *potential* blink point. In a sense, by cutting, by this sudden displacement of the visual field, you are blinking *for* the audience: you achieve the immediate juxtaposition of two concepts for them—what they achieve in the real world by blinking.

Your job is partly to anticipate, partly to control the thought processes of the audience. To give them what they want and/or what they need just before they have to "ask" for it—to be surprising yet self-evident at the same time. If you are too far behind or ahead of them, you create problems, but if you are right with them, leading them ever so slightly, the flow of events feels natural and exciting at the same time.

A GALAXY OF WINKING DOTS

Along these lines, it would be fascinating to take an infrared film of an audience and find out when and in what patterns people blink when they are watching a movie. My hunch is that if an audience is really in the grip of a film, they are going to be thinking (and therefore blinking) with the rhythm of the film.

There is a wonderful effect that you can produce if you shine infrared light directly out in line with the lens of a camera. All animal eyes (including human eyes) will bounce a portion of that light directly back into the camera, and you will see bright glowing dots where the eyes are: it is a version of the "red-eye" effect in family snapshots taken with flashbulbs.

If you took a high-contrast infrared motion picture of an audience watching a film, placing the camera on stage and aligning the light source directly with the camera, you would see a galaxy of these dots against a field of black. And when someone in the audience blinked, you would see a momentary interruption in a pair of these dots.

If it were true, if there *were* times when those thousand dots winked more or less in unison, the filmmaker would have an extremely powerful tool at his disposal. Coherent blinking would be a strong indication that the audience was thinking together and that the film was working. But when the blinking became scattered, it would indicate that he may have lost his audience, that they had begun to think about where to go for dinner, or whether their car was parked in a safe place, etc.

When people are deeply "in" a film, you'll notice that nobody coughs at certain moments, even though they may have a cold. If the coughing were purely an autonomic response to smoke or congestion, it would be randomly constant, no matter what was happening onscreen. But the audience holds back at certain moments, and I'm suggesting that blinking is something like coughing in this sense. There is a famous live recording of pianist Sviatoslav Richter playing Mussorgsky's *Pictures at an Exhibition* during a flu epidemic in Bulgaria many years ago. It is just as plain as day what's going on: while he was playing certain passages, no one coughed. At those moments, he was able to suppress, with his artistry, the coughing impulse of 1,500 sick people.

I think this subconscious attention to the blink is also something that you would probably find as a hidden factor in everyday life. One thing that may make you nervous about a particular person is that you feel, without knowing it, that his blinking is wrong. "He's blinking too much" or "He's not blinking enough" or "He's blinking at the wrong time." Which means he is not really listening to you, thinking along with you.

Whereas somebody who is really focused on what you are saying will blink at the "right" places at the "right" rate, and you will feel comfortable in this person's presence. I think we know these things intuitively, subconsciously, without having to be told, and I wouldn't be surprised to find that it is part of our built-in strategy for dealing with each other.

When we suggest that someone is a bad actor, we are certainly not saying that he is a bad human being; we are just saying that this person is not as fully *in* the character as he wants us to believe, and he's nervous about it. You can see this clearly in political campaigns, where there is sometimes a vivid distinction between who somebody is and who they want the voters to believe they are: something will always be "wrong" with the rate and moment that these people blink.

That brings me back to one of the central responsibilities of the editor, which is to establish an interesting, coherent rhythm of emotion and thought—on the tiniest and the largest scales—that allows the audience to trust, to give themselves to the film. Without their knowing why, a poorly edited film will cause the audience to hold back, unconsciously saying to themselves, "There's something scattered and nervous about the way the film is thinking, the way it presents itself. I don't want to think that way; therefore, I'm not going to give as much of myself to the film as I might." Whereas a good film that is well edited seems like an exciting extension and elaboration of the audience's own feelings and thoughts, and they will therefore give themselves to it, as it gives itself to them.

"One Hang, We All Hang":
High Plains Drifter

Richard Hutson

n his biography of Clint Eastwood, Richard Schickel tends to defend and champion Eastwood on the basis of a statement he made about deciding to star in Don Siegel's *Dirty Harry*. After the script had been turned down by Paul Newman "on political grounds," Eastwood was asked if he was interested, to which he replied, "Well, I don't have any political affiliations . . . so send it over."[1] Nevertheless, hardly any critic has been able to refrain from interpreting, criticizing, or defending Eastwood's highly politically charged films. Paul Smith noted that, from around 1970, with a couple of Dirty Harry films and Eastwood's own early directorial efforts in *High Plains Drifter*, critics were characterizing Eastwood as a fascist, and right-wing commentators were championing Eastwood as one of their own.[2] Eastwood more or less always claimed that he was merely trying to entertain, and clearly one of his basic motives was to set himself up, like Harry Callahan, as an "in-your-face" adversary to whatever he and his co-workers perceived as the cultural hype of the times. Eastwood, clearly sensitive to the politically left critics, spent time in the early seventies defending himself against the charge of fascism that was coming from many different sources. Schickel quotes a dictionary definition of fascism (Schickel, *Clint Eastwood*, 274) to prove that Dirty Harry could not possibly be a fascist character, but the concept is defined so narrowly and vaguely as to be of little use in American culture of the late sixties and early seventies. The utter contempt that the lone Eastwood character displays for whatever establishment he encounters could also be an American form of fascism, with its hatred of women and of the middle class, what proto-Nazis referred to, according to Klaus Theweleit, as "'the slimy mire of bourgeois life.'"[3] The individual, who performs police work on his own, against the bureaucracy, presents himself, in fact, as the heroic defender of the bourgeois status quo. In this perspective, the central authority of the status quo needs the outsider who is also, it turns out, the insider. Schickel goes on to suggest precisely this point—that the lone-outsider type of superhero belongs to the official, perhaps "covert," dominant culture of mainstream America (Schickel, *Clint Eastwood*, 275). Don Siegel's and Clint Eastwood's films, in the popular response, could serve as a preface to the right-wing takeover of US politics with Ronald Reagan's becoming president in 1980.

But by starring in and making genre films, such as detective stories or Westerns, Eastwood also indicated his knowledge of the traditions of American popular culture. Genre films refer to two different realities: the genre tradition, with its cast of characters and story structures, and, if they are to be seen as historically important, the external world of the cultural discourses from the era of their production. And to claim that Eastwood has always been perceived politically entails understanding that his films have been seen as important.

In a 1984 interview with the French scholar and critic Michael Henry [Wilson], Eastwood claims that "the starting point" for the screenplay of *High Plains Drifter* was: "'What would have happened if the sheriff [*sic*] of *High Noon* had been killed? What would have happened afterwards?' In the treatment by Ernest Tidyman, the sheriff's brother came back to avenge the sheriff[,] and the villagers were as contemptible and selfish as in *High Noon*." Eastwood adds that he changed the concept of the brother so that "you would never know whether the brother in question is a diabolic being or a kind of archangel. It's up to the audience to draw their own conclusions."[4] In this view, Eastwood conceived of his film as a counterfactual sequel to *High Noon*, with additional inspiration from Sergio Leone's Dollars trilogy. Tidyman and Eastwood could also have had Anthony Mann's *The Man from Laramie* (1955) in mind, a narrative about a military brother, a captain, who comes into a frontier community to investigate the circumstances in which his brother was killed. In addition, there appear to be references to William S. Hart's *Hell's Hinges* (1916) and to other films as well.

The interviewer, Henry, had suggested that "visually and thematically[,] *High Plains Drifter* evokes the Sergio Leone Westerns, but you appear to have wanted to exorcise this past while going even further in excess and cruelty." But Eastwood claims that he wanted a narrative that would be "less fragmented" than Leone's. He saw Leone's films as a "series of vignettes that were rather loosely linked."[5] Eastwood could base his narrative on a specific previous narrative, *High Noon*, and then, fugue-like or pastiche-like, allude to or appropriate details from different films.

High Noon pits a heroic marshal, Will Kane, against a community of good citizens unwilling to support him when a killer who had promised to kill the marshal returns. The film brilliantly turned the conventional drama in Westerns between a good guy and a bad guy into a conflict between the town's highly respected citizen-marshal and the town itself. Once the killer, Frank Miller, is released from jail, the community of citizens hides behind the fallacy of misplaced concreteness and refuses to help Kane, claiming that the conflict is strictly between Kane and Miller, and advises Kane to leave town quickly, before Miller arrives. The important drama is between hero and community, with the film questioning the nature and motives of the community rather than emphasizing the hero. Scholar-critics have been tempted to focus on the figure that Eastwood represents both in *High Plains Drifter* and in his Leone trilogy, "the mysterious kind of character who has everything under control."[6] No doubt, that character, with his "insolence of confidence," is what a moviegoer sees primarily.[7] But I think that, like *High Noon*, *High Plains Drifter* presents a portrait of a community that has an amazingly rich and complicated resonance in the history of Westerns in the United States, not to mention the fact that the theme and practice of community in America, its hopes and liability to disintegration, hark back to the very beginning of European settlement in America, as in William Bradford's *Of Plymouth Plantation* (ca. 1650), for instance. It was the portrait of the community and of Will Kane throwing down his badge at the end of the film that generated John Wayne's famous diatribe that *High Noon* was "the most un-American thing I've ever seen in my whole life. . . . I'll never regret having helped run Foreman [Carl Foreman, the screenwriter] out of this country."[8] But Wayne seems to have had a severely limited grasp of American history and American cinema.

What stands out in *High Plains Drifter* is the devastating portrait of a frontier community, despite the perspective of the film forcing spectators to be on the side of the isolated drifter, the catalyst, if not the destroyer, of a corrupt social entity. Not even Robert Altman, usually considered the filmmaker most negative about the United States in this era, in *McCabe and Mrs. Miller* (1971), presented such a negative portrait of a frontier town. Something was going on in American culture at the time that generated serious critiques of a fundamental mythology about American identity (the Turner thesis, for instance), that American democracy was founded, maintained, and continually renewed in these frontier communities. For Altman as for Eastwood, these communities represent the decadent, business-dominated, greed-driven motives of frontier communities.

The three murderous thugs, the pathological Stacy Bridges and his cousins, are members of this community, although as Mordecai, the town dwarf, remembers on the night of the murder, they ride into town in the dark, whip the marshal to death, and ride out again, so that the town can claim, as Sheriff Sam does, that the murderer "wasn't anybody from this town" and that the citizens of Lago are "good people," "god-fearin' people" living in "a god-fearin' town." And now the thugs are returning to Lago from their year in prison to demand a year's back wages, having carried out the orders of the company officials. As we learn from Sheriff Sam, Stacy and the Carlin brothers were hired by the Lago Mining Company as "what you call 'trouble shooters.'" Callie Travers, now living with Morg Allen, one of the company owners, had been Stacy's woman before he was sent to jail. Stacy and his cousins expose the inner sadistic criminal motives of the community because their minds can imagine justice or recompense only as violence against the people who used them, just as the company would respond to the threat of exposure only with violence. This primitive horde of men with a family relationship can be found in Westerns as far back as James Fenimore Cooper's *The Prairie*, and became especially common in post–World War II Westerns such as *Wagonmaster*, *High Noon*, *Shane*, and, most grippingly, *Man of the West*.

At issue here is what we are to make of such a community or society. As a social entity, Lago might have been built as a viable social project, as having the primary features of a successful community. It is a community based on rationality, economic self-interest. There is no reason for anyone being here without the Lago Mining Company. In addition, the community, in looking out for its survival, has entered into a clear criminal conspiracy, so that it has the affective bond to tie the citizens together: guilt and fear. Utopian social solidarities, according to theorists of community, should have minimally this combination of rationality and affect for success.[9] The portrait of the community in *High Plains Drifter* displays the power of this combination. In theory, citizens ought to be willing to restrain their mere self-interest for the good of the community, and the business people do so by obeying the sheriff's and mayor's demand that the drifter can have everything he wishes, free of charge, an idea suggested and validated by the two leaders of the company, Dave Drake and Morg Allen. It appears that these two men are the true authorities for all actions by the Lago citizens.

In Eastwood's depiction, the film will make the people who live in the communal conspiracy look passive, conspiratorial, and incompetent, partners in crime. The townspeople are made to look absurd for sticking so closely (and abjectly) together as well as for not being able to hold the community together. Stacy Bridges and his cousins, according to Sheriff Sam, "got too big for their britches" and started "ordering people around, takin' over the town." Since they were the ones hired to kill the marshal, they apparently use their insider information to bully people, and so they threaten to expose the leading citizens and owners of the Lago Mining Company. They have performed the killing for "the good of the community," as it were, and they ought to have blended back into the community, lived within the social bonding of what was, in effect, a communal crime, necessary, as the citizens think, for the survival of the economic and social entity. The marshal, who had been hired by Morgan Allen, had found out about the encroachment of the company on government property and is a convenient sacrificial victim. But the film especially demonizes the people who take matters into their own hands, like the sadistic Stacy Bridges or the aggressive Callie Travers or the business partner Morgan Allen. Each person breaks away from the community to act on his or her own (although Bridges needs his two cousins, and Morg needs three henchmen to go with him to murder the drifter). Only Callie truly acts on her own, but the film construes her as a despicable person who, once put in a dangerous position, will cower and cringe like any of the other citizens. Her association with the other two rebels of the community suggests that she is the center of the "good-for-nothings," people who inherently resist obeying explicit and implicit rules of social order.

What looks like social bonding at the beginning of the narrative derives from the solidarity of a group in the grip of fear plus guilt. In a sense, this kind of social bonding, with its questionable foundation, somewhat transcends the idea of society (mere self-interested association). Because guilt and fear and collective crime cannot serve for long as the building blocks of a genuine community, the social group is subject to disintegration and, with the turmoil over the hired thugs, had begun to dissolve even before the drifter had arrived. A citizenry motivated by economic self-interest carries its self-destructive potentiality within it. But the paranoid community is always looking over its collective shoulder to defend itself against intrusion, whether real or imagined. The arrival of the drifter/stranger reveals both the power of the town's unity in paranoia and its inherent liability toward disunity. A citizenry motivated by fear of exposure and/or guilt is also subject to coming apart.[10]

The drifter eventually accepts the sheriff's offer to take anything he wants from any of the townspeople, who may begrudge being forced to pay such a tax but consent to the proposal. For the citizens of Lago, fear trumps economic self-interest and generates their sacrifices—in effect, an ad hoc tax. Even when the drifter hands over the two most important positions of authority to the town dwarf, thereby inverting as in a carnival the previous social and political order (if one can call it that), everyone sticks together, for the moment at least. The citizens of Lago feel that they are in danger of being exposed to exposure, violence, or death. Although the citizens of Lago have intensified their isolation from the rest of the world after the "trouble" with the marshal and Bridges, sharply dividing the world between citizens and outsiders, they immediately hire the drifter/stranger as their defender after he has killed the three newly hired defenders. He can take on the role of a kind of Hobbesian monarch, hiding somewhat behind the dwarf's titles of authority, also apparently unaware that the owners of the company are still dictating town policies and supporting actions that appear to derive from the stranger. Even the stranger is liable to become, for a time, a puppet of the company.

It's true that the thugs who whipped the marshal to death in the middle of the street in the middle of town were eventually arrested, convicted, and jailed. But they were convicted not for their murder of the marshal, but on quite possibly trumped-up charges of robbery. At their trial, they claim to have been "railroaded." But now the thugs are returning to claim back pay against the people who sent them to prison for carrying out corporate policy. The company officials might have wanted them silenced for the murder. Or, more likely, as Sheriff Sam explains, they "started pushing people around," like the second three-some of gunmen, hired to replace the imprisoned troubleshooters. It is clear that the town has some difficulty getting everyone to act in solidarity to protect "the company's interests and the interests of the town, which are identical," as Dave Drake, the boss of the company, explains. The leading citizens have all witnessed the murder, so every-one also has to live with the fact of exposure, and possible guilt, just as they conspired to convict the thugs of a lesser crime. The company's illegal encroachment on government property is hidden by the mar-shal's murder, and the crime of murder is hidden and displaced by the trumped-up crime of robbery. In this community, the citizens find a number of devices to shift a crime around, like a pea under a nutshell, with the hope that the most damaging crimes will be overlooked or forgotten. In fact, various Lago citizens appear to know only part of the story of the company's crimes. Most of them witnessed the murder of the marshal without knowing the background of this incident. Sheriff Sam seems to be the person most in the dark about everything involved in the various crimes, with the exception of the preacher. But any hint that would expose the truth behind the marshal's murder entails Dave Drake's wisdom: "One hang, we all hang." As he clarifies, "The whole town had a hand in what happened," even as his partner complains that "this whole business has gone sour" since the murder. The citizens are caught in a dilemma that renders them helpless.

And so the citizens live in a paranoid state, fearing exposure or the return of the thugs, which could still bring disclosure or violence or, most likely, both. A stranger enters the town and will eventually expose all the lies and the crimes. As in Sergio Leone's *Fistful of Dollars*, as in Akira Kurosawa's *Yojimbo* (*Fistful* being a remake of *Yojimbo*), Eastwood's drifter, the Man With No Name (or the lone samurai warrior), could just be drifting when we first see him, as he drifts into the town of Lago to get a drink and a shave and a bath. He shoots the three overly aggressive hired gunmen in the opening moments of his arrival. In these films, which are echoes of each other, the killings establish a number of important ideas almost immediately. This lone figure is not exactly a heroic savior of a community, but the killings establish him as someone who has to be taken into account, a man capable of "the god damndest shooting I ever even heard of," as one citizen recounts. The shootings get everyone's, including the audience's, attention.[11]

What does not get the attention of the townspeople is the drifter's rape of the town beauty, Callie, who deliberately bumped against him in an aggressive welcoming. She challenges his manhood in her insulting remarks to him, and the drifter tells her that she has to be taught some manners, as he drags her into a barn and rapes her. Unlike the other men of Lago, the drifter does not accept insults or challenges to his manhood without a counter-response. Callie at first resists the rape and then appears to realize that there is a genuine man on top of her and becomes his sexual partner as she moves from resistance to acceptance.[12] Shortly after, Callie shoots at him while he is taking a bath, and when the drifter wonders why it took her so long to get mad, Mordecai suggests that maybe it was because he had not gone back for more. (He does later, when she agrees to have dinner and sex with him, in an eating scene reminiscent of *Tom Jones*, although Callie has also conspired with her present male partner, Morg Allen, to have Morg enter the hotel room and kill the drifter.)

In fact, Callie's initial aggression is subject to various possible interpretations. Is she paranoid, like the rest of the town? Does she see a chance to provoke this man into disclosing his intention for being in town, or into acting masculine? Is she really "asking for" a rape? Is she so cynical about men that she wants to humiliate the drifter to prove that he is no different from the other men in the town? The fact that Callie seems to be acting as a lone individual raises questions about the nature of this community and her personality. The narrative constructs this woman as a scapegoat, representing the disloyalty and dishonesty of the community. Or, her initial challenge to the drifter may be a supplement to the hired gunmen's role of protecting the town from strangers. In effect, by lunging into the drifter, she is usurping a male role of testing him. Her usurpation suggests that, in her view, the men of the town are ineffective and need a resolute agent. She may be a woman who has illegitimately overreached her position within the community and has to be put back in her place by the drifter. What becomes clear after the rape is that, in this town, a woman has to defend her own honor and cannot depend upon any local man to do it. She has to take the role of her own avenger in a town of men whom she screamingly chastises for ignoring a rape in "broad daylight." The town's men not only fail to protect their women; they prefer to ignore women entirely. They appear not to care or even to have known about the rape. Later, the wife of the hotelkeeper, in a gentler repetition of the drifter's rape, seems to be liberated by being forced into bed with the drifter, realizing that her husband is so cowardly, looking out solely for his business interests, as to undermine his sexual, in addition to his political, appeal. What is implied here is a fairly archaic view that a man's duty is to protect the women of the community from such molestation and also to keep women in subordination. The women may feel the humiliation of rape, but the military premise is that the fact of rape exposes the powerlessness or cowardice of the men. If Callie had taken on the role as the representative of the community in her initial, seemingly unprovoked attack on the drifter, then her rape is a rape of the community at large. But as her partner, Morg, advises her when she screams at him to do something about the rape, she should learn to live with it and be quiet, subordinate herself to the general good of the community.

Or is it possible that the drifter is insecure about his masculinity and forces the rape in order to prove that he is a man, because he is paranoid about his masculinity?[13] It would appear that Eastwood wishes to put a woman tempted to act as an autonomous individual back in her place.[14] Equally interesting is the fact that Callie, like others from time to time, appears to break out of the social solidarity and act as an individual. Despite the restraints on individuality here, people keep acting on their own; though they are not necessarily acting in rebellion against the social entity, they take upon themselves the responsibility to perform some act "for the good of everybody." In this view, social solidarity and conformity have their limits, even among the paranoid.

The scope of the drifter's humiliation of the town becomes massive when he strips Sam, the local sheriff, of his badge and places it on Mordecai, the town dwarf, referred to by the townspeople as the "runt," and, in addition, crowns Mordecai as the mayor of the town. Here is the kind of parody of communal authority that probably derives from Sergio Leone's spaghetti Westerns. In their cowardice, in being awed by his gunplay, the leading townspeople accept the drifter's one-man revolution and offer him "anything he wants, free of charge" from the local merchants and saloon and hotelkeepers. Here is an absurd act for an absurd community with egregiously abject leaders and followers; the drifter's dark humor in his unchallenged coup d'état generates a revision of the community's self-image. As Lewis Belding, the hotel owner, claims at a town meeting, the drifter is "making a mock of this whole town." The drifter takes advantage of the offers, without much enthusiasm. No rules or regulations apply to him in the town of Lago. The community of men has ceded all power and violence to a man who has already proven his abilities in the three killings, not to speak of the confidence of his arrogance. The men in Lago have a highly reduced set of values—profit, safety, fear of exposure—as do the women, it seems—sexual satisfaction, resolute male individuals. These values can be critiqued by a masculine individual who still has the confidence and ability to engage in sex, as well as non-vicarious killing. The drifter, unlike the townspeople, is a rapist who does his own killing.[15]

The drifter treats the whole town as militantly traitorous. Throughout the narrative, we see that the townspeople are now just as craven before the new stranger as they were before the murderous violence against the marshal. With such abjectness in the town, we can understand how it was possible for hired gunmen to start dictating orders there insofar as Sheriff Sam tells the drifter that "everybody in town is more or less at your orders." It's as if the drifter knows in advance that this community is utterly spineless before economic power in combination with brute violence. In this view, once shown to be craven, the town, perhaps now with the supplement of guilt, will continue in its cowardly ways. This is an extraordinarily nasty portrait of a community, even nastier than that of the frontier town that William S. Hart burns down in *Hell's Hinges* (1916). The town of Hell's Hinges is so paranoid in its fear of conversion to Christianity and domesticated life that it rises up against the new minister and his sister, burns down the newly built church, and engages in a pitched gun battle against the parishioners, only to be destroyed by the lone Blaze Tracy, formerly a member of the saloon society, but now, with his conversion to Christianity, a man of Old Testament–style vengeance. It is also a nastier portrait of a frontier citizenry than the one we see in *High Noon*.

For Eastwood, the drama is almost completely about the inner weakness of a community that allows a figure like the drifter/stranger to come in and take over. What enables him to do this is a simple will to take action. Compared to the town, he seems to be a figure with no values, determined only to assert his will against the community, as if he knows that it has no iron in its soul and that the communal cohesion is ultimately unstable. He enters with an unfathomable cynicism, although we find out in the end that he is perhaps wreaking punishment on the community for failing to protect the lawman who may have been his brother. Or it may be that he is himself the ghost of the murdered marshal. Despite his claim to Sarah Belding that he drifted into town "just stopping by for a bottle of whiskey and a nice hot bath," he becomes for the town a figure of retribution, a violent ghost of the community's repressed conscience.

It's true that the drifter tries to educate or drill the men of the community into self-defense, but the citizens are incapable of hitting targets or of standing up to resolute gunmen, as they prove when Stacy and the Carlins enter Lago. Remembering the issues about communal self-protection in *High Noon* and *Rio Bravo* (1959), one might agree with Sheriff John T. Chance (the John Wayne character in *Rio Bravo*) that he doesn't want ordinary citizens to get involved with helping the sheriff and his deputies because citizens will just get in the way and have to be protected from the bad men. John Wayne must have forgotten his remarks as Sheriff John T. Chance indicating his skepticism about citizen defenders when he wrote to Eastwood and "launched into a gratuitous critique of *High Plains Drifter*. Its townspeople, he said, did not represent the true spirit of the American pioneer, the spirit that had made America great."[16]

As in Anthony Mann's *The Man from Laramie*, the newly arrived stranger who decides to stay on in the community generates paranoia and crazed violence, and, less brutally, a strong aura of mystery, especially for the patriarch, who runs the country even as he is going blind. The patriarch thinks that the stranger is a figure he has seen in a dream who is coming to kill his son and take everything away from him. The stranger is, in fact, an undercover captain in the cavalry, trying to find out exactly how his younger brother, also in the military, was killed. What he finds is that the patriarch's son has been selling repeating rifles to the Apaches, a dangerous operation that could even destroy the patriarch and other settlers.

The stranger consistently refuses to give inquirers his name. He is the man with no name, the figure from Sergio Leone's Westerns. When he fires from a distance upon Stacy Bridges and his cousins as they are returning to Lago, he generates Stacy's anger against the whole town because Stacy does not know who his attacker is. All he can do is speculate that the shooter might be Drake, the partner in charge of the company, after Stacy has just stabbed to death the other partner, Morg Allen. In his frustration with the shooting, Stacy threatens to kill every man in town. A man with no name is disturbing to everyone. His namelessness reverberates into a vague generality, even the inhuman, because without his name, no one can make up a reliable story about him and so cannot even begin to understand him. He is not only a stranger; he is an ongoing mystery. As Sarah Belding says to him, "You make people afraid." The drifter replies, "It's what people know about themselves inside that makes them afraid." It would be highly speculative to suggest that the drifter is the buried conscience of the town, just as Stacy and his cousins represent the sadistic interior of the town or as Callie, in her sexual availability, represents the town's potential for disloyalty. But a man with no name becomes an object of projection for everyone. Thus, the stranger really serves as a catalyst that is always a danger in that he is liable to dissolve the false solidarity of the community, as individuals project their inner demons of one sort or another on him. He exposes the inner life of the citizens, generates anxiety that leads to the fear that he's "got everybody in this town at each other's throats," as the hotelkeeper Belding says to the group meeting. But the narrative emphasizes that the power of the stranger derives from the inner anxieties of the community for its crimes of commission and omission. The mystery of his confidence makes the citizens superstitious about him, as if he is an avenging angel who has entered their lives to punish them. Belding claims that he has got everyone "snake fascinated." Given what the narrative understands to be the inner weakness of a communal solidarity composed of individuals with their own weaknesses, anyone who stands outside that paranoia will be spiritually stronger than the people in their collective being. This might well be a libertarian fantasy. There is no need, in this view, for a superhero; there is only the presence of an autonomous human being who, given the abjectness and paranoia of the community, will come to look like a hero or a ghost.

The stranger's self-confidence serves as a mirror image for the community, which can either generate the individual initiative of the citizens or, in their fear, force them to hover back upon the solidarity of a social entity trying to defend itself against an impending dissolution. For instance, the little outbreaks of individual initiative, like Morg Allen's plan to kill the drifter against the advice of his partner and with the help of his woman, Callie, stands a chance of redeeming the community—and Morg—in the eyes of Callie and in the community, which would certainly welcome the drifter's death. As the confident and autonomous individual, the stranger is always able to outwit such moves toward individual decision, just as his wisdom about people's inner fears allows him to anticipate the abjectness of most people. But the solidarity of the community is, from the stranger's point of view, always in danger of coming apart because he knows that at the heart of everyone's life there is the possibility or the instinct to become autonomous. Richard Schickel quotes Eastwood: "Man is always dreaming of being an individual, but man is really a flock animal."[17]

What would it mean to try to figure out who this character is? Obviously, the film plays blatantly with this idea, as he never answers the questions of the dying Stacy Bridges, "Who are you?" Earlier, as he comes into the town of Lago, he refuses to sign his name in the hotel register. He might be like Shane, a ghost from a violent past. This drifter may be the embodiment of all the heroes of former Western films, a ghost of a genre that, like Shane, is still likely to drop into the world unannounced but somehow mysteriously anticipated. Or maybe

85

he is an echo of John Ford's Wyatt Earp, a legend that is almost as powerful as a ghost. Did Jim Duncan actually die? Is the drifter a brother, or is he a reincarnation, or is he a ghost created by the townspeople in their guilt from having witnessed the whipping death of the marshal? If he is the latter, if he is the return of the repressed spirit of heroic resoluteness that was somehow buried in the town's fear of exposure, then it might make sense to see him as the representative of this resoluteness in his sexual exploits with the women. They, in effect, become the measure of a value that has, seemingly, vanished from the town in the fear of extinction. This ghost is a different idea from the dream figure who arrives in *The Man from Laramie*, but this possibility of a vague and unknowable spirituality has something to do with Westerns invoking the culture at large.

Paul Smith quotes Leone as saying about Eastwood, "I looked at him and didn't see any character . . . just a physical figure." Leone subtracts "from the interiority of character, offering instead the placid and almost spectral presence that finds its ideal owner in the figure and face of Clint Eastwood."[18] But his physical being signifies more than mere physical being. It stands for something associated with the West, sort of like William S. Hart, Gary Cooper, Randolph Scott, or Henry Fonda, although the spectral sense of the figure is crucial to the drifter. He arrives and departs in the haze of desert light and heat, accompanied by eerie, otherworldly music, but, of course, he may be the ghost of the whipped marshal, come back to haunt the citizens of the town and seek revenge for his murder.

As for spirituality, the narrative is especially harsh in its view of the preacher. When the preacher invokes the brotherhood of man, in his one instance of standing up for something in the community, the drifter denies that he is the preacher's brother, just as the only other possible upright figure in the town, Sarah Belding, claims that her "neighbors" make her "sick hiding behind words like 'faith,' 'peace' and 'trust'" when they "hid a murder behind them." This film wants nothing to do with the falsity of the idealism of "good words." For some reason, going back to James Fenimore Cooper and Owen Wister (and right down to *Deadwood*), ministers get a bad rap in Westerns, perhaps because they are seen as offering an idealistic view of the world, spouting ideas such as the brotherhood of man that do not seem pertinent in the Western or frontier setting, where violence is the ultimate law. However, the presence of the minister in the West is a sign of at least a pretension toward a higher civilization. In this instance, the men of the town want nothing to do with the preacher, as he seems to remind them of their own commitment to vicarious violence, inhumanity. At the moment when the men are debating whether or not to hire the newly arrived drifter as their protector, the preacher finds that he has an appointment at a sickbed when he is told to shut up or get out. The businessmen do not want to hear about values that they profess but don't believe in. Still, this preacher is a figure quite in consonance with the rest of the community, displaying a lack of charity by charging people for rooms in his parsonage when the drifter orders them out of the hotel.

The drifter/stranger resembles the returning veteran of the Vietnam War who becomes "a threat to the American Dream."[19] The mining venture of the town of Lago is an expression of the possibilities of this dream. But there really is no image of domesticity in this whole village, no indication that anyone lives in a family house with a family. In fact, in this mining town, as in Hell's Hinges, there are no miners present, an indication of the strictly allegorical conception of the town of Lago. All the townspeople seem to live in a hotel (except the preacher). Marriages are either nonexistent or dysfunctional. The reference to the citizens of Lago as a community is severely qualified by the fact that there are no families present. The cynicism of the narrative is so profound that the very motive of willing the American Dream has become corrupt, based on illegalities piled one on top of the other. The drifter's confidence may lie in the fact that he is a war veteran who has already faced enemy fire and is not intimidated by violence or the threat of violence.

The drifter's presence undermines any idealism in an official faith in such ventures of ordinary people. The only person who has a chance of being admirable is the dwarf, a totally powerless and marginal figure whom the drifter raises to an unstable position of authority and centrality. In his marginality, the dwarf could be excused for being merely a spectator because his marginality often gives him a privileged vantage from which to see actions, such as the whipping death or the rape scene. In fact, the drifter seems to realize that the dwarf is the true representative of the town; thus, the drifter makes him into the sheriff and the mayor. There has been in the town of Lago a dwarfing of all possibilities for genuine human life.

As in Dashiell Hammett's *Red Harvest*, the basis for Sergio Leone's *Fistful of Dollars* (because it is the basis for Kurosawa's *Yojimbo*), the stranger's very presence sets a dysfunctional community into the deeper disintegration of people warring against each other. Life in such a state of nature had moved far enough into civilization to suppress the perpetual war of people against people, but the stranger upsets what has been only a false community all along. In this view, the mere motive of greed—money and power—is not sufficient to sustain a genuine social bonding. The frontier minimalization, or dwarfing, of human motive is an obstacle to the possibility of building a community, if the narrative even suggests that such an idea is possible. This corrupt motive has infested everyone. Even the stranger seems rather shocked at the fact that the preacher announces he will charge the guests the same price as the hotel did, refusing the very charity for his "brothers" that he had just invoked. This is a profoundly sick social group that makes up the citizenry of Lago. And this level of sickness makes the community all the more vulnerable to the resolute individual.

The drifter may look to some viewers like a superhuman hero who easily dominates ordinary human beings, but Eastwood and Tidyman understand that such a primitive state of human collective endeavor is so weak that a fairly ordinary man who does not waver before the many temptations thrown his way to test his resolve, as with Will Kane or Wyatt Earp, can, in a social vacuum, take over all positions of authority and control such a community, with perhaps only the minimum of super-heroism. Yet, despite the fact that this narrative offers many ways to undermine the pure idea that the drifter is a superhuman hero, Eastwood understood that a male working-class spectator would probably see his character as superhuman: "My appeal is the characters I play. A superhuman character who has all the answers is double cool, exists on his own without society or the help of society's police forces." A twenty-five-year-old worker, Eastwood claims, "wants to have that self-sufficient thing he sees up there on the screen."[20] A mirror image, in this view, is easy for a projected audience to fathom, especially because Eastwood has been careful to make the drifter/stranger a rather unattractive person. Perhaps one might argue that the community is dwarfed only in the view of the drifter, who wishes to see himself as always knowing in advance what others will do, as always superior in his thinking and action. Such a perspective constructs the inadequacy of all other human beings before one's own fantasy of superiority. Eastwood is willing to make his favorite spectators into pathetic figures who need a fantasy figure they can never be.

Either the stranger is a resolute figure who dominates a community because of the citizens' abjectness, because something is wrong with such a community, or the drifter (Eastwood) is so insecure in his own sense of superiority that he has to demean all people around him in order to make himself look superior, admirable. His presenting the dwarf with positions of authority can be read in these two ways: the dwarf is either the true representative of this social group, or he derives from the drifter's own need to project everyone in this dwarfish manner in order to construct his own superiority. There is the possibility that Eastwood was highly aware of both of these possibilities, and that as actor and director he made sure that these two ideas exist together so that there is a built-in irony in the relationship between the drifter and the community. Those viewers who need a hero can construe the drifter as superhuman. Viewers less interested in a hero can see the film as a statement about a defective social entity.[21] Whether one takes the view that, at the end of the Vietnam War, when it became clear that the United States had been humiliated, Eastwood felt that the country needed a hero who could win, or whether one takes the view that Eastwood felt that this foundational image of the United States as a frontier community had failed, both possibilities belong to the Vietnam War era, to the post-1965 era that brought about a "sense of pervasive national malaise, decadence, and social failure."[22] *High Plains Drifter* presents a certain sign of history in the early seventies, something of the passions of a historical moment, confusing and even contradictory as they might have been. But the experience of this historical moment also derives from the genre's memory of its many instances throughout the twentieth century.

Of course, one might argue that the depiction of the Lago citizens serves to promote the stranger's heroism. The belittlement makes the stranger look perhaps transcendent in his confidence and abilities. William Beard construes the character as utterly spiritual and transcendental.[23] François Guérif thinks that the figure is the egotistical Eastwood himself.[24]

Eastwood could have learned from his work in spaghetti Westerns that what makes a Western plausible or entertaining at this late date is pastiche. *High Plains Drifter*, like Leone's films, echoes a number of former Westerns. The more Westerns one sees, the more shadows of other Westerns one sees in a film like *High Plains Drifter* or *Once Upon a Time in the West*, as if the latest instance of the genre is a kind of summary or anthology of what has already been shown. Actually, a well-defined genre like the Western has a built-in pastiche, a generic intertextuality. Eastwood might have learned a lot from Leone and his screenwriters, but he also could have learned a lot from simply viewing other Westerns by the important American directors: Ford, Hawks, Mann, Sturges, and others.[25] The Italian or spaghetti Westerns, however, brought to the making of Westerns a new self-consciousness and inclusiveness (including Kurosawa's translations of American Westerns), and Eastwood inherits this self-consciousness, picking his screenwriters carefully and effectively. This is not to claim that the film is not original, only that it achieves significance because it is so deeply inscribed within the tradition of the genre.

The spaghetti Western style here is to exaggerate every feature of the genre. William S. Hart makes his case against the town of Hell's Hinges with heavy melodrama, an instance of the moralism in the service of Progressive Era reform. Carl Foreman, *High Noon*'s screenwriter, indicates his sense of the American people's failure to stand up against the terror of McCarthyism. Eastwood makes a much more exaggerated case for his sense of the severely compromised moral issues at stake within the culture, as if he distrusts social solidarity, as if he distrusts humanity. Eastwood offers a heavy misanthropic message, apparently disgusted with everyone and everything. The film has a nihilistic tinge. Robin Wood refers to this period in filmmaking wherein every film directed by major directors presented a desolate portrait of the United States, a country either deeply confused or disintegrating, morally and intellectually.[26] The lone individual with a resolute will serves, then, as a critique of the community as a whole, of citizens who are able to act only as a whole or mass, with a few individual pathetic gestures of autonomy.

The more general point I am trying to argue is that a Western that is so tightly controlled by historical generic terms is important and challenging for a cultural historian because it is able to comment upon a cultural moment and also is so abstract, in its echoes of a long history of a genre, as to commit its comment to irrelevance. A number of historians of the American era in which the country was involved in a controversial and losing war in Vietnam have emphasized that the primary, albeit vague, causes of the war can be found in American history, as far back as the ideologies of the original Puritan settlers, with their "errand into the wilderness."[27] Likewise, whether or not a traditionally well-established popular genre like the Western could offer a serious critique of a precise historical moment is also in question. In the case of *High Plains Drifter*, the very abstractness of this version of the genre, its emphasis on a lone avenger, is seductive, and its own sense of its ghostly presence is the product of a serious self-consciousness. Within the history of a genre we find the continuity of a culture, despite its many transformations.

Without mentioning all the instances of Westerns as criticizing the inadequacy of the communities, *High Plains Drifter* lies in this tradition of a pervasive generic theme. What makes genre interesting is that a particular instance can comment on a cultural moment by commenting on other instances of the genre in the long history of the genre. Eastwood is not committed to a parody of the genre. If there is any literary parallel, it might be the punishing form of satire made famous by Jonathan Swift. Eastwood uses the genre to reject the community as corrupt, narrow-minded, incompetent, irresolute. The question is how to try to understand the attitude of a projected actual audience for such a portrait in 1973. It seems obvious that only the Vietnam War era could account for viewer expectations, especially as the war was ending. If Lago can be saved, that possibility can only come about if it is destroyed. One remembers what is probably a folklore item from the war era, about a US field commander in Vietnam who claimed that "we had to destroy that village in order to save it." There was a historical moment in the United States when such a statement might have seemed hopeful. This may be the message of *High Plains Drifter*.

Notes

1. Richard Schickel, *Clint Eastwood: A Biography* (New York: Alfred A. Knopf, 1996), 257.
2. Paul Smith, *Clint Eastwood: A Cultural Production* (Minneapolis: University of Minnesota Press, 1993), 85–135.
3. Klaus Theweleit, *Male Fantasies,* vol. 1, trans. Stephen Conway (Minneapolis: University of Minnesota Press, 1987), 22.
4. Michael Henry, "Interview with Clint Eastwood," in *Clint Eastwood: Interviews,* ed. Robert E. Kapsis and Kathie Coblentz (Jackson: University Press of Mississippi, 1999), 99–100.
5. Michael Henry, "Interview with Clint Eastwood," 99.
6. David Thomson, "Cop on a Hot *Tightrope*," in *Clint Eastwood: Interviews,* ed. Kapsis and Coblentz, 86.
7. David Thomson, "Cop on a Hot *Tightrope*," 83.
8. Quote from Randy Roberts and James S. Olson, *John Wayne American* (New York: Free Press, 1995), 349.
9. A good introduction to theories of community is Graham Crow, *Social Solidarities: Theories, Identities and Social Change* (Philadelphia: Open University Press, 2002). For theories and histories of the practice of community in American history, a good introduction is Thomas Bender, *Community and Social Change in America* (Baltimore: Johns Hopkins University Press, 1978).
10. Historians of the sixties and early seventies wrote of American society as "coming apart." See William L. O'Neill, *Coming Apart* (Chicago: Quadrangle, 1971).
11. Leone truly believed in the three (or four) killings as an opening to his Westerns, in *Fistful of Dollars,* and perhaps most famously in the opening sequence of *Once Upon a Time in the West.* Jim Kitses notes that the opening killings construct a "signature scene that goes through all the spaghettis to its source in Kurosawa" (i.e., *Yojimbo*). *Horizons West,* rev. ed. (London: British Film Institute, 2004), 294.
12. Richard Schickel writes that the rape scene of Callie "plays gratuitously as Clint now admits: 'I might do it differently if I were making it now. I might omit that.' Even at the time, he knew it was (as he anachronistically puts it) 'politically incorrect.' He has no good explanation for why he went ahead with the sequence anyway." *Clint Eastwood: A Biography,* 192. However, Jim Kitses sees Callie as Eastwood's version of *High Noon*'s Mrs. Ramirez, who had a relationship with the killer, Frank Miller, and with the marshal, Will Kane. *Horizons West,* 296. Kitses's reading of *High Plains Drifter* is especially valuable for the manner in which he sees Eastwood's film as a continuous echo of *High Noon,* just as *Pale Rider* continuously echoes *Shane.* To think of Callie as the new version of the Mrs. Ramirez character speaks volumes about Eastwood's perspective on women and society at the time.

13. Christopher Frayling notes that Sergio Leone, for the young Clint Eastwood, "wanted to make him look more virile, to harden him" for the role of the "Mysterious Stranger" in *Fistful of Dollars*. *Sergio Leone* (London: Faber & Faber, 2000), 137. Eastwood, Leone thought, looked "a little 'light,'" "a little sophisticated." As Paul Smith emphasizes, Eastwood is a "cultural production." *Clint Eastwood: A Cultural Production*.

14. We might note that, by 1973, the feminist movement was perhaps gaining the height of its cultural prestige in the United States so that, by 1975, "*Time* declared that its Man of the Year for 1975 would be American Women." Philip Jenkins, *Decade of Nightmares* (New York: Oxford University Press, 2006), 28. Eastwood's ambivalent position on women is a continuing issue for his viewers right up to, and including, *Million Dollar Baby*.

15. As a confessed rapist claimed in an interview from the early seventies, "The image of a man in this society is violent and hypersexual, so I just put those two things together." Quote from Jack Fremont, "Rapists Speak for Themselves," in Diana E. H. Russell, *The Politics of Rape* (New York: Stein & Day, 1975), 250. This statement provides a definition of the masculine hero that Eastwood represents in the drifter.

16. Quote from Schickel, *Clint Eastwood: A Biography*, 291.

17. Schickel, *Clint Eastwood: A Biography*, 231.

18. Smith, *Clint Eastwood: A Cultural Production*, 12.

19. Rick Berg, "Losing Vietnam: Covering the War in an Age of Technology," in *From Hanoi to Hollywood: The Vietnam War in American Film*, ed. Linda Dittmar and Gene Michaud (New Brunswick: Rutgers University Press, 1990), 58.

20. Richard Schickel, *Clint Eastwood: A Biography*, 231.

21. The film would be an example of what Forrest G. Robinson has referred to as "having it both ways." See *Having It Both Ways: Self-Subversion in Western Popular Classics* (Albuquerque: University of New Mexico Press, 1993).

22. Philip Jenkins, *Decade of Nightmares*, 16.

23. William Beard, *Persistence of Double Vision* (Edmonton: University of Alberta Press, 2000): Eastwood "abandons realism, while emphasizing the transcendent power of both protagonist and narrative. The film's most crucial activity, in other words, is to denaturalize its story and its hero, and to move both of them towards an occult and transcendental realm" (25).

24. François Guérif, *Clint Eastwood* (Paris: Henri Veyrier, 1983): "*L'Homme des hautes plaines* est un film incontestablement narcissique, à la limite de la megalomanie." Guérif quotes Jacques Zimmer, who defends the film against a number of French critics who saw Eastwood as "the handsome blond Aryan" hero in "typically Nazi ideology," depicting the film itself as the "*Mein Kampf* of the West" (102). Zimmer claims that "it is curious to see a film maligned as extreme right-wing ideology, if not Nazi, which takes up the good old theme of the lone individual who comes into town to

correct an injustice and gets the community, which has named him marshal out of fear, to obey the law. I will not burden these pages with a list of Westerns that revolve around these two themes" (my translation). Richard Abel offers a long list of Westerns made before World War I alone that take up the theme of the community and hero. "The 'Imagined' Community of the Western, 1910–1913," in *American Cinema's Transitional Era: Audiences, Institutions, Practices*, ed. Charlie Keil and Shelley Stamp (Berkeley: University of California Press, 2004), 131–70.

25. The Kapsis and Coblentz collection, *Clint Eastwood: Interviews*, shows that Eastwood has a comprehensive knowledge of Westerns and films in general. He is a less obvious example, perhaps, of what Michael Pye and Lynda Myles referred to as a "movie brat" in *The Movie Brats* (New York: Holt, Rinehart & Winston, 1979). They have in mind movie directors like George Lucas, Francis Ford Coppola, or Martin Scorsese, who incorporate their extensive knowledge of film history into their productions.

26. Robin Wood, *Hollywood from Vietnam to Reagan* (New York: Columbia University Press, 1986), 28.

27. The bibliography on this issue is immense, but a student looking for cultural perspectives on the US involvement in the Vietnam conflict might begin with Loren Baritz, *Backfire* (New York: William Morrow, 1985); John Hellman, *American Myth and the Legacy of Vietnam* (New York: Columbia University Press, 1986); and Milton J. Bates, *The Wars We Took to Vietnam: Cultural Conflict and Storytelling* (Berkeley: University of California Press, 1996). A much more comprehensive view of the era of the late sixties and the early seventies is Philip Jenkins, *Decade of Nightmares*.

Lynch on Lynch

(selection)

Chris Rodley, interview with David Lynch

Chris Rodley: Did you now regard yourself primarily as a filmmaker?

David Lynch: I didn't really think about it; I was making this film [*Eraserhead*]. But I always felt there were these filmmakers out there, and I wasn't part of that. I was separate from that. I never really considered myself in the system at all.

CR: But, with the facilities at the Centre, are you now looking at the work of other filmmakers? You've often mentioned Fellini, a director who not only seems to have been fascinated with physical strangeness on occasion, but who also loves his own locale.

DL: Like *Roma*? Yeah. I love Fellini. And we've got the same birthday, so if you believe in astrology . . . His is a totally different time, and an Italian take on life. But there's something about his films. There's a mood. They make you dream. They're so magical and lyrical and surprising and inventive. The guy was unique. If you took his films away, there would be a giant chunk of cinema missing. There's nothing else around like that. I like Bergman, but his films are so different. Sparse. Sparse dreams.

And I think Herzog is one of the all-time greats. *Really* great. When I was in England once I saw *Stroszek* on TV. I'd missed the beginning of it so I thought it was, like, some real documentary. I was just captivated in the first *two seconds*. I'd never seen anything like it.

Later I met him in New York and he showed me a journal that he'd kept for the past year: *Walking the Perimeter of Germany*. He'd notated every single day, and I said he must have had the world's sharpest pencil! Because this writing was *crystal* clear, but so small you'd need a magnifying glass to read it. The journal was very small—about two inches by two inches—and each page was *filled* with, you know, four or five hundred sentences. It was *unbelievable*!

CR: He can be pretty crazy. He's threatened to shoot people on set!

DL: That's not crazy! Get real, Chris!

CR: All are European directors. Was European cinema more interesting to you all the time?

DL: Yeah, for the kind of thing I wanted to do. You go to films for different reasons: just to go, and then there are ones that get down and thrill your soul. And probably most of those came from Europe.

CR: Is that something to do with the fact that they're not so driven by narrative as American films?

DL: Yes. Exactly. I think so.

CR: What about Jacques Tati? You've mentioned him on occasion.

DL: I *love* that guy. His whole style, and how he sees things. And again, you know, the guy's an inventor, visually, *and* with the sound, choreography, and music. Then there's his childlike love of his characters; I really dig it. I met his daughter. But, you know, I hear these stories, how he died a bitter man, and he wasn't really that loved in his own country. And it *kills* me.

CR: What about the prologue to *Eraserhead* with the Man in the Planet? Obviously, it's very important. How does that relate to Henry's story and the rest of the film?

DL: Oh, it relates. I've got to tell you, it relates. "Prologue" means what goes before, right? That's exactly what it is. It's very important what goes on there. And no one has ever really written about that front part. This Canadian guy, George Godwin, wrote something on it. He came and talked to me and interviewed Jack Nance and wrote his take on it.

I wouldn't really talk about it, but I answered some questions for him. But there's certain things that happen in that sequence that are a key to the rest. And, er . . . that's all.

CR: Which are . . . ?

DL: They're right there, you know. [Laughs.]

CR: Many readings of aspects of *Eraserhead* inevitably end up in the Freudian zone because there are so many obvious . . .

DL: Things you can latch on to—psychological things, yeah.

CR: Does it bother you that people will come to the movie with an orthodoxy? Any kind of orthodoxy? You seem very resistant to any single meaning being placed on your work—particularly by yourself!

DL: No. See, the thing is, I love the idea that one thing can be different for different people. Everything's that way. Like the O. J. Simpson trial. Everybody hears the same words, they see the same faces, the same expressions, the same anger or frustration or evidence, and they come away with absolutely different verdicts in their minds. Even with a standard spoon-fed film, people see it differently. It's just the way it is.

And then there are films or writings that you could read once and then ten years later read again and get way more from. You've changed; the work stays the same. But suddenly it's got way more meaning for you, depending on where you are. I like things that have a kernel of something in them. They have to be abstract. The more concrete they are, the less likely that this thing will happen. The maker has to feel it and know it in a certain way and be honest to it. Every single decision passes through this one person, and if they judge it and do it correctly, then the work holds together for that one person, and they feel it's honest and it's right. And then it's released, and from that point on there's not *one thing* you can do about it. You can talk about it—try to defend it or try to do this or that. It doesn't work. People still hate it. They hate it. It doesn't work for them. And you've lost them. You're not going to get them back. Maybe twenty years later they'll say, "My God! I was wrong." Or maybe, twenty years later, they'll hate it when at first they loved it. Who knows? It's out of your control.

Certain things are just so beautiful to me, and I don't know why. Certain things make so much sense, and it's hard to explain. I *felt* *Eraserhead*, I didn't think it. It was a quiet process: going from inside me to the screen. I'd get something on film, get it paced a certain way, add the right sounds, and then I'd be able to say if it worked or not. Now, just to get to that point, there's a million times more talking. And in Hollywood, if you can't write your ideas down, or if you can't pitch them, or if they're so abstract they can't be pitched properly, then they don't have a chance of surviving. Abstract things are important to a film, but very few people get the chance to really go all out with cinema. Creations are an extension of yourself, and you go out on a limb whenever you create anything. It's a risk.

CR: Isn't the problem with, say, Freudian analysis for you that, inscribed within such an approach, is the tendency to say, "This *does* mean that, because we're all part of the same . . . ?"

DL: Collective subconscious thing. Yes, but the thing is, if a couple of different psychoanalysts got together they wouldn't agree on everything either. There may be an exact science, but it isn't psychiatry. The whole picture's not locked in yet.

CR: Can we talk a bit about the scenes in the radiator? Years later, when the Man from Another Place turned up unexpectedly in *Twin Peaks,* he seemed very much like the Lady in the Radiator. They appear to come from a similar place. Is that true?

DL: Yes. The floor pattern in Henry's apartment lobby is the same pattern as the floor in the Red Room in *Twin Peaks.* That's one similar factor. The Lady in the Radiator wasn't in the original script for *Eraserhead.* I was sitting in the food room one day and I drew a picture of the Lady in the Radiator, but I didn't know where it came from. But it was meaningful to me when I saw it finally drawn. And then I saw the radiator in my head. And it was an instrument for producing warmth in a room; it made me sort of happy—like me as Henry, say. I saw this opening to another place. So I ran into the set and looked at the radiator more closely. You know, there are many different types of radiators, but I'd never seen another radiator like this. It had a little kind of chamber, like a stage in it. I'm not kidding you. It was right there, and it just changed everything. So then I had to build the doors and the stage, and do the whole thing. One thing led to another, and suddenly there she was.

The Lady in the Radiator had bad skin. I think she had bad acne as a child and used a lot of pancake makeup to smooth that out. But inside is where the happiness in her comes from. Her outward appearance is not the thing.

So a film isn't finished until it's finished. Anything can come along and you realize that it's almost like the thing *knows* how it will be one day. You might discover some parts of it at first—become excited and fall in love and go—but the thing knows that you haven't seen the whole yet. Will the person discover those other things? The only way is to stay in there, and be watchful and feel it. And maybe they'll pop into your conscious mind. But they've always been there, somewhere.

PERFORMING

PERFORMING

The characters we see onscreen and the actors who portray them are central to our experience of film watching. But who *are* film stars? And how do they exist beyond the screen? The pieces in this section explore notions of performance and consider how portrayal is inextricably bound with questions of truth and deception.

In her essay "John Wayne: A Love Song" (1965), **Joan Didion** recounts her expectations of the legendary actor and the image of him that she had built in her mind over years of movie viewing.

Adam Mars-Jones, in "Nonstop Action: Why Hollywood's Aging Heroes Won't Give Up the Gun" (2015), takes a less enchanted view of film legends and questions the discrepancies in behavior and expectations between male and female film stars as they grow older.

Lorrie Moore's short story "Willing" (1998) captures the malaise of a former film actress and how her previous lifestyle continues to influence her daily behavior.

Jess Zimmerman's piece, "Furiosa: The Virago of *Mad Max: Fury Road*" (2017), focuses on recent examples of women action heroes in Hollywood films. As these women overturn numerous gendered expectations, their performances have attracted both admiration and ire.

John Wayne: A Love Song

Joan Didion

n the summer of 1943 I was eight, and my father and mother and small brother and I were at Peterson Field in Colorado Springs. A hot wind blew through that summer, blew until it seemed that before August broke, all the dust in Kansas would be in Colorado, would have drifted over the tarpaper barracks and the temporary strip and stopped only when it hit Pikes Peak. There was not much to do, a summer like that: there was the day they brought in the first B-29, an event to remember but scarcely a vacation program. There was an Officers' Club, but no swimming pool; all the Officers' Club had of interest was artificial blue rain behind the bar. The rain interested me a good deal, but I could not spend the summer watching it, and so we went, my brother and I, to the movies.

We went three and four afternoons a week, sat on folding chairs in the darkened Quonset hut which served as a theater, and it was there, that summer of 1943 while the hot wind blew outside, that I first saw John Wayne. Saw the walk, heard the voice. Heard him tell the girl in a picture called *War of the Wildcats* that he would build her a house, "at the bend in the river where the cottonwoods grow." As it happened I did not grow up to be the kind of woman who is the heroine in a Western, and although the men I have known have had many virtues and have taken me to live in many places I have come to love, they have never been John Wayne, and they have never taken me to that bend in the river where the cottonwoods grow. Deep in that part of my heart where the artificial rain forever falls, that is still the line I wait to hear.

I tell you this neither in a spirit of self-revelation nor as an exercise in total recall, but simply to demonstrate that when John Wayne rode through my childhood, and perhaps through yours, he determined forever the shape of certain of our dreams. It did not seem possible that such a man could fall ill, could carry within him that most inexplicable and ungovernable of diseases. The rumor struck some obscure anxiety, threw our very childhoods into question. In John Wayne's world, John Wayne was supposed to give the orders. "Let's ride," he said, and "Saddle up." "Forward *ho*," and "A man's gotta do what he's got to do." "Hello, there," he said when he first saw the girl, in a construction camp or on a train or just standing around on the front porch waiting for somebody to ride up through the tall grass. When John Wayne spoke, there was no mistaking his intentions; he had a sexual authority so strong that even a child could perceive it. And in a world we understood early to be characterized by venality and doubt and paralyzing ambiguities, he suggested another world, one which may or may not have existed ever but in any case existed no more: a place where a man could move free, could make his own code and live by it; a world in which, if a man did what he had to do, he could one day take the girl and go riding through the draw and find himself home free, not in a hospital with something going wrong inside, not in a high bed with the flowers and the drugs and the forced smiles, but there at the bend in the bright river, the cottonwoods shimmering in the early morning sun.

"Hello, there." Where did he come from, before the tall grass? Even his history seemed right, for it was no history at all, nothing to intrude upon the dream. Born Marion Morrison in Winterset, Iowa, the son of a druggist. Moved as a child to Lancaster, California, part of the migration to that promised land sometimes called "the west coast of Iowa." Not that Lancaster was the promise fulfilled; Lancaster was a town on the Mojave where the dust blew through. But Lancaster was still California, and it was only a year from there to Glendale, where desolation had a different flavor: antimacassars among the orange groves, a middle-class prelude to Forest Lawn. Imagine Marion Morrison in Glendale. A Boy Scout, then a student at Glendale High. A tackle for USC, a Sigma Chi. Summer vacations, a job moving props on the old Fox lot. There, a meeting with John Ford, one of the several directors who were to sense that into this perfect mold might be poured the inarticulate longings of a nation wondering at just what pass the trail had been lost. "Dammit," said Raoul Walsh later, "the son of a bitch looked like a man." And so after a while the boy from Glendale became a star. He did not become an actor, as he has always been careful to point out to interviewers ("How many times do I gotta tell you, I don't act at all, I *re*-act"), but a star, and the star called John Wayne would spend most of the rest of his life with one or another of those directors, out on some forsaken location, in search of the dream.

> *Out where the skies are a trifle bluer*
> *Out where friendship's a little truer*
> *That's where the West begins.*

Nothing very bad could happen in the dream, nothing a man could not face down. But something did. There it was, the rumor, and after a while the headlines. "I licked the Big C," John Wayne announced, as John Wayne would, reducing those outlaw cells to the level of any other outlaws, but even so we all sensed that this would be the one unpredictable confrontation, the one shootout Wayne could lose. I have as much trouble as the next person with illusion and reality, and I did not much want to see John Wayne when he must be (or so I thought) having some trouble with it himself, but I did, and it was down in Mexico when he was making the picture his illness had so long delayed, down in the very country of the dream.

It was John Wayne's 165th picture. It was Henry Hathaway's 84th. It was number 34 for Dean Martin, who was working off an old contract to Hal Wallis, for whom it was independent production number 65. It was called *The Sons of Katie Elder*, and it was a Western, and after the three-month delay they had finally shot the exteriors up in Durango, and now they were in the waning days of interior shooting at Estudio Churubusco outside Mexico City, and the sun was hot and the air was clear and it was lunchtime. Out under the pepper trees the boys from the Mexican crew sat around sucking caramels, and down the road some of the technical men sat around a place which served a stuffed lobster and a glass of tequila for one dollar American, but it was inside the cavernous empty commissary where the talent sat around, the reasons for the exercise, all sitting around the big table picking at *huevos con queso* and Carta Blanca beer. Dean Martin, unshaven. Mack Gray, who goes where Martin goes. Bob Goodfried, who was in charge of Paramount publicity and who had flown down to arrange for a trailer and who had a delicate stomach. "Tea and toast," he warned repeatedly. "That's the ticket. You can't trust the lettuce." And Henry Hathaway, the director, who did not seem to be listening to Goodfried. And John Wayne, who did not seem to be listening to anyone.

"This week's gone slow," Dean Martin said, for the third time.

"How can you say that?" Mack Gray demanded.

"*This . . . week's . . . gone . . . slow,* that's how I can say it."

"You don't mean you want it to end."

"I'll say it right out, Mack, I want it to *end.* Tomorrow night I shave this beard, I head for the airport, I say *adiós amigos!* Bye-bye *muchachos!*"

Henry Hathaway lit a cigar and patted Martin's arm fondly. "Not tomorrow, Dino."

"Henry, what are you planning to add? A world war?"

Hathaway patted Martin's arm again and gazed into the middle distance. At the end of the table someone mentioned a man who, some years before, had tried unsuccessfully to blow up an airplane.

"He's still in jail," Hathaway said suddenly.

"In jail?" Martin was momentarily distracted from the question whether to send his golf clubs back with Bob Goodfried or consign them to Mack Gray. "What's he in jail for if nobody got killed?"

"Attempted murder, Dino," Hathaway said gently. "A felony."

"You mean some guy just *tried* to kill me he'd end up in jail?"

Hathaway removed the cigar from his mouth and looked across the table. "Some guy just tried to kill *me* he wouldn't end up in jail. How about you, Duke?"

Very slowly, the object of Hathaway's query wiped his mouth, pushed back his chair, and stood up. It was the real thing, the authentic article, the move which had climaxed a thousand scenes on 165 flickering frontiers and phantasmagoric battlefields before, and it was about to climax this one, in the commissary at Estudio Churubusco outside Mexico City. "Right," John Wayne drawled. "I'd kill him."

Almost all the cast of *Katie Elder* had gone home, that last week; only the principals were left, Wayne, and Martin, and Earl Holliman, and

Michael Anderson Jr., and Martha Hyer. Martha Hyer was not around much, but every now and then someone referred to her, usually as "the girl." They had all been together nine weeks, six of them in Durango. Mexico City was not quite Durango; wives like to come along to places like Mexico City, like to shop for handbags, go to parties at Merle Oberon Pagliai's, like to look at her paintings. But Durango. The very name hallucinates. Man's country. Out where the West begins. There had been ahuehuete trees in Durango; a waterfall, rattlesnakes. There had been weather, nights so cold that they had postponed one or two exteriors until they could shoot inside at Churubusco. "It was the girl," they explained. "You couldn't keep the girl out in cold like that." Henry Hathaway had cooked in Durango, gazpacho and ribs and the steaks that Dean Martin had ordered flown down from the Sands; he had wanted to cook in Mexico City, but the management of the Hotel Bamer refused to let him set up a brick barbecue in his room. "You really missed something, *Durango*," they would say, sometimes joking and sometimes not, until it became a refrain, Eden lost.

But if Mexico City was not Durango, neither was it Beverly Hills. No one else was using Churubusco that week, and there inside the big sound stage that said LOS HIJOS DE KATIE ELDER on the door, there with the pepper trees and the bright sun outside, they could still, for just so long as the picture lasted, maintain a world peculiar to men who like to make Westerns, a world of loyalties and fond raillery, of sentiment and shared cigars, of interminable desultory recollections; campfire talk, its only point to keep a human voice raised against the night, the wind, the rustlings in the brush.

"Stuntman got hit accidentally on a picture of mine once," Hathaway would say between takes of an elaborately choreographed fight scene. "What was his name, married Estelle Taylor, met her down in Arizona."

The circle would close around him, the cigars would be fingered. The delicate art of the staged fight was to be contemplated.

"I only hit one guy in my life," Wayne would say. "Accidentally, I mean. That was Mike Mazurki."

"Some choice." Murmurings, assent.

"It wasn't a choice, it was an accident."

"I can believe it."

"You bet."

"Oh boy. Mike Mazurki."

And so it would go. There was Web Overlander, Wayne's makeup man for twenty years, hunched in a blue windbreaker, passing out sticks of Juicy Fruit. "*Insect* spray," he would say. "Don't tell us about insect spray. We saw insect spray in Africa, all right. Remember Africa?" Or, "*Steamer* clams. Don't tell us about steamer clams. We got our fill of steamer clams all right, on the *Hatari!* appearance tour. Remember Bookbinder's?" There was Ralph Volkie, Wayne's trainer for eleven years, wearing a red baseball cap and carrying around a clipping from Hedda Hopper, a tribute to Wayne. "This Hopper's some lady," he would say again and again. "Not like some of these guys, all they write is sick, sick, sick, how can you call that guy *sick*, when he's got pains, coughs, works all day, *never complains*. That guy's got the best hook since Dempsey, not *sick*."

And there was Wayne himself, fighting through number 165. There was Wayne, in his thirty-three-year-old spurs, his dusty neckerchief, his blue shirt. "You don't have too many worries about what to wear in these things," he said. "You can wear a blue shirt, or, if you're down in Monument Valley, you can wear a yellow shirt." There was Wayne, in a relatively new hat, a hat which made him look curiously like William S. Hart. "I had this old cavalry hat I loved, but I lent it to Sammy Davis. I got it back, it was unwearable. I think they all pushed it down on his head and said *OK, John Wayne*—you know, a joke."

There was Wayne, working too soon, finishing the picture with a bad cold and a racking cough, so tired by late afternoon that he kept an oxygen inhalator on the set. And still nothing mattered but the Code. "That guy," he muttered of a reporter who had incurred his displeasure. "I admit I'm balding. I admit I got a tire around my middle. What man fifty-seven doesn't? Big news. Anyway, that guy."

He paused, about to expose the heart of the matter, the root of the distaste, the fracture of the rules that bothered him more than the alleged misquotations, more than the intimation that he was no longer the Ringo Kid. "He comes down, uninvited, but I ask him over anyway. So we're sitting around drinking mescal out of a water jug."

He paused again and looked meaningfully at Hathaway, readying him for the unthinkable denouement. "He had to be *assisted* to his room."

They argued about the virtues of various prizefighters, they argued about the price of J&B in pesos. They argued about dialogue.

"As rough a guy as he is, Henry, I still don't think he'd raffle off his mother's *Bible*."

"I like a shocker, Duke."

They exchanged endless training-table jokes. "You know why they call this memory sauce?" Martin asked, holding up a bowl of chili.

"Why?"

"Because you *remember it in the morning*."

"Hear that, Duke? Hear why they call this memory sauce?"

They delighted one another by blocking out minute variations in the free-for-all fight which is a set piece in Wayne pictures; motivated or totally gratuitous, the fight sequence has to be in the picture, because they so enjoy making it. "Listen—this'll really be funny. Duke picks up the kid, see, and then it takes both Dino and Earl to throw him out the door—*how's that?*"

They communicated by sharing old jokes; they sealed their camaraderie by making gentle, old-fashioned fun of wives, those civilizers, those tamers. "So Señora Wayne takes it into her head to stay up and have one brandy. So for the rest of the night it's 'Yes, Pilar, you're right, dear. I'm a bully, Pilar, you're right, I'm impossible.'"

"You hear that? Duke says Pilar threw a table at him."

"Hey, Duke, here's something funny. That finger you hurt today, get the doc to bandage it up, go home tonight, show it to Pilar, tell her she did it when she threw the table. You know, make her think she was really cutting up."

They treated the oldest among them respectfully; they treated the youngest fondly. "You see that kid?" they said of Michael Anderson Jr. "What a kid."

"He don't act, it's right from the heart," said Hathaway, patting his heart.

"Hey kid," Martin said. "You're gonna be in my next picture. We'll have the whole thing, no beards. The striped shirts, the girls, the hi-fi, the eye lights."

They ordered Michael Anderson his own chair, with "BIG MIKE" tooled on the back. When it arrived on the set, Hathaway hugged him. "You see that?" Anderson asked Wayne, suddenly too shy to look him in the eye. Wayne gave him the smile, the nod, the final accolade. "I saw it, kid."

On the morning of the day they were to finish *Katie Elder*, Web Overlander showed up not in his windbreaker but in a blue blazer. "Home, Mama," he said, passing out the last of his Juicy Fruit. "I got on my getaway clothes." But he was subdued. At noon, Henry Hathaway's wife dropped by the commissary to tell him that she might fly over to Acapulco. "Go ahead," he told her. "I get through here, all I'm gonna do is take Seconal to a point just this side of suicide." They were all subdued. After Mrs. Hathaway left, there were desultory attempts at reminiscing, but man's country was receding fast; they were already halfway home, and all they could call up was the 1961 Bel Air fire, during which Henry Hathaway had ordered the Los Angeles Fire Department off his property and saved the place himself by, among other measures, throwing everything flammable into the swimming pool. "Those fire guys might've just given it up," Wayne said. "Just let it burn." In fact this was a good story, and one incorporating several of their favorite themes, but a Bel Air story was still not a Durango story.

In the early afternoon they began the last scene, and although they spent as much time as possible setting it up, the moment finally came when there was nothing to do but shoot it. "Second team out, first team in, *doors closed*," the assistant director shouted one last time. The stand-ins walked off the set, John Wayne and Martha Hyer walked on. "All right, boys, *silencio*, this is a picture." They took it twice. Twice the girl offered John Wayne the tattered Bible. Twice John Wayne told her that "there's a lot of places I go where that wouldn't fit in." Everyone was very still. And at 2:30 that Friday afternoon Henry Hathaway turned away from the camera, and in the hush that followed he ground out his cigar in a sand bucket. "OK," he said. "That's it."

Since that summer of 1943 I had thought of John Wayne in a number of ways. I had thought of him driving cattle up from Texas, and bringing airplanes in on a single engine, thought of him telling the girl at the Alamo that "Republic is a beautiful word." I had never thought of him having dinner with his family and with me and my husband in an expensive restaurant in Chapultepec Park, but time brings odd mutations, and there we were, one night that last week in Mexico. For a while it was only a nice evening, an evening anywhere. We had a lot of drinks and I lost the sense that the face across the table was in certain ways more familiar than my husband's.

And then something happened. Suddenly the room seemed suffused with the dream, and I could not think why. Three men appeared out of nowhere, playing guitars. Pilar Wayne leaned slightly forward, and John Wayne lifted his glass almost imperceptibly toward her. "We'll need some Pouilly-Fuissé for the rest of the table," he said, "and some red Bordeaux for the Duke." We all smiled, and drank the Pouilly-Fuissé for the rest of the table and the red Bordeaux for the Duke, and all the while the men with the guitars kept playing, until finally I realized what they were playing, what they had been playing all along: "The Red River Valley" and the theme from *The High and the Mighty*. They did not quite get the beat right, but even now I can hear them, in another country and a long time later, even as I tell you this.

Nonstop Action: Why Hollywood's Aging Heroes Won't Give Up the Gun

Adam Mars-Jones

Male careers in the movies have always been longer than female ones, but until recently there was only one real route to onscreen immortality—to the certified, gold-standard agelessness of, say, Cary Grant. (In *North by Northwest*, Grant, then fifty-five, not only appeared opposite a woman twenty years younger than him, Eva Marie Saint, [but] his screen mother was played by someone only seven years his senior.) The key principle is suavity: the refusal to break a sweat; sophistication with the faintest hint of self-mockery; the actor letting us know that he is old enough to know how silly this all is.

There are still disciples following that path up the mountain to the sunny uplands of longevity—perhaps we should think of this as Mount Rushmore being reconfigured to include a huge stone likeness of Grant himself, like the ones he scrambled over so urbanely in *North by Northwest*. Over there, do you see? There are George Clooney and Hugh Grant (both fifty-four) in their hiking shorts, clambering for dear life as the career shadows fall, and a little further down is Colin Firth (also fifty-four), trying to make sense of the map. Richard Gere (sixty-five) is sitting cross-legged on a boulder and seems to be meditating, though he may just be taking a nap. Suddenly they all freeze (though with Gere it is hard to tell). What's that sound? Gunfire. But it seems to be coming from further up the mountain, where the old-timers are plainly not putting their feet up.

There is now apparently no age limit to an action career in Hollywood. The expendables are no longer unemployables, and actors in their sixties and even seventies are high-kicking in can-can routines of choreographed violence. After making a third *Indiana Jones* sequel in his mid-sixties, Harrison Ford was over seventy when he joined the grizzled crew of *The Expendables 3* (with Sylvester Stallone weighing in at sixty-eight and Arnold Schwarzenegger at sixty-seven), in which the mercenary group does battle with its founder, who is now resolved to destroy them. In *Indiana Jones and the Kingdom of the Crystal Skull*, the camera keeps its distance from Ford's stunt doubles—the charisma of an aging action star has more to fear from obvious fakery in fights than from facial close-ups, since not much more is required of him than rugged scowls and glares of baleful defiance. Ford's return as Han Solo in a forthcoming installment of *Star Wars* after a third of a century is a melancholy prospect, like someone dressing up in late life to match a graduation photograph.

Tom Cruise, now fifty-three and strongly committed to stunt work, has just appeared in a fifth *Mission Impossible* film and has signed up for another. By the time of its scheduled release, in 2017, he will be as old as Bruce Willis was in the first *RED* film, when he was Retired (though allegedly also Extremely Dangerous, to complete the acronym of the film's title). For Cruise it seems that the real mission impossible would be calling it a day.

A loophole seems to have opened up, almost a wormhole in the fabric of Hollywood space-time. Through this portal an entire generation of veterans is currently trooping—and it is Liam Neeson, sixty-three, who has made the most drastic and yet the smoothest journey across the genre universe, with *Taken* and its sequels. Steven Spielberg's Schindler, agonizing over whether he might have managed to save one more life, has been made over into a killing machine.

Neeson's *Taken* character is a civilian whose unending mission is to rescue and secure his family, which gives him the moral stature to justify any amount of bloodshed. At the beginning of the story, Neeson's character, Bryan Mills, was presented as an overprotective father, unable to move on from a broken marriage and spending altogether too much time worrying about the safety of his teenage daughter, Kim, seeking to control her movements. This could be a psychological drama of divorce, but then it strays into *Bodyguard* territory when Bryan agrees to help out some old friends, who have been hired to provide security for a moppet pop star's gala concert but are a man short. In due course, there is a murder attempt, fitting the Kevin Costner/ Whitney Houston template, and a moment of intimacy in its aftermath, but this too is a false trail, revealing the hero's combat skills but not yet explaining them (he is an ex–CIA operative). Two genre feints in a running time of only ninety-three minutes—that's not bad going. Only when Kim (Maggie Grace) goes to Paris and is abducted does the film move up decisively in terms of octane rating. Neeson plays it grim and straight. As *Gladiator* showed, audiences attuned to romantic self-sacrifice (a traditionally female character arc) will accept a fair amount of violence, and it also works the other way around, with the stereotypically male element willing to identify ungrumblingly with a man who has lost the love of his life and never looks for a replacement.

What's Neeson's secret? His physique? Hardly—he has never been one of Hollywood's Shirtless Ones, hasn't even spent much screen time in a singlet. No doubt he has a fitness regimen beyond what most civilians would contemplate, but he seems to have no interest in projecting bolts of testosterone to the back of the auditorium. He moves like a big man who has learned to be light on his feet.

He has had the advantage of a late start, though it can hardly have seemed like an advantage at the time. There were plenty of male stars from Hollywood's classic period who could not easily be imagined young, among them the ones who most seem to symbolize integrity: Humphrey Bogart and Spencer Tracy. A young actor can embody idealism easily enough (James Spader, say, in *sex, lies, and videotape*, Steven Soderbergh's 1989 drama of fetishism and repression), but integrity is something that needs to have been tested over time, if not actually by time. For actors such as Bogart and Tracy (plus James Cagney and Edward G. Robinson, though less reliably virtuous), their heyday was middle age. Wrinkles formed part of their appeal, rather than undermining it. Maturity was their present tense, and they had no visual history, lacking Facebook pages to plunder their own lives and archive the mistakes of adolescence.

The fact that more people are living long lives does not necessarily make aging easier, and stardom has become a complicated business, with any amount of toxic undercurrent, ripples of projected narcissism, and rancor. Stardom has changed because fandom has changed. Fandom in cinema increasingly follows the model of Kathy Bates's Annie Wilkes in Stephen King's *Misery*, which reveals devotion as something essentially raging and vengeful. Obsessive love becomes malign stalking. Fame has always had its drawbacks, but now it seems all downside. To be a celebrity these days is to be beleaguered and outgunned, to feel at the mercy of every stranger's Twitter feed. Perhaps that's part of the appeal of action roles to the mature performer. In a world of stalkers, it is tempting for the world-weary to fire the first shot.

Celebrity has become an incurable condition, without remission. I can almost find it in my heart to sympathize with film stars who ban eye contact on set or from their staff. Fame is a treadmill, and having your own gym does not seem to make the legwork any easier.

When Charlie Chaplin was the most famous person in the world, he could get rid of his moustache and go more or less anywhere he wanted. When the Beatles were the most famous people in the world, they had to dodge the crowds, naturally, but that did not stop them taking time off without worrying too much about it. Publicity then was still a dog that could be brought to heel—but now thousands of the world's most famous people have no possibility of escape from the spotlight they once ran towards so trustingly. Even seemingly contrived experiments in leading a normal life, such as Paul McCartney sending his children to state schools, would be impractical nowadays. The time when a world-famous film star could announce her retirement, as Greta Garbo did in 1941, and live out her life in New York without being bothered, even though anyone who wanted to could discover her whereabouts, are long gone. Only death can break the spell.

When Gore Vidal said of Truman Capote that his death was a good career move, it was mere waspish provocation, but the same assertion could be made without irony about Jean Harlow, James Dean, Marilyn Monroe. The flesh-and-blood person is surplus to requirements once an icon has been created, and often becomes an active embarrassment.

The prophetic document of the transformation of fame from safe haven into torture chamber was Robert Aldrich's hideous 1962 film *What Ever Happened to Baby Jane?*, in which a former child actor, now an angry old woman, imprisons her disabled sister. There had been conscious ugliness in films before, but if this was meant to be a star vehicle for Bette Davis and Joan Crawford, then the vehicle it most resembled was a hearse driven off a bridge. The film's greatest effect lay in its sadistic gloating over the aging of the actors, whose faces and bodies were showing the effects of the passing of time, which female film stars are not allowed to undergo. Davis, in particular, seemed punished by being put in childish clothing and portrayed as being trapped in the past, when in fact her screen persona had always been nonstandard and her choices often inventive—her fading actor Margo Channing in *All About Eve*, for instance, was by Hollywood standards a stingingly honest portrait of vanity made monstrous by despair.

It is easy to feel that the main event of celebrity culture is now the showing-up of the failing flesh, and all the acclaim of youth and freshness that goes before is only a pretext. When identification fails, when the idol fails to retire gracefully, things can turn nasty. Films are so centrally about youth and beauty that aging onscreen is a real taboo. We do not feel sympathetic when our idols reveal themselves as mortal —we feel betrayed. They have let down their side of the bargain, and unless they find a way to negotiate a new contract with a degree of energy and grace, fans become feral.

This used to be primarily the experience of women in films, but these days there is almost as full a range of options and delusions available to male movie stars as to their female counterparts. We have seen male stars go too far down the path of plastic surgery and others who have relied too much on what they were born with. There is the temptation to have a lot of work done, as revealed by Mickey Rourke to gasps of audience horror in *The Wrestler*. And there is the temptation to put your faith in Mother Nature and let it all hang out, as exemplified by Gérard Depardieu to gasps of audience horror in *Welcome to New York*.

There are pages on the internet about "celebrities aging disgustingly." One of the prime exhibits in this rogues' gallery of blasphemers against approved self-presentation is Macaulay Culkin. What has this disgusting brute done? He just stopped being ten years old, as he was at the time of *Home Alone*—a bit of bad behavior he shares with everyone else who was born in 1980. Culkin has not even forced himself on the world's attention with any great energy, unless voice-overs for *Robot Chicken* on TV count. He looks a bit rough, it's true. It is enough that he was once the defining image of youth and innocence and now falls short of it. In the aftermath of celebrity, privacy is not an option.

The current incarnation of youth in films is not in the equivalent of a John Hughes comedy, but in Richard Linklater's high-concept movie *Boyhood*, in which Ellar Coltrane is made to age convincingly from child to man by the drastic decision to film him over twelve years. Linklater's film seems to have outwitted the enemy, containing and controlling the poignancy of the passage of time, but that is just how it looks now. There is no inoculation against mortality on film, except, strangely, tragic early death. If Coltrane is spared that, then one day soon he will be snapped unshaven and with bags under his eyes, and then he will be all over the media world, with the shaming image appearing alongside the dewiest frame of him from *Boyhood*.

What is it about Liam Neeson that gives him durability while those around him are derided for the solecism of getting older? If it isn't his physique, then perhaps it is worth considering his face. A broken nose can have a whole range of overlapping meanings. It suggests a bad boy rather than someone who abides by the rules, though there are many ways of suffering a facial impact, and relatively few of them corroborate such a character sketch. The decision not to have the nose straightened seems to offer more reliable testimony of a character indifferent to vanity. Even if this is a false impression, a broken nose takes away the potential stigma of prettiness from a male face. It is certainly a mark of experience of some sort and an imperfection that can somehow enhance appeal.

There is no facial characteristic that communicates, however misleadingly, fearlessness and lack of vanity in women. In film terms, experience seems to add to a man but subtract from a woman. Men can have been around the block a few times, but women are condemned to the repetition of freshness. It is as if a man can live off the interest of the time and effort invested in making movies, with a real prospect of earning the adjective "distinguished," while a woman is always spending the capital of her looks, jeered at when she runs into debt or has to buy back her youth from a surgeon.

Heavyweight dramatic actors often venture into comedy as a way of extending their durability in the marketplace. Meryl Streep has turned herself, with some effort and after a fair few duds, into a performer who can raise a laugh, while Robert De Niro has by now spent more time spoofing his persona than exploring it. Self-parody has existed in the movies at least since Marlene Dietrich's performance in *Destry Rides Again* (a 1939 Western in which she stars as a crime boss's girlfriend who is won over by earnest, nonviolent James Stewart while he tries to impose order on a lawless town), but it is a new development for it to be a whole career in itself. Of course, it is tempting for writers and directors to protect their films against laughter by preempting it.

Liam Neeson may or may not have a sense of humor—certainly his appearance on Ricky Gervais and Stephen Merchant's *Life's Too Short* on television was as excruciating as anything since De Niro's turn as the deluded would-be chat show host in Martin Scorsese's *The King of Comedy*, but that was the desired effect. Comic relief is certainly not part of the organizing principle of *Taken* and its sequels, though the incongruity of Neeson as a skilled assassin was built into the structure of the first film—something impossible to carry over into subsequent installments of what has become a successful franchise.

The level of brutality in *Taken* is modest by Quentin Tarantino's standards and is excused in plot terms by a number of factors: the hero being far from home, one against many, racing against time, and so on. But not every actor can make an audience accept the hero leaving a villain plugged into the mains after he has no more information to give, or shooting a woman without warning to make sure her husband understands the gravity of his situation. "It's only a flesh wound," growls Neeson, as if he had done no more than spill red wine on his hostess's dress.

Bruce Willis, an actor reliant on wisecracks, can make sure that a film such as *RED* seems like light entertainment with added gunplay and punch-throwing, but there is an awkward moment when Willis produces a bag full of severed fingers in order to identify the bodies of the men who have rashly just ambushed him. Liam Neeson's Bryan Mills does not do anything quite as cold-blooded as mutilating corpses, but if he did, we would not be shielded from it by the directors of the *Taken* series—Pierre Morel, replaced in the sequels by the wonderfully named Olivier Megaton, both protégés of Luc Besson, Frenchmen shrewdly recycling American film tropes for the US market. Willis has been quipping his way out of moral ambiguity since the romantic comedy TV series *Moonlighting* three decades ago. Neeson is much less of a known quantity, certainly in action roles, and at their best the *Taken* films move him back and forth across the boundary between defensible and indefensible violence, never quite losing sympathy, nor ever quite taking it for granted.

What quality can turn an earnest middle-aged actor into an action hero? Gravitas is the indispensable element in this context: the moral stature that can complement physical power and even make it irrelevant, which seems to be viewed culturally as a male preserve. This quality is hard to define, though, even as it applies to men. Perhaps it is simplest to describe it in negative terms, as "what Tom Cruise will never have." Some have gravitas and some do not. Boyishness and gravitas do not go together, and an eager-beaver manner kills it stone dead. The script of the 1992 film *Far and Away*, for instance, required Cruise, in desperate straits, to assert his authority over a horse by punching it (the setting is the Oklahoma land rush, and he is in a hurry to stake a claim). As a bit of business, it simply didn't come off. There were film actors at the time who could have made it work, and they are the same ones who could get away with it today, nearly a quarter century on: Clint Eastwood, Sean Connery, Harrison Ford. It is not a matter of physical strength—after all, no horse is actually being hit. It is down to gravitas: old-style stardom without benefit of moisturizer.

Gravitas is an accumulated heroic presence that can act as both armor and arsenal. How many people, for instance, watching Clint Eastwood in *The Gauntlet* in 1976, noticed that, while protecting a key witness in a mob trial, he never shoots anyone? Gravitas is a sort of abstract firepower that does not need to pull the trigger.

Is gravitas even possible for women in the movies? A woman in public life can embrace the physical signs of seniority as a badge of her seriousness, like Christine Lagarde of the IMF, who does not dye her hair and, as a result, appears to stand above the distractions of vanity. That, however, is not a possible strategy for an actor who wants to be cast in films. Even going ash blonde is a bit of a risk. Of the possible claimants, in terms of seniority and eminence (all of them older than Lagarde), Meryl Streep more or less disqualifies herself by her reliance on acting technique, her disinclination to establish a consistent persona across a range of roles. Helen Mirren relies on a disarming insolence, and her confidence that she will never run short of desirability seems justified so far. She can have a love interest her own age or, in *RED*, even fractionally older, and she is so offhand about it that nobody even notices how exceptional this is. Of this select group, only Judi Dench is defined not by being looked at but by looking. In her best work she out-stares the viewer, astringent, judging, refusing even the admiration she has earned with her rejection of conventional approval. Female gravitas necessarily has a charge of wariness, and an actor who waited until after her sixtieth birthday for a leading role on the big screen (*Mrs. Brown*, in which she plays the newly widowed Queen Victoria) will be warier than most. Dench escaped the workings of Stephen Sondheim's law of female destiny in show business, as spelled out in "I'm Still Here" from the musical *Follies* ("First you're another sloe-eyed vamp / Then someone's mother, then you're camp"), and that doesn't happen by taking anything for granted.

There seems to be a shortage of intelligent presentations of older women to a grown-up audience. Anyone who has seen Pedro Almodóvar's *Women on the Verge of a Nervous Breakdown* will have seen the director's cheeky casting of Francisca Caballero—his mother—as a television newsreader. Women who work in front of a television camera and are unwise enough to pass their fortieth birthdays are losing their jobs all the time, but one look at Almodóvar's film should convince any sensible person that newsreaders in their forties are not slightly too old, but much too young. What you want, when it is time to hear about the day's events, is not some glamorpuss but someone who has been around for a bit, someone who has seen a few things in her time, a few wars, floods, and Oscar nominations. It gives a bit of context, a sense of proportion.

Filmmaking, of course, is not about proportion. Stardom has strange acoustical properties that variously amplify, suppress, and distort the frequencies of the personality involved. It is hard to turn such an apparatus into a loudspeaker for consciously conveying messages, though it has sometimes been tried. Subtext needs to stay buried.

When Mark Rydell's *On Golden Pond* brought Jane and Henry Fonda together onscreen in 1981, the family reunion seemed to stand in for something more ambitious, the rehabilitation of a prodigal daughter. The star who had aligned herself most intensely with the counterculture of the 1960s, Hanoi Jane herself, was sending the message, using her father as a stand-in, that all she had ever wanted was to be loved and accepted by conservative America. No wonder the film felt strained—it had an agenda as fraught as the AGM [annual general meeting] of a failing company.

Film stars, offering themselves as screens on to which audiences can project their fantasies, cannot expect to control the process, except in the most indirect way. A shrewd film star is both a work of art and its curator. The supreme practitioner in this line must be Marlene Dietrich—when you hired her, you got her lighting man, too, so that she retained full control over the product. Alongside the erotic mystique, she had a strong hausfrau side, which did not show up on film, but she certainly kept her glamour swept and dusted. That professionalism extended to her home, where she received visitors in a chair placed under a spotlight, with a silver stripe painted down her nose to correct the proportions that did not meet her standards. Without any such crude mechanisms, Cary Grant maintained an astonishingly consistent persona over the decades, defending his narrow range (stylized ease, controlling suavity) against any possible challenge.

It can happen that stardom simply evaporates, leaving talent intact, which would be one way of describing Al Pacino's career—he is still a performer with magnetism but has shed what made him so fascinating in the 1970s, a physicality with elements of both the innocent and the wild. And sometimes a star persona takes a dogleg, moving into new territory without an actual break. John Wayne's last starring role, in *The Shootist* (1976), for instance, was enriched by the cancer diagnosis shared by the actor and the character he played. Sometimes a film star can have two different and contrasting heydays, as happened with James Stewart. In his early career, up to *The Philadelphia Story* in 1940, he embodied an idealism that did not necessarily exclude slyness (in *The Philadelphia Story*, as the reporter at the society wedding, he makes divorced roué Cary Grant seem smug and obvious). When he started making films again after his distinguished military service, he had changed. He was like a bell with a hairline crack, the fundamental note unchanged, the overtones tending to jangle, and offering rich new resonances of uncertainty (*Vertigo*), strained folksiness (*Anatomy of a Murder*), and despair (*It's a Wonderful Life*) to the directors he worked with.

The first *Taken* film was made before Neeson's wife, Natasha Richardson, died suddenly in 2009. If it seems crass to connect a film star's changing persona with his life experiences, then it is a crassness that was built into the workings of stardom even before modern communications made sure that there was no such thing as a secret sorrow. Film is porous. An event such as Neeson's bereavement echoes backward in time, filling his segment of *Love Actually* (widowed father tries to teach his son how to approach the girl he is besotted with) with new associations, though it is anything but classic material in itself. His persona has been enriched with pain and the guilt of the survivor, which adds depth to the action hero's trump card, the willingness to take punishment. He wins not because he is the better fighter, but because he doesn't care about himself. Neeson's presence was always somber rather than blithe, so that the sorrow and strain we project on to it only accentuates what was there before. To have gravitas means to inhabit your history and not to be diminished by your losses. And if that isn't quite the same thing as real-world maturity, on the big screen it is the best we are going to get.

Willing

Lorrie Moore

How can I live my life without committing an act with giant scissors?

—Joyce Carol Oates, "An Interior Monologue"

n her last picture, the camera had lingered at the hip, the naked hip, and even though it wasn't her hip, she acquired a reputation for being willing.

"You have the body," studio heads told her over lunch at Chasen's. She looked away. "Habeas corpus," she said, not smiling.

"Pardon me?" A hip that knew Latin. Christ.

"Nothing," she said. They smiled at her and dropped names. Scorsese, Brando. Work was all playtime to them, playtime with gel in their hair. At times, she felt bad that it *wasn't* her hip. It should have been her hip. A mediocre picture, a picture queasy with pornography: these, she knew, eroticized the unavailable. The doctored and false. The stand-in. Unwittingly, she had participated. Let a hip come between. A false, unavailable, anonymous hip. She herself was true as a goddamn dairy product; available as lunch whenever.

But she was pushing forty.

She began to linger in juice bars. Sit for entire afternoons in places called I Love Juicy or Orange-U-Sweet. She drank juice and, outside, smoked a cigarette now and then. She'd been taken seriously—once—she knew that. Projects were discussed: Nina. Portia. Mother Courage with makeup. Now her hands trembled too much, even drinking juice, *especially* drinking juice, a Vantage wobbling between her fingers like a compass dial. She was sent scripts in which she was supposed to say lines she would never say, not wear clothes she would never not wear. She began to get obscene phone calls, and postcards signed, "Oh yeah, baby." Her boyfriend, a director with a growing reputation for expensive flops, a man who twice a week glowered at her Fancy Sunburst guppy and told it to get a job, became a Catholic and went back to his wife.

"Just when we were working out the bumps and chops and rocks," she said. Then she wept.

"I know," he said. "I know."

And so she left Hollywood. Phoned her agent and apologized. Went home to Chicago, rented a room by the week at the Days Inn, drank sherry, and grew a little plump. She let her life get dull—dull, but with Hostess cakes. There were moments bristling with deadness, when she looked out at her life and went "*What?*" Or worse, feeling interrupted and tired, "Wha—?" It had taken on the shape of a terrible mistake. She hadn't been given the proper tools to make a real life with, she decided, that was it. She'd been given a can of gravy and a hairbrush and told, "There you go." She'd stood there for years, blinking and befuddled, brushing the can with the brush.

Still, she was a minor movie star, once nominated for a major award. Mail came to her indirectly. A notice. A bill. A Thanksgiving card. But there was never a party, a dinner, an opening, an iced tea. One of the problems with people in Chicago, she remembered, was that they were never lonely at the same time. Their sadnesses occurred in isolation, lurched and spazzed, sent them spinning fizzily back into empty, padded corners, disconnected and alone.

She watched cable and ordered in a lot from a pizza place. A life of obscurity and radical calm. She rented a piano and practiced scales. She invested in the stock market. She wrote down her dreams in the morning to locate clues as to what to trade. *Disney*, her dreams said once. *St. Jude's Medical*. She made a little extra money. She got obsessed. The words *cash cow* nestled in the side of her mouth like a cud. She tried to be original—not a good thing with stocks—and she began to lose. When a stock went down, she bought more of it, to catch it on the way back up. She got confused. She took to staring out the window at Lake Michigan, the rippled slate of it like a blackboard gone bad.

"Sidra, *what* are you doing there?" shrieked her friend Tommy long distance over the phone. "Where are you? You're living in some state that borders on North Dakota!" He was a screenwriter in Santa Monica and once, a long time ago and depressed on Ecstasy, they had slept together. He was gay, but they had liked each other very much.

"Maybe I'll get married," she said. She didn't mind Chicago. She thought of it as a cross between London and Queens, with a dash of Cleveland.

"Oh, *please*," he shrieked again. "What are you *really* doing?"

"Listening to seashore and self-esteem tapes," she said. She blew air into the mouth of the phone.

"Sounds like dust on the needle," he said. "Maybe you should get the squawking crickets tape. Have you *heard* the squawking crickets tape?"

"I got a bad perm today," she said. "When I was only halfway through with the rod part, the building the salon's in had a blackout. There were men drilling out front who'd struck a cable."

"How awful for you," he said. She could hear him tap his fingers. He had made himself the make-believe author of a make-believe book of essays called *One Man's Opinion*, and when he was bored or inspired, he quoted from it. "I was once in a rock band called Bad Perm," he said instead.

"Get out." She laughed.

His voice went hushed and worried. "What *are* you *doing* there?" he asked again.

Her room was a corner room where a piano was allowed. It was L-shaped, like a life veering off suddenly to become something else. It had a couch and two maple dressers and was never as neat as she might have wanted. She always had the DO NOT DISTURB sign on when the maids came by, and so things got a little out of hand. Wispy motes of dust and hair the size of small heads bumped around in the corners. Smudge began to darken the moldings and cloud the mirrors. The bathroom faucet dripped, and, too tired to phone anyone, she tied a string around the end of it, guiding the drip quietly into the drain, so it wouldn't bother her anymore. Her only plant, facing east in the window, hung over the popcorn popper and dried to a brown crunch. On the ledge, a jack-o'-lantern she had carved for Halloween had rotted, melted, froze, and now looked like a collapsed basketball—one she might have been saving for sentimental reasons, one from the *big game*! The man who brought her room service each morning—two poached eggs and a pot of coffee—reported her to the assistant manager, and she received a written warning slid under her door.

On Fridays, she visited her parents in Elmhurst. It was still hard for her father to look her in the eyes. He was seventy now. Ten years ago, he had gone to the first movie she had ever been in, saw her remove her clothes and dive into a pool. The movie was rated PG, but he never went to another one. Her mother went to all of them and searched later for encouraging things to say. Even something small. She refused to lie. "I liked the way you said the line about leaving home, your eyes wide and your hands fussing with your dress buttons," she wrote. "That red dress was so becoming. You should wear bright colors!"

"My father takes naps a lot when I visit," she said to Tommy.

"Naps?"

"I embarrass him. He thinks I'm a whore hippie. A hippie whore."

"That's ridiculous. As I said in *One Man's Opinion*, you're the most sexually conservative person I know."

"Yeah, well."

Her mother always greeted her warmly, puddle-eyed. These days, she was reading thin paperback books by a man named Robert Valleys, a man who said that after observing all the suffering in the world—war, starvation, greed—he had discovered the cure: hugs.

Hugs, hugs, hugs, hugs, hugs.

Her mother believed him. She squeezed so long and hard that Sidra, like an infant or a lover, became lost in the feel and smell of her—her sweet, dry skin, the gray peach fuzz on her neck. "I'm so glad you left that den of iniquity," her mother said softly.

But Sidra still got calls from the den. At night, sometimes, the director phoned from a phone booth, desiring to be forgiven as well as to direct. "I think of all the things you might be thinking, and I say, 'Oh Christ.' I mean, do you think the things I sometimes think you do?"

"Of course," said Sidra. "Of course I think those things."

"*Of course! Of course* is a term that has no place in this conversation!"

When Tommy phoned, she often felt a pleasure so sudden and flooding, it startled her.

"God, I'm so glad it's you!"

"You have no right to abandon American filmmaking this way!" he would say affectionately, and she would laugh loudly, for minutes without stopping. She was starting to have two speeds: Coma and Hysteria. Two meals: breakfast and popcorn. Two friends: Charlotte Peveril and Tommy. She could hear the clink of his bourbon glass. "You are too gifted a person to be living in a state that borders on North Dakota."

"Iowa."

"Holy bejesus, it's worse than I thought. I'll bet they say that there. I'll bet they say 'Bejesus.'"

"I live downtown. They don't say that here."

"Are you anywhere near Champaign-Urbana?"

"No."

"I went there once. I thought from its name that it would be a different kind of place. I kept saying it to myself, 'Champagne, ur*bah* na, *champagne*, ur*bah* na! Champagne! Urbana!'" He sighed. "It was just this thing in the middle of a field. I went to a Chinese restaurant there and ordered my entire dinner with *extra* MSG."

"I'm in Chicago. It's not so bad."

"Not so bad. There are no movie people there. Sidra, what about your *acting talent*?"

"I have no acting talent."

"Hello?"

"You heard me."

"I'm not sure. For a minute there, I thought maybe you had that dizziness thing again, that inner-ear imbalance."

"Talent. I don't have *talent*. I have willingness. What *talent*?" As a kid, she had always told the raunchiest jokes. As an adult, she could rip open a bone and speak out of it. Simple, clear. There was never anything to stop her. Why was there never anything to stop her? "I can stretch out the neck of a sweater to point at a freckle on my shoulder. Anyone who didn't get enough attention in nursery school can do that. Talent is something else."

"Excuse me, okay? I'm only a screenwriter. But someone's got you thinking you went from serious actress to aging bimbo. That's ridiculous. You just have to weather things a little out here. Besides. I think willing yourself to do a thing is brave, and the very essence of talent."

Sidra looked at her hands, already chapped and honeycombed with bad weather, bad soap, bad life. She needed to listen to the crickets tape. "But I *don't* will myself," she said. "I'm just already willing."

She began to go to blues bars at night. Sometimes she called Charlotte Peveril, her one friend left from high school.

"Siddy, how are you?" In Chicago, Sidra was thought of as a hillbilly name. But in LA, people had thought it was beautiful and assumed she'd made it up.

"I'm fine. Let's go get drunk and listen to music."

Sometimes she just went by herself.

"Don't I know you from the movies?" a man might ask at one of the breaks, smiling, leering in a twinkly way.

"Maybe," she'd say, and he would look suddenly panicked and back away.

One night, a handsome man in a poncho, a bad poncho—though was there such a thing as a good poncho? asked Charlotte—sat down next to her with an extra glass of beer. "You look like you should be in the movies," he said. Sidra nodded wearily. "But I don't go to the movies. So if you *were* in the movies, I would never have gotten to set my eyes on you."

She turned her gaze from his poncho to her sherry, then back. Perhaps he had spent some time in Mexico or Peru. "What do you do?"

"I'm an auto mechanic." He looked at her carefully. "My name's Walter. Walt." He pushed the second beer her way. "The drinks here are okay as long as you don't ask them to mix anything. Just don't ask them to mix anything!"

She picked it up and took a sip. There was something about him she liked: something earthy beneath the act. In LA, beneath the act you got nougat or Styrofoam. Or glass. Sidra's mouth was lined with sherry. Walt's lips shone with beer. "What's the last movie you saw?" she asked him.

"The last movie I saw. Let's see." He was thinking, but she could tell he wasn't good at it. She watched with curiosity the folded-in mouth, the tilted head: at last, a guy who didn't go to the movies. His eyes rolled back like the casters on a clerk's chair, searching. "You know what I saw?"

"No. What?" She was getting drunk.

"It was this cartoon movie." Animation. She felt relieved. At least it wasn't one of those bad art films starring what's-her-name. "A man is asleep, having a dream about a beautiful little country full of little people." Walt sat back, looked around the room, as if that were all.

"*And?*" She was going to have to push and pull with this guy.

"'And?'" he repeated. He leaned forward again. "And one day the people realize that they are only creatures in this man's dream. Dream people! And if the man wakes up, they will no longer exist!"

Now she hoped he wouldn't go on. She had changed her mind a little.

"So they all get together at a town meeting and devise a plan," he continued. Perhaps the band would be back soon. "They will burst into the man's bedroom and bring him back to a padded, insulated room in the town—the town of his own dream—and there they will keep watch over him to make sure he stays asleep. And they do just that. Forever and ever, everyone guarding him carefully, but apprehensively, making sure he never wakes up." He smiled. "I forgot what the name of it was."

"And he never wakes up."

"Nope." He grinned at her. She liked him. She could tell he could tell. He took a sip of his beer. He looked around the bar, then back at her. "Is this a great country or what?" he said.

She smiled at him, with longing. "Where do you live," she asked, "and how do I get there?"

"I met a man," she told Tommy on the phone. "His name is Walter."

"A forced relationship. You're in a state of stress—you're in a *syndrome*, I can tell. You're going to force this romance. What does he do?"

"Something with cars." She sighed. "I want to sleep with someone. When I'm sleeping with someone, I'm less obsessed with the mail."

"But perhaps you should just be alone, be by yourself for a while."

"Like you've ever been alone," said Sidra. "I mean, have you *ever* been alone?"

"I've been alone."

"Yeah, and for how long?"

"Hours," said Tommy. He sighed. "At least it felt like hours."

"Right," she said, "so don't go lecturing me about inner resources."

"Okay. So I sold the mineral rights to my body years ago, but, hey, at least *I* got good money for mine."

"I got some money," said Sidra. "I got some."

Walter leaned her against his parked car. His mouth was slightly lop-sided, paisley-shaped, his lips anneloid and full, and he kissed her hard. There was something numb and on hold in her. There were small dark pits of annihilation she discovered in her heart, in the loosening fist of it, and she threw herself into them, falling. She went home with him, slept with him. She told him who she was. A minor movie star once nominated for a major award. She told him she lived at the Days Inn. He had been there once, to the top, for a drink. But he did not seem to know her name.

"Never thought I'd sleep with a movie star," he did say. "I suppose that's every man's dream." He laughed—lightly, nervously.

"Just don't wake up," she said. Then she pulled the covers to her chin.

"Or change the dream," he added seriously. "I mean, in the movie I saw, everything is fine until the sleeping guy begins to dream about something else. I don't think he wills it or anything; it just happens."

"You didn't tell me about that part."

"That's right," he said. "You see, the guy starts dreaming about fla-mingos and then all the little people turn into flamingos and fly away."

"Really?" said Sidra.

"I *think* it was flamingos. I'm not too expert with birds."

"You're *not*?" She was trying to tease him, but it came out wrong, like a lizard with a little hat on.

"To tell you the truth, I really don't think I ever saw a single movie you were in."

"Good." She was drifting, indifferent, no longer paying attention.

He hitched his arm behind his head, wrist to nape. His chest heaved up and down. "I think I may of *heard* of you, though."

Django Reinhardt was on the radio. She listened, carefully. "Aston-ishing sounds came from that man's hands," Sidra murmured.

Walter tried to kiss her, tried to get her attention back. He wasn't that interested in music, though at times he tried to be.

"'Astonishing sounds'?" he said. "Like this?" He cupped his palms together, making little pops and suction noises.

"Yeah," she murmured. But she was elsewhere, letting a dry wind sweep across the plain of her to sleep. "Like that."

He began to realize, soon, that she did not respect him. A bug could sense it. A doorknob could figure it out. She never quite took him seriously. She would talk about films and film directors, then look at him and say, "Oh, never mind." She was part of some other world. A world she no longer liked.

And now she was somewhere else. Another world she no longer liked.

But she was willing. Willing to give it a whirl. Once in a while, though she tried not to, she asked him about children, about having children, about turning kith to kin. How did he feel about all that? It seemed to her that if she were ever going to have a life of children and lawn mowers and grass clippings, it would be best to have it with someone who was not demeaned or trivialized by discussions of them. Did he like those big fertilized lawns? How about a nice rock garden? How did he feel deep down about those combination storm windows with the built-in screens?

"Yeah, I like them all right," he said, and she would nod slyly and drink a little too much. She would try then not to think too strenuously about her *whole life*. She would try to live life one day at a time, like an alcoholic—drink, don't drink, drink. Perhaps she should take drugs.

"I always thought someday I would have a little girl and name her after my grandmother." Sidra sighed, peered wistfully into her sherry.

"What was your grandmother's name?"

Sidra looked at his paisley mouth. "Grandma. Her name was Grandma." Walter laughed in a honking sort of way. "Oh, thank you," murmured Sidra. "Thank you for laughing."

Walter had a subscription to *Autoweek*. He flipped through it in bed. He also liked to read repair manuals for new cars, particularly the Toyotas. He knew a lot about control panels, light-up panels, side panels.

"You're so obviously wrong for each other," said Charlotte over tapas at a tapas bar.

"Hey, please," said Sidra. "I think my taste's a little subtler than that." The thing with tapas bars was that you just kept stuffing things into your mouth. "Obviously wrong is just the beginning. That's where I *always* begin. At obviously wrong." In theory, she liked the idea of mismatched couples, the wrangling and retangling, like a comedy by Shakespeare.

"I can't imagine you with someone like him. He's just not special." Charlotte had met him only once. But she had heard of him from a girlfriend of hers. He had slept around, she'd said. "Into the pudding" is how she phrased it, and there were some boring stories. "Just don't let him humiliate you. Don't mistake a lack of sophistication for sweetness," she added.

"I'm supposed to wait around for someone special, while every other girl in this town gets to have a life?"

"I don't know, Sidra."

It was true. Men could be with whomever they pleased. But women had to date better, kinder, richer, and bright, bright, bright, or else people got embarrassed. It suggested sexual things. "I'm a very average person," she said desperately, somehow detecting that Charlotte already knew that, knew the deep, dark, wildly obvious secret of that, and how it made Sidra slightly pathetic, unseemly—*inferior*, when you got right down to it. Charlotte studied Sidra's face, headlights caught in the stare of a deer. Guns don't kill people, thought Sidra fizzily. Deer kill people.

"Maybe it's that we all used to envy you so much," Charlotte said a little bitterly. "You were so talented. You got all the lead parts in the plays. You were everyone's dream of what *they* wanted."

Sidra poked around at the appetizer in front of her, gardening it like a patch of land. She was unequal to anyone's wistfulness. She had made too little of her life. Its loneliness shamed her like a crime. "Envy," said Sidra. "That's a lot like hate, isn't it." But Charlotte didn't say anything. Probably she wanted Sidra to change the subject. Sidra stuffed her mouth full of feta cheese and onions, and looked up. "Well, all I can say is, I'm glad to be back." A piece of feta dropped from her lips.

Charlotte looked down at it and smiled. "I know what you mean," she said. She opened her mouth wide and let all the food inside fall out onto the table.

Charlotte could be funny like that. Sidra had forgotten that about her.

Walter had found some of her old movies in the video-rental place. She had a key. She went over one night and discovered him asleep in front of *Recluse with Roommate*. It was about a woman named Rose who rarely went out, because when she did, she was afraid of people. They seemed like alien life-forms—soulless, joyless, speaking asyntactically. Rose quickly became loosened from reality. Walter had it freeze-framed at the funny part, where Rose phones the psych ward to have them come take her away, but they refuse. She lay down next to him and tried to sleep, too, but began to cry a little. He stirred. "What's wrong?" he asked.

"Nothing. You fell asleep. Watching me."

"I was tired," he said.

"I guess so."

"Let me kiss you. Let me find your panels." His eyes were closed. She could be anybody.

"Did you like the beginning part of the movie?" This need in her was new. Frightening. It made her hair curl. When had she ever needed so much?

"It was okay," he said.

"So what is this guy, a racecar driver?" asked Tommy.

"No, he's a mechanic."

"Ugh! Quit him like a music lesson!"

"Like *a music lesson*? What is this, *Similes from the Middle Class*? *One Man's Opinion*?" She was irritated.

"Sidra. This is not right! You need to go out with someone really smart for a change."

"I've been out with smart. I've been out with someone who had two PhDs. We spent all of our time in bed with the light on, proofreading his vita." She sighed. "Every little thing he'd ever done, every little, little, little. I mean, have you ever seen a vita?"

Tommy sighed, too. He had heard this story of Sidra's before. "Yes," he said. "I thought Patti LuPone was great."

"Besides," she said. "Who says he's not smart?"

The Japanese cars were the most interesting. Though the Americans were getting sexier, trying to keep up with them. *Those Japs!*

"Let's talk about my world," she said.

"What world?"

"Well, something *I'm* interested in. Something where there's something in it for me."

"Okay." He turned and dimmed the lights, romantically. "Got a stock tip for you," he said.

She was horrified, dispirited, interested.

He told her the name of a company somebody at work invested in. AutVis.

"What is it?"

"I don't know. But some guy at work said buy this week. They're going to make some announcement. If I had money, I'd buy."

She bought, the very next morning. A thousand shares. By the afternoon, the stock had plummeted 10 percent; by the following morning, 50. She watched the ticker tape go by on the bottom of the TV news channel. She had become the major stockholder. The major stockholder of a dying company! Soon they were going to be calling her, wearily, to ask what she wanted done with the forklift.

"You're a neater eater than I am," Walter said to her over dinner at the Palmer House.

She looked at him darkly. "What the hell were you thinking of, recommending that stock?" she asked. "How could you be such an irresponsible idiot?" She saw it now, how their life would be together. She would yell; then he would yell. He would have an affair; then she would have an affair. And then they would be gone and gone, and they would live in that gone.

"I got the name wrong," he said. "Sorry."

"You what?"

"It wasn't AutVis. It was AutDrive. I kept thinking it was vis for vision."

"'Vis for vision,'" she repeated.

"I'm not that good with names," confessed Walter. "I do better with concepts."

"'Concepts,'" she repeated as well.

The concept of anger. The concept of bills. The concept of flightless, dodo love.

Outside, there was a watery gust from the direction of the lake. "Chicago," said Walter. "The Windy City. Is this the Windy City or what?" He looked at her hopefully, which made her despise him more.

She shook her head. "I don't even know why we're together," she said. "I mean, why are we even together?"

He looked at her hard. "I can't answer that for you," he yelled. He took two steps back, away from her. "You've got to answer that for yourself!" And he hailed his own cab, got in, and rode away.

She walked back to the Days Inn alone. She played scales soundlessly, on the tops of the piano keys, her thin-jointed fingers lifting and falling quietly like the tines of a music box or the legs of a spider. When she tired, she turned on the television, moved through the channels, and discovered an old movie she'd been in, a love story–murder mystery called *Finishing Touches*. It was the kind of performance she had become, briefly, known for: a patched-together intimacy with the audience, half cartoon, half revelation; a cross between shyness and derision. She had not given a damn back then, sort of like now, only then it had been a style, a way of being, not a diagnosis or demise.

Perhaps she should have a baby.

In the morning, she went to visit her parents in Elmhurst. For winter, they had plastic-wrapped their home—the windows, the doors—so that it looked like a piece of avant-garde art. "Saves on heating bills," they said.

They had taken to discussing her in front of her. "It was a movie, Don. It was a movie about adventure. Nudity can be art."

"That's not how I saw it! That's not how I saw it at all!" said her father, red-faced, leaving the room. Naptime.

"How are you doing?" asked her mother, with what seemed like concern but was really an opening for something else. She had made tea.

"I'm okay, really," said Sidra. Everything she said about herself now sounded like a lie. If she was bad, it sounded like a lie; if she was fine— also a lie.

Her mother fiddled with a spoon. "I was envious of you." Her mother sighed. "I was always so envious of you! My own daughter!" She was shrieking it, saying it softly at first and then shrieking. It was exactly like Sidra's childhood: just when she thought life had become simple again, her mother gave her a new portion of the world to organize.

"I have to go," said Sidra. She had only just gotten there, but she wanted to go. She didn't want to visit her parents anymore. She didn't want to look at their lives.

She went back to the Days Inn and phoned Tommy. She and Tommy understood each other. "I *get* you," he used to say. His childhood had been full of sisters. He'd spent large portions of it drawing pictures of women in bathing suits—Miss Kenya from Nairobi!—and then asking one of the sisters to pick the most beautiful. If he disagreed, he asked another sister.

The connection was bad, and suddenly she felt too tired. "Darling, are you okay?" he said faintly.

"I'm okay."

"I think I'm hard of hearing," he said.

"I think I'm hard of talking," she said. "I'll phone you tomorrow."

She phoned Walter instead. "I need to see you," she said.

"Oh, really?" he said skeptically, and then added, with a sweetness he seemed to have plucked expertly from the air like a fly, "Is this a great country or what?"

She felt grateful to be with him again. "Let's never be apart," she whispered, rubbing his stomach. He had the physical inclinations of a dog: he liked stomach, ears, excited greetings.

"Fine by me," he said.

"Tomorrow, let's go out to dinner somewhere really expensive. My treat."

"Uh," said Walter, "tomorrow's no good."

"Oh."

"How about Sunday?"

"What's wrong with tomorrow?"

"I've got. Well, I've gotta work and I'll be tired, first of all."

"What's second of all?"

"I'm getting together with this woman I know."

"Oh?"

"It's not big deal. It's nothing. It's nothing. It's not a date or anything."

"Who is she?"

"Someone whose car I fixed. Loose mountings in the exhaust system. She wants to get together and talk about it some more. She wants to know about catalytic converters. You know, women are afraid of getting taken advantage of."

"Really!"

"Yeah, well, so Sunday would be better."

"Is she attractive?"

Walter scrinched up his face and made a sound of unenthusiasm. "Enh," he said, and placed his land laterally in the air, rotating it up and down a little.

Before he left in the morning, she said, "Just don't sleep with her."

"*Sidra*," he said, scolding her for lack of trust or for attempted supervision—she wasn't sure which.

That night, he didn't come home. She phoned and phoned and then drank a six-pack and fell asleep. In the morning, she phoned again. Finally, at eleven o'clock, he answered.

She hung up.

At 11:30, her phone rang. "Hi," he said cheerfully. He was in a good mood.

"So where were you all night?" asked Sidra. This was what she had become. She felt shorter and squatter and badly coiffed.

There was some silence. "What do you mean?" he said cautiously.

"You know what I mean."

More silence. "Look, I didn't call this morning to get into a heavy conversation."

"Well, then," said Sidra, "you certainly called the wrong number." She slammed down the phone.

She spent the day trembling and sad. She felt like a cross between Anna Karenina and Amy Liverhaus, who used to shout from the fourth-grade cloakroom, "I just don't feel *appreciated*." She walked over to Marshall Field's to buy new makeup. "You're much more of a cream beige than an ivory," said the young woman working the cosmetics counter.

But Sidra clutched at the ivory. "People are always telling me that," she said, "and it makes me very cross."

She phoned him later that night and he was there. "We need to talk," she said.

"I want my key back," he said.

"Look. Can you just come over here so that we can talk?"

He arrived bearing flowers—white roses and irises. They seemed wilted and ironic; she leaned them against the wall in a dry glass, no water.

"All right, I admit it," he said. "I went out on a date. But I'm not saying I slept with her."

She could feel, suddenly, the promiscuity in him. It was a heat, a creature, a tenant twin. "I already know you slept with her."

"How can you know that?"

"Get a life! What am I, an idiot?" She glared at him and tried not to cry. She hadn't loved him enough and he had sensed it. She hadn't really loved him at all, not really.

But she had liked him a lot!

So it still seemed unfair. A bone in her opened up, gleaming and pale, and she held it to the light and spoke from it. "I want to know one thing." She paused, not really for effect, but it had one. "Did you have oral sex?"

He looked stunned. "What kind of question is that? I don't have to answer a question like that."

"*You don't have to answer a question like that.* You don't have any rights here!" she began to yell. She was dehydrated. "You're the one who did this. Now I want the truth. I just want to know. Yes or no!"

He threw his gloves across the room.

"Yes or no," she said.

He flung himself onto the couch, pounded the cushion with his fist, placed an arm up over his eyes.

"Yes or no," she repeated.

He breathed deeply into his shirtsleeve.

"Yes or no."

"Yes," he said.

She sat down on the piano bench. Something dark and coagulated moved through her, up from the feet. Something light and breathing fled through her head, the house of her plastic-wrapped and burned down to tar. She heard him give a moan, and some fleeing hope in her, surrounded but alive on the roof, said perhaps he would beg her forgiveness. Promise to be a new man. She might find him attractive as a new, begging man. Though at some point, he would have to stop begging. He would just have to be normal. And then she would dislike him again.

He stayed on the sofa, did not move to comfort or be comforted, and the darkness in her cleaned her out, hollowed her like acid or a wind.

"I don't know what to do," she said, something palsied in her voice. She felt cheated of all the simple things—the radical calm of obscurity, of routine, of blah domestic bliss. "I don't want to go back to LA," she said. She began to stroke the tops of the piano keys, pushing against one and finding it broken—thudding and pitchless, shiny and mocking like an opened bone. She hated, hated her life. Perhaps she had always hated it.

He sat up on the sofa, looked distraught and false—his face badly arranged. He should practice in a mirror, she thought. He did not know how to break up with a movie actress. It was boys' rules: don't break up with a movie actress. Not in Chicago. If *she* left *him*, he would be better able to explain it, to himself, in the future, to anyone who asked. His voice shifted into something meant to sound imploring. "I know" was what he said, in a tone approximating hope, faith, some charity or other. "I know you might not *want* to."

"For your own good," he was saying. "Might be willing . . ." he was saying. But she was already turning into something else, a bird—a flamingo, a hawk, a flamingo-hawk—and was flying up and away, toward the filmy pane of the window, then back again, circling, meanly, with a squint.

He began, suddenly, to cry—loudly at first, with lots of *oh*s, then tiredly, as if from a deep sleep, his face buried in the poncho he'd thrown over the couch arm, his body sinking into the plush of the cushions—a man held hostage by the anxious cast of his dream.

"What can I do?" he asked.

But his dream had now changed, and she was gone, gone out the window, gone, gone.

Furiosa: The Virago of
Mad Max: Fury Road

Jess Zimmerman

One of the earliest reviews of *Mad Max: Fury Road* (2015) came from a man who'd never seen it and never intended to. Shortly before the film's general release—in a blog post eventually reported on and mocked by outlets from *Hollywood Reporter* to *Wired* to the *Guardian*—a contributor to the virulently anti-woman website Return of Kings decried the newest installment of the Australian post-apocalypse movie series as "feminist propaganda" based on its trailer and called for a boycott.

The target of his bile was Imperator Furiosa, played by a shaven and grease-smudged Charlize Theron (who tried several hairstyles for the film but says that the character didn't jell until she had the idea to cut it all off). The Return of Kings contributor was incensed by seeing trailers from the film featuring Furiosa doing masculine things like sweating, punching, aiming a gun, and saying, "Let's go!" ("Nobody barks orders to Mad Max," he sputtered.) "This is the Trojan Horse feminists and Hollywood leftists will use to (vainly) insist on the trope women are equal to men in all things, including physique, strength, and logic," he wrote. "And this is the subterfuge they will use to blur the lines between masculinity and femininity, further ruining women for men, and men for women."

By that writer's lights, *Fury Road* was even worse than he'd imagined, although by the terms of his self-imposed boycott he presumably never found out. The central plot involves the escape of a dystopian despot's "wives"—really sex slaves who are expected to birth his heirs. (The film briefly shows other, less desirable women being milked like livestock to feed those heirs.) In another film this setup might be played for titillation, with the camera lingering on the young women's sexual trauma. But in *Fury Road*, our introduction to the wives comes when the despot, Immortan Joe, stalks into their quarters looking for his missing harem. The camera lingers on the words the women have written on the floor: "Our babies will not be warlords." And on the wall: "We are not things." The wives' manifesto precedes them; they are introduced by what they refuse to be, and what they refuse to be is property.

"Where is she taking them?" Immortan Joe demands of the women's minder, Miss Giddy, who shouts back, "She didn't take them, they begged her to go." "She" is Furiosa, whom we've already seen driving her massive "war rig," giving orders to men who jump to obey her without question. Over a tight and barely scripted two hours (the movie has fewer than 4,000 words of dialogue, while in *Die Hard*, for comparison, Bruce Willis alone has more), Furiosa will rescue the wives, evade pursuers, drive like crazy, and fight with fists and guns. She will lead her charges to the promised land and, when they realize it no longer exists, all the way back. By taking on the roles of commander, savior, warrior, and (though it's left ambiguous) perhaps eventual ruler of Immortan Joe's defeated empire, Furiosa fulfills a number of functions typically reserved for male action heroes. The wives, by refusing to be seen as possessions, turn their backs on the meager acreage usually given to women in film. Furiosa takes this a step further, by annexing the territory of men.

Return of Kings has a small audience; the vaunted "boycott" never materialized, or if it did it had no measurable effect on the movie's box office take of $379 million. (*Fury Road* was the highest-grossing film of the series and won six Academy Awards.) But that angry writer was right, to some extent: *Fury Road* does "blur the lines between masculinity and femininity." What he didn't understand is that it benefits from doing so—that, indeed, film as a whole can benefit from this blurring.

Though it is the fourth installment of a series historically fronted not only by a man but by a male actor who has been openly misogynistic and abusive, *Fury Road* instead foregrounds a female character who troubles the artificial line between men's and women's roles. Furiosa is part of a sisterhood of warrior women that stretches back centuries. These women snatch so-called masculine attributes from the clutches of masculinity, where they never deserved to be caged. She's a virago. And she won't be the last.

Many of the words we use to insult brash women have their roots in animals, monsters, or the supernatural: *shrew, vixen, old bat; harpy, gorgon, crone. Harridan,* like *nag,* probably meant an old horse.

Virago is different. It's a feminine suffix added to the Latin *vir,* which means "man"—not "man" as in male human being (that's *homo*), but "man" as in possessing the manly quality of *virtus,* of courage and valor. The word itself is a grudging acknowledgment that manliness can be womanly.

Eventually, of course, *virago* became an insult—a domineering woman, a scold. But before that, it was a term of (sometimes backhanded) praise; women named as viragos were also called noble, stout, worthy. Like Furiosa, they incorporated the traits thought to exemplify masculine success but expressed them in a body that was, if not feminine, then at least female. (Historically, the word was also sometimes used to mean a woman with physically masculine traits, like a beard.)

As a character, the female hero may not defy expectations so much as reshape them. We know how a champion behaves, after all; we just don't expect him to look like her. But the true viragos—Furiosa among them—are not just male fighters with plastered-on breasts. They are female vessels of *virtus,* now no longer the realm of men: courageous, valorous women whose courage and valor exist in addition to their other traits, not in contrast to them or substitution for them. Furiosa, after all, is defined not only by her toughness and resilience but by her compassion and even her pain. Her defining moment comes after she has led the wives, and some male hangers-on, through a perilous desert to the "Green Place" where she was born, only to discover that it's no longer green at all. When she realizes the full magnitude of what she's lost—the paradise of her memories, the safe place of her imagination, most of her kin—Furiosa staggers away from her friends to drop to her knees and howl.

Indeed, director and co-writer George Miller—who also co-wrote and directed the earlier, Mel Gibson–fronted Mad Max films, but who was so committed to a different vision for *Fury Road* that he asked his wife to edit it because "if a guy did it, it would look like every other action movie"—wasn't willing to put a man in the Furiosa role. The rescuer "had to be female," he told the *New York Times*, "because if it was male, it's a male stealing the wives of another male. That's a different story." Furiosa has an action hero's grit, but she uses it for a purpose only a woman can fulfill.

The virago is not a variation of conventional femininity, a Barbie who stole G.I. Joe's gun. She's not a tomboy, either, deliberately rejecting conventional femininity in favor of macho pursuits. Rather, the virago lays bare the fact that "feminine" and "masculine" are consensual fictions, designed to keep both women and men in their place.

This is disorienting for people who use those fictions as a compass. The virago slips the bonds of femininity rather than rejecting femininity itself. But by dodging feminized categories, she makes herself unsettlingly uncategorizable for people who depend on those boundaries. For this reason, viragos typically show up in fantasy and science fiction, places where uncanniness is par for the course and categorical disruption is expected or at least tolerable.

Even in the uncharted territory of science fiction, though, gender expectations are often so deeply ingrained that the virago still noticeably troubles anticipated categories. Here's science fiction writer John Scalzi on how one of the inaugural viragos in sci-fi movies, Ellen Ripley of the *Alien* series, stubbornly refuses the limited lady-character roles available to her:

> Ripley isn't a fantasy version of a woman. Science fiction film is filled with hot kickass women doing impossible things with guns and melee weapons while they spin about like a gymnast in a dryer. As fun as that is to watch, at the end of the day it's still giving women short shrift, since what they are then are idealized killer fembots rather than actual human beings. Ripley, on the other hand, is pushy, aggressive, rude, injured, suffering from post-traumatic

syndrome, not wearing makeup, tired, smart, maternal, angry, empathetic, and determined to save others, even at great cost to herself. All without being a spinny killbot.

The last few years have seen a gradual and incomplete erosion of the artificial norms of gender, which have historically been treated—by the kind of men who fear Furiosa—as incontrovertible biological fact. Though it's still a personal risk to openly change, reject, or bridge genders, it's a risk more people are taking. Even more are ceasing to treat gender as a prepackaged, preordained set of roles, goals, and accessories. We still tend to be handed a metaphorical pink or blue knapsack at birth, stocked with "appropriate" clothes and books and props and unattainable ideals. (For a real person, the knapsack is stuffed to the brim; for a character it's sparser, the pink pack holding only slivers of costume labeled "vamp," "damsel," "sidekick," "spinny killbot.") But for a while now, women have been increasingly comfortable opening up the men's knapsack and poking around—maybe you don't want to swap packs completely, but there's some good gear in there.

The virago offers one model (among many possible ones) for picking and choosing—for constructing a form of womanhood that's not dictated by courting expectations of femininity, or conspicuously flouting them, but simply by setting them aside. The message of the woman fighter is not that women *have* to fight. It's that fighting does not belong to men. Heroism does not belong to men. Being central to the story, acting instead of being acted upon, being something other than "beautiful enough" or "insufficiently beautiful": these are not privileges accorded to men alone. *Virtus* does not require *vir*.

She has a long pedigree, this female vessel of *virtus*. My personal favorite virago figure is Britomart, a female knight in Edmund Spenser's epic sixteenth-century poem *The Faerie Queene*. Spenser's description of Britomart—"For she was full of amiable grace / And manly terrour mixed therewithall"—may be the purest expression of the virago. But Britomart herself is based on Bradamante from an earlier epic poem, Ludovico Ariosto's *Orlando Furioso*, and both evoke warrior women of folklore and history: the Valkyrie, the Amazon, the goddess Artemis, the legendary queen Boadicea, and any number of queens, knights, and goddesses from around the world. From Britomart, there's a direct line to other literary characters who expand the role that women are allowed to play—for instance, Tamora Pierce's 1983 young adult novel *Alanna*, about a girl who dresses as a boy in order to train as a knight.

The virago of film is a newer creature, though by no means brand-new. One reason for this is obvious: film is still a new medium, covering only a sliver of the lifespan of human art. But the visual nature of film, the way it literally recapitulates the gaze of the (until recently, virtually always male) director and the (until recently, presumptively male) viewer, also complicates the virago character. Even if she's as bold and brave as a man, a female character's access to *virtus* can be undermined by presenting her as an object of sexual interest. (Take Wonder Woman, for example, or Lara Croft, or even Beatrix Kiddo.)

For one thing, male characters (particularly in action films) are not objects of sexual anything; they are subjects, actors, doers-to. Passively portraying a woman as a projection screen for desire—and by "passively" I mean that this effect can be achieved entirely with images, without anything explicit in the script—automatically bars her from heroism equal to a man's.

But "virtue" is also a double-edged sword. The viragos of myth and literature and history took masculine-inflected *virtus* and made it female. This meant embodying the male virtues in a female body but simultaneously embodying the concept of "virtue" as it was used to apply to women. Such viragos were, in short, sexually pure. Britomart is the knight of chastity, Artemis the goddess who turns would-be suitors into stags. Semiramis, an Assyrian warrior queen of legend, is even credited with inventing the chastity belt. *Virtus* often means virginity.

Furiosa and Ripley aren't sexualized, and that's a blessing and a relief. They are excused from the roles usually designated for women—trophy, love interest, vamp—and they are spared the visual objectification that mars the heroism of many a spinny killbot. But that exemption comes at a price: in order to dodge objectification, they are constrained entirely to the realm of the nonsexual, a whole area of common human experience neatly scythed out. Female moviegoers might have sighed over Tom Hardy's suspiciously moisturized-looking lips, but Furiosa was unmoved. The only fluid she shares with him is a blood transfusion.

The virago of literature, myth, and history—and so far, of film as well—may appear to straddle the illusory wall that separates men's roles from women's and enjoy the best of both worlds. But on closer examination, this position comes at the expense of being literally unsexed, removed not only from sexual objectification but from sexual action. Our culture has not yet developed a vision of female sexuality divorced from the male gaze and male expectations.

There's no question that culture will demand more viragos, even in a political context that aims to reinstate "traditional" and restrictive roles for women, promising to denigrate both women's heroism and the blurring of gender. Maybe especially in that age we'll want our art to see further than we do. The next stage of virago evolution may give us a central and heroic female figure who is also a fully realized sexual being (television's Jessica Jones is getting there). Until then, it's revolutionary to have a character who does not capitulate to the male gaze, who stands outside or on top of it and takes whatever she wants.

It's no surprise that the virago character is frightening to a certain type of man—the type of man who does not practice *virtus* but hoards it as his birthright. If the positive aspects of masculinity are no longer these men's sole province, what do they have left? If they relax their grip on their knapsack, they'll wind up empty-handed. But the idea of embracing the positive aspects of femininity, of blurring that artificial line further, is even more anathema.

"If . . . *Fury Road* is a blockbuster, then you, me, and all the other men (and real women) in the world will never be able to see a real action movie ever again that doesn't contain some damn political lecture or moray [*sic*] about feminism," wrote the Return of Kings contributor. *Fury Road* was indeed a blockbuster by any measure, so it's a point worth discussing: What's next for the virago?

Some of the answers may lie in a more recent film to draw ire for its overly powerful women: the 2016 woman-powered remake of *Ghostbusters*, which sent men's rights commentators into a veritable tailspin. If there's a way forward for movie viragos to avoid sexual objectification without avoiding sex or love entirely, it may start with a character like Jillian Holtzmann. Holtzmann is a fount of *virtus*—courageous, adept, and brimming with swagger, which might be the primary virago trait.

And while she doesn't get a romantic interest or subplot, she does—without ever once pandering to the male gaze—exude a knuckle-biting sex appeal so powerful that its effect is something like a neurotoxin. (There are now dozens of stories on the fan-fiction site Archive of Our Own that feature Holtzmann having an affair with the reader.)

Less spectacular, but no less real, is the precedent that the rebooted *Ghostbusters* offers for the virago's opposite number, the male character inhabiting a feminine role. Lunkheaded Kevin manages to check off several of the slots usually assigned to female characters: the sexy secretary, the unwitting lust object, the damsel in distress. The role-bending is obvious and broad, played for laughs—but it could also herald a more nuanced type of male character for the future, one who can lay aside some of the constraints of masculinity and take up the traits that have long defined feminine characters.

The 2016 *Ghostbusters* didn't have anything close to *Fury Road*'s box office success, but taken together, the two films are an indication that we may be moving, gradually, toward a more robust vision of what a female hero might mean. A line drawn from *Alien* to *Fury Road* and the *Ghostbusters* remake will point to whatever comes next: perhaps a culture in which shedding the artificial constraints of gender doesn't mean giving up sex, a world in which women can be warriors and men can be caregivers.

Even in a political climate of misogyny, chauvinism, and gender policing, art moves forward; art moves faster than politics, always. Furiosa came before we were all ready for her, as the reaction of some on the internet makes clear. But the kind of heroism she represents, the so-called masculine virtues decanted into a female character, is hardly a new idea. Furiosa is the latest in a long line of artistic, literary, and cinematic viragos—and the first in a longer line.

WATCHING

WATCHING

Watching a film—in a theater or at home, on a mobile device or outside on a summer evening—can be a transformative experience. How does the experience of viewing a movie bring forth such a wide range of ideas, beliefs, and associations? The pieces in this section consider the nature of watching and how it inspires diverse and multilayered emotional responses.

Kim Addonizio's poem "Scary Movies" (2004) takes the reader back to childhood and the thrill and terror of a recently watched film seeming to reach out into real life.

Manuel Muñoz, in his piece "Skyshot" (2003), explores how films and the discussions they inspire can be the catalyst for major life changes.

In the poem "Edward Hopper's *New York Movie*" (1989), **Joseph Stanton** reflects on Hopper's painting of a midcentury cinema usherette and the unspoken thoughts and memories captured in the scene.

Stephen King, in "Why We Crave Horror Movies" (1981), considers the primal need of the audience for frightening experiences. His claims for the horror film's relevance elevate it beyond cheap thrills and argue for the emotional and intellectual apparatus viewers bring to any film, whatever the genre.

Robert Coover's story "Matinée" (2011) plays with the notion of screen as removed from reality and builds layer upon layer of existence, moving in and out of the silver screen. Watching a film in Coover's story becomes an act of complex and complicit blurring.

In her poem "The Last Movie" (1981), **Rachel Hadas** relates movie watching to an all-to-real and painful experience, as the cinema becomes the marker of a life and its passing.

Sheryl St. Germain's poem "Some Months After My Father's Death" (2007) continues that line of thought, as she sees a lost loved one in the film she watches.

Scary Movies

Kim Addonizio

Today the cloud shapes are terrifying,
and I keep expecting some enormous
black-and-white B-movie Cyclops
to appear at the end of the horizon,

to come striding over the ocean
and drag me from my kitchen
to the deep cave that flickered
into my young brain one Saturday

at the Baronet Theater where I sat helpless
between my older brothers, pumped up
on candy and horror—that cave,
the litter of human bones

gnawed on and flung toward the entrance,
I can smell their stench as clearly
as the bacon fat from breakfast. This
is how it feels to lose it—

not sanity, I mean, but whatever it is
that helps you get up in the morning
and actually leave the house
on those days when it seems like death

in his brown uniform
is cruising his panel truck
of packages through your neighborhood.
I think of a friend's voice

on her answering machine—
Hi, I'm not here—
the morning of her funeral,
the calls filling up the tape

and the mail still arriving,
and I feel as afraid as I was
after all those vampire movies
when I'd come home and lie awake

all night, rigid in my bed,
unable to get up
even to pee because the undead
were waiting underneath it;

if I so much as stuck a bare
foot out there in the unprotected air
they'd grab me by the ankle and pull me
under. And my parents said there was

nothing there, when I was older
I would know better, and now
they're dead, and I'm older,
and I know better.

Skyshot

Manuel Muñoz

tell my friend Quetz, "Count as soon as the screen lights up. See how far you can get."

Sometimes we're lucky. Quetz says, "Music doesn't matter, does it?" and I shake my head no, waiting for voices. We can count to twenty or thirty when it's a movie we like. Even Quetz says, "It's too easy to have someone speak." Even Quetz says that.

I say, "I don't like voices in the dark, and then the face showing up."

Neither does Quetz. "The voice never matches the face. It's disappointing."

We've come to like: orchestrations by Miklos Rozsa; inventive title designs, like the office building and the arrows in *North by Northwest*; what we think are Joan Crawford's legs turning at the carport gate. Quetz detests bland landscape shots and credits typed over open fields. I hate John Williams.

What's best are the aerial shots, even the sloppy ones from helicopters and their dragonfly shadows skimming along the terrain. We like the way that the camera descends from nowhere like a sudden cloud. Everywhere below is just rigid lines and intersections until the camera gets closer and closer, or the scene clips to the real story, and all that geometry suddenly means something.

So how to begin this, without a camera? Just yesterday I was flying back home after seeing my mom in LA and all below me was the giant square of Fresno. And all around it more squares—orchards and vineyards and farmers' cattle grounds. How to begin a story out of this mess of order? (Quetz and I have been taking classes at Fresno State from an old crudgy professor. Abstract art. He says a couple things about the impossibilities of geometry. He says, Geometry, not figures. He says, Shapes, not stories. And then he looks blankly at all of us when we stare back.)

I flew in yesterday and saw where I lived. I want to be able to say that it's like the Robert Altman movie I rented where an army of helicopters is spraying for medflies over LA. It made LA seem dangerous, contaminated. But LA is where a lot of us say we will go someday, four hours south of the Central Valley, crossing the Grapevine on I-5 and descending straight into a city of limousines and lights. In winter, when the entire floor of the Valley is shrouded in the thickest fog, only the rising of the freeway breaks through into the mountains, and then suddenly Los Angeles and you're reminded that there's sun after all.

From way up, even in my descending plane, I would have never guessed that the trees hide things. Small things: Robert Altman didn't show the tiny triangular flytraps put out by the farmers. But we have traps here and the farmers look at them, sometimes with a local television crew filming as they open a triangle and see if a black speck is stuck to the lining. We've been lucky. None of them has been trapped here.

Quetz is in his twenties just like me. We go to school together. Each semester, we look over the class schedules for Fresno State and try to arrange our courses so we can save on gas. Sometimes it works, sometimes it doesn't. He took the course on abstract art just for the hell of it, so he could keep his financial aid for the semester. He's a mechanic, and when his technical classes cancel out on him, he sits next to me and wonders what the hell he's doing. I write his essays for him.

Quetz is one of those kids whose parents were hung up on Chicano nationalism back in the sixties and named their children after Aztec gods. Quetz spells his name Quetzalcoatl, but he freely tells me, "I've never been able to say it and I don't give a shit either." He's been wanting to leave our town for years now and he thinks he's missed his chance. I say, "We can leave once we get our degrees," and he turns to me without saying anything and I know what he wants to tell me: What will we do in Los Angeles with these kids from UCLA and USC and the ones who've come down from Stanford?

He is not rational: when I remind him he can work as a mechanic, he says no way and then he says, out of the blue, "You know, LA is nothing but cars," and in the same spirit, he believes I can pick up my own love by simply moving to Hollywood. "You can break into movies," he tells me.

I ignore him. Quetz suggests this because I make him spend so much time watching movies with me, and he sits still even through the ones he doesn't like. We know Robert Altman because no one rents his movies in our town and so he gets onto the ninety-nine-cent shelf along with the old videotapes from before 1980—the big bulky boxes with curling cellophane covers. We discovered Hal Ashby this way and Sidney Lumet. Quetz likes William Friedkin and I liked Martin Ritt best, until I saw Altman.

At the end of *Nashville*, Quetz says, "You don't even like country music," but I tell him that I really liked it, that it wasn't like any of the movies we had seen before.

"No," he says. "How come all those people don't know each other after three hours?" and I shake my head at him because I don't know, either.

I tell him: people and city, how they make up a city. But he doesn't go for it. He says to me, "They didn't talk to each other and they kept talking at the same time," and he shakes his head as he lights up a joint.

Sometimes I'll have the joint with him and sometimes not. This time I do because he says, "So no more Martin Ritt, huh?" and his tone implies that I don't care anymore about how Sally Field reminded us of the people at the tomato-packing plant on our side of town.

"I liked *Nashville*," I say again.

He tries, "I think people should talk to each other in movies, and that's it," and he moves over to where I am sitting on my couch. Before I know it, he's kissing me, the both of us in my living room, and I don't worry that my father will walk in. I used to, but I don't anymore, because it doesn't matter. What consequences, when nothing matters in a town this small, if you leave.

I wish I could say this takes place over five days in this little town, and there will be this many people who are part of my story, and this many of them matter. But I can't, because me and Quetz and my father and

Quetz's parents and Mrs. Santos are all scattered. I wish I could sit the way my aunts do at the kitchen table and tell my father, This is why I'm leaving. But I don't know how to put it together and I wish everything important in my life had happened in just the past five days, so it would be fresh. And all I would have to do would be to say, Here, this is why this means this and that means that. Because it all happened so close together, and time, at least, can help me close the distances.

My mother left. She is in Los Angeles without my father, and I have stayed with him because, behind his olive and beige clothes—shirts and pants and shorts (my father is no longer in the military after thirty years)—my father is alone. I see now that he wants to look fresh out of the army, wearing white T-shirts sometimes. He wants to look strong but is angry and hurt whenever I travel to see my mother. He is either angry or not angry.

"Come here," my father said one day. He was standing at our living room window, which faces the street, the curtains pulled back because it was late afternoon and the sun didn't hit that side of the house. "Look," he said, with a faint gesture toward the shady street.

I got up from watching a movie and walked over. "What?" I asked, and looked out, seeing only an older neighbor as she slowly walked along. In the late afternoons and early evenings, as long as it was warm out, she circled the block to get her exercise.

"What about her?" I asked my father.

"You notice how she never looked up in this direction?"

"Yeah."

"And we have this big window."

"What about it?" I asked him as she left our sight.

He said bluntly, "When her husband wasn't around. Mrs. Santos. I had an affair with that woman."

"Mrs. Santos? When?"

"When her husband went to Texas for a month. His little brother got killed in Vietnam, and they shipped him back to San Antonio for burial."

I didn't say much because I wanted to do the math—maybe twenty-five years, when my father was my age, in his twenties. And that woman, maybe forty or so.

My father looked up at me. He was wearing his olive shorts and was barefoot, and this made me think that he'd been on his way out to water the grass and then stopped. I thought if someone had been looking through the window at us, staring at each other, they would have known exactly what was happening and what the problem was: he was on the verge of telling me and I was on the verge of asking. If someone had been looking through that window, they might have shouted to us to speak.

Mrs. Santos came down the block while the two of us continued standing by the window, and she passed by without making a twitch toward the house. My father stopped watching me.

"It's always been like that. She went her way. I went mine."

Lily Tomlin plays a wife and she goes to a barbecue or a fundraiser and she sits talking to a woman, the way my aunts do, telling stories, telling them well. She never gets to the whole story, and I never know why she's telling it in the first place. She circles around a motorcycle accident and a woman with a bump on her head. There are mentions of motorcycles and beautiful boys, how she walked into a whole ward full of them and every single one was paralyzed.

I think another director would have shown that ward—I know I would have—because it made me sad to think of so many clean beds and legs wrapped in casts and boys with shaved heads to make way for stitches. What Lily Tomlin said had nothing to do with anything, but the way she told it, the way my aunts tell stories—something matters even when the pieces don't quite fit. I couldn't stop thinking of a whole hospital floor of beautiful boys, all of them mangled, and what they might have done to deserve such a fate.

Time seems like it's running out on me and Quetz, and yet we don't know what to compare it against. There is only now. This is August, and our registration dates for Fresno State have come and gone, neither of us with classes, and now we are broke.

We sit in the bakery in the middle of downtown, splitting a whole lunch between us. Quetz takes a bite of his sandwich, and I can't help but think about the money he is swallowing. I can tell he's not thinking right.

He says, "Let's just go to LA. Tomorrow."

I stare out the window because it does not feel immediate. It does not feel like a tension. There is nowhere to work; I haven't told my father that we screwed up registration for school and my money is gone. What would change about home, me always watching movies and us not talking?

"My dad," I tell Quetz. "I can't leave my dad," but can't say why.

Quetz scoffs, pushes his plate away. He is clearing the space between us. He says, "Give me your hand," and he stretches his arm on the table, reaching for me.

I look at him. He isn't fearful.

"Just hold my hand," he insists.

Ned Beatty is wearing a tight brown polyester shirt. He is wearing it the way only Ned Beatty can. It's beige rather than brown. He is listening. He is playing a man who is able to listen, but doesn't, not when his deaf son signs to him. His son tries to tell him a simple story about swimming, about diving to the bottom of the pool, touching that space. It's hard to figure out exactly what his son is saying, but it's easy at the same time. It's easy to see he's talking about going down, and then farther down. He even breaks it down, to the individual letters, his fingers quick. That's all he wants: to tell his father about touching bottom. But Ned Beatty doesn't listen.

The last conversation I had with my father before I left was about Altman. While I was watching *Nashville* for the second time, my father came into the room. He said, though he spoke perfectly good English, "I hate movies that aren't in Spanish" as he picked up the box.

"Altman—that's German, right? Like *alemán*? That's 'German' in Spanish," and before I knew it he started explaining the German-Mexican alliances during the wars and how Mexico would have been screwed if they followed through with anything. "Do you know a German offered your grandpa money to blow up buildings in Los Angeles?" he asked.

"The movie's almost over," I told him, and he watched with me as Ronee Blakley sang a song about Idaho, an enormous American flag fluttering across the screen.

"Look at Argentina," my father said suddenly. "And Uruguay. Where are they now, for helping out those fuckers?" I nodded my head, my father stepping outside to water the lawn in his olive shorts and bare feet, and I had absolutely no idea what he was angry about.

I'll say one good thing about that art professor—at least he taught me to study things. Since I've been shelling out my spare change for cheap movies, I've been ignoring the plots and the stars and the music and noticing how the director looks at things. Robert Altman does it best, I think. He likes to look at people and likes you to do the same and make some judgments about them—why they do things, like the waitress who can't sing.

I like those moments when the camera sneaks up on someone. Or, it's just two people talking, and then suddenly you notice that the camera is moving closer and closer and closer until it's right on one person's face and suddenly everything that person says could be terrible and devastating. It is just that person's face, the roundness of the cheekbones and the eyes knowing that what happens next could make a horrific kind of difference. It means listening very hard.

I am not naive. From the supermarket, my father brings home tabloid magazines, and these same faces are in fancy clothes and dark ties. I like to think that Robert Altman is not like them, that he sits at a park bench or an airport lounge and waits for people to walk by with their lives impossible to hide. Or that Sidney Lumet walks the streets of New York trying to memorize every stretch of sidewalk. I know that Martin Ritt doesn't think about how Melvyn Douglas has to kill all his cattle and be left with nothing, or how Patricia Neal would be one of the few people to run away from Paul Newman. He doesn't sit there and cry into his hands. But I like to think that he does.

The first time I ever really looked at Quetz was at the Sunflower Festival in our town a couple of days ago, a whole bevy of queens and princesses selling raffle tickets downtown or at the supermarket, trying to win a crown. We have a large park in the center of our town, the tallest trees around, and they gave us shade all day as we mingled around the amphitheater and the food booths.

It was at night that I first looked at him, during the intermission for the beauty pageant. We were on the Ferris wheel, a rickety and groaning one, moving up into the dark. Below us, a line of couples inched along the gate, watching. I let my legs dangle, spread open, my wrists hanging over the safety bar with as much nonchalance as I could give.

Quetz didn't seem to care. He let his leg touch mine, and he didn't laugh and point out at anything, the way some people did. On our way up, he said nothing and stared straight ahead to the darker outskirts of town, visible past the yellow lights and blue neon of the festival. He looked at the fields he had to work in as a kid and how these people did all the harvesting and then came here to spend their money.

Down below, a whole group of girls ran dizzy, cotton candy in their hands—they were rushing to catch their friends in the pageant who could dance or sing. Each one of them seemed pretty as they raced by.

"Hey," Quetz said to me, and I braced myself for him to say something too loudly with these people watching us, our legs touching in the dark. "What are we waiting for?" he asked.

On the stage, we could see (and then hear) a ranchera being sung by a tiny girl in a green dress. The sequins caught the light of camera bulbs and twinkled at us. I didn't know what Quetz was asking me, so I listened to the tiny girl and the way the audience applauded her.

I was afraid Quetz would turn to me and say, "I love you," that he wouldn't care about being in a public park with so many people around. That he would hand the ride operator a twenty-dollar bill and tell him, "Keep us spinning," until the carnival had to pack its tents and the soothsayers went home.

He did not continue, would not explain. I think he was looking at the horizon as if Los Angeles were that close. I saw his eyes tense, his mouth narrow against what occupied him. He was angry, though I still don't know about what, and he made me think of my father—how so many people here behave the same way. They say things and don't finish, maybe because they don't know what comes next.

Right then, I wished I had a camera. I wished I had it so Quetz could see, somehow, his face in profile and how his anger came across even though he didn't mean it. There, closer, and closer, until the sheer proximity made him act and say, "It's this town, don't you see?" Or, "I need out." Or, "Why don't you come with me?"

They were crowning a winner down below, and the crowd applauded on command when the master of ceremonies came forward and told them, "*Un fuerte aplauso por estas muñecas, por favor.*" They proclaimed the tiny girl in the green dress the winner. Her face, even from where we sat on the Ferris wheel, broke into a grin as bright as any of the lights at the carnival.

"That country music movie we watched the other day," Quetz said, "didn't it end with someone getting shot? That's what this needs."

"Quetz, that's a shitty thing to say," I told him. Though I pictured him doing it, I know he would never do such a thing. He was just being mean. In the movie, it was a way to end things. I knew Quetz could do more than just end things.

Shelley Duvall is a bad niece and walks around Nashville in wigs and tight shorts and even changes her name. She fucks every man in the movie, just about, and it doesn't matter that she's skinny and looks ridiculous. You have to wonder what makes someone do that. Why she's a niece and not a daughter, and why it's only about her shallowness. She never gets to speak, never gets to say, only her uncle running after her, desperate for some explanation about why she missed her aunt's funeral. She never gets to say.

What to make of Quetz's room: a tiny shed of planks in the backyard of his cousin's house. What to think of how I went over there in broad daylight and shut the door behind me. Or, in the cold of winter, how we piled blankets onto his slender bed and camped out there, smoking pot. I think, because he is not afraid, that I have become too brazen, that I'm forgetting how small this town is, that we're old enough to know what we're doing.

Quetz isn't afraid: not of what we're doing, not of his parents, not of the cold. I admire him.

His parents know. I sometimes run into them at the grocery store or buying Mexican bread at the bakery. They put their money down angrily.

I wonder if my father ever runs into them. He used to be good friends with them; so did my mother. But my father never mentions a word.

"Just hold my hand," Quetz insists, and he keeps his arm stretched on the table, reaching for me and he is not afraid.

I tell him, "I wish I had a camera," and I know he's thinking a Kodak, a throwaway roll of film. But I want a real camera, one that could circle around us. How else to describe the rush inside of me, the questions that don't matter anymore—telling my father that I want to leave and how he'll react, if my mother will take me in. The exhilaration of the moment is what is most important, and I want to see my own face. I close my eyes to see it, from far away and then closer, how I must look, Quetz waiting for me to say yes.

The people around us don't matter anymore. And we don't know where we're going in LA or how. So it is our hands—as if a camera really were above us—the space Quetz cleared on the table. It is, for now, just our hands clasped, the spoons and the lips of the round coffee cups, the mismatched butter knives. There are two plates and the half-finished sandwiches.

What Altman did at the end of *Nashville* was right on the money: if you look up at the sky in the middle of the afternoon, it isn't blue. It isn't a happy ending. It washes out with the terrible brightness of the sun. I look out the bakery window, my decision made to go to LA, holding Quetz's hand, and I can hear people clearing their throats.

But what's behind all of this is not the leaving. Or the things making me go. I cannot explain, the way movies can with their happy endings. This is not a happy ending just because of our clasped hands. When I look up at the sky, it hurts, but rather than close my eyes to fade it out, I come back down to the street. My town's main street. It doesn't look cramped anymore. I don't want it to look that way. I want the looking up, the open space sudden, mine.

Edward Hopper's
New York Movie

Joseph Stanton

We can have our pick of seats.
Though the movie's already moving,
the theater's almost an empty shell.
    All we can see on our side
of the room is one man and one woman—
as neat, respectable, and distinct
    as the empty chairs that come
between them. But distinctions do not surprise,
fresh as we are from sullen street and subway
    where loneliness crowded
about us like unquiet memories
that may have loved us once or known our love.
    Here we are an accidental
fellowship, sheltering from the city's
obscure bereavements to face a screened,
    imaginary living,
as if it were a destination
we were moving toward. Leaning to our right
    and suspended before us
is a bored, smartly uniformed usherette.
Staring beyond her lighted corner, she finds
    a reverie that moves through
and beyond the shine of the silver screening.

But we can see what she will never see—
    that she's the star of Hopper's scene.
For the artist she's a play of light,
and a play of light is all about her.
    Whether the future she is
dreaming is the future she will have
we have no way of knowing. Whatever
    it will prove to be
it has already been. The usherette
Hopper saw might now be seventy,
    hunched before a Hitachi
in an old home or a home for the old.
She might be dreaming now a New York movie,
    Fred Astaire dancing and kissing
Ginger Rogers, who high kicks across New York
City skylines, raising possibilities
    that time has served to lower.
We are watching the usherette, and the subtle
shadows her boredom makes across her not-quite-
    impassive face beneath
the three red-shaded lamps and beside
the stairs that lead, somehow, to dark streets
    that go on and on and on.
But we are no safer here than she.
Despite the semblance of luxury—
    gilt edges, red plush,
and patterned carpet—this is no palace,
and we do not reign here, except in dreams.
    This picture tells us much
about various textures of lighted air,
but at the center Hopper has placed
a slab of darkness and an empty chair.

Why We Crave Horror Movies

Stephen King

I f you're a genuine fan of horror films, you develop the same sort of sophistication that a follower of the ballet develops; you get a feeling for the depth and the texture of the genre. Your ear develops with your eye, and the sound of quality always come through to the keen ear. There is fine Waterford crystal that rings delicately when struck, no matter how thick and chunky it may look; and then there are Flintstone jelly glasses. You can drink your Dom Perignon out of either one, but, friends, there is a difference.

The difference here is between horror for horror's sake and art. There is art in a horror film when the audience gets more than it gives. Not when our fears are milked just to drive us crazy but when an actual liaison is found between our fantasy fears and our real fears.

Few horror movies are conceived with art in mind; most are conceived for profit. The art is not consciously created but, rather, is thrown off, as an atomic pile throws off radiation. There are films that skate right up to the border where art ceases be thrown off and exploitation begins, and those films are often the field's most striking successes. *The Texas Chain Saw Massacre* is one of those. I would happily testify to its redeeming social merit in any court in the country. I would not do so for *The Ghastly Ones*, a 1968 film in which we are treated to the charming sight of a woman being cut open with a two-handed bucksaw; the camera lingers as her intestines spew out onto the floor. The difference is more than the difference between a chain saw and a bucksaw; it is something like 70 million light years. The *Chain Saw Massacre* is done with taste and conscience. *The Ghastly Ones* is the work of morons with cameras.

If horror movies have redeeming social merit, it is because of that ability to form liaisons between the real and the unreal. In many cases—particularly in the fifties and then again in the early seventies—the fears expressed are sociopolitical in nature, a fact that gives such disparate pictures as Don Siegel's *Invasion of the Body Snatchers* and William Friedkin's *The Exorcist* a crazily convincing documentary feel. When the horror movies wear their various sociopolitical hats—the B picture as tabloid editorial—they often serve as an extraordinarily accurate barometer of those things that trouble the night thoughts of a whole society.

But horror movies don't always wear a hat that identifies them as disguised comments on the social or political scene (as David Cronenberg's *The Brood* comments on the disintegration of the generational family, or as his *They Came from Within* deals with the more cannibalistic side effects of Erica Jong's "zipless fuck"). More often the horror movie points farther inward, looking for those deep-seated personal fears, those pressure points we all must cope with. This adds an element of universality to the proceedings and may produce an even truer sort of art.

This second kind of horror film has more in common with the Brothers Grimm than with the op-ed pages of the tabloid newspapers. It is the B picture as fairy tale. It doesn't want to score political points but, rather, to scare the hell out of us by crossing certain taboo lines. So if my idea about art is correct (it giveth more than it receiveth), this sort of film is of value to the audience by helping it better understand what those taboos and fears are, and why it feels so uneasy about them.

I think we'd all agree that one of the great fears with which all of us must deal on a purely personal level is the fear of dying; without good old death to fall back on, the horror movies would be in bad shape. A corollary to this is that there are "good" deaths and "bad" deaths; most of us would like to die peacefully in our beds at the age of eighty (preferably after a good meal, a bottle of really fine vino, and a really super lay), but very few of us are interested in finding out how it might feel to get slowly crushed under an automobile lift while crankcase oil drips slowly onto our foreheads.

Lots of horror films derive their best effects from the fear of the bad death (as in *The Abominable Dr. Phibes*, in which Phibes dispatches his victims one at a time using the twelve plagues of Egypt, slightly updated, a gimmick worthy of the *Batman* comics during their palmiest days). Who can forget the lethal binoculars in *Black Zoo*, for instance? They came equipped with spring-loaded six-inch prongs, so that when the victim put them to her eyes and then attempted to adjust the field of focus . . .

Others derive their horror simply from the fact of death itself and the decay that follows death. In a society in which such a great store is placed in the fragile commodities of youth, health, and beauty, death and decay become inevitably horrible—and inevitably taboo. If you don't think so, ask yourself why the second grade doesn't get to tour the local mortuary along with the police department, the fire department, and the nearest McDonald's. One can imagine—or I can in my more morbid moments—the mortuary and McDonald's combined; the highlight of the tour, of course, would be a viewing of the McCorpse.

No, the funeral parlor is taboo. Morticians are modern priests, working their arcane magic of cosmetics and preservation in rooms that are clearly marked off-limits. Who washes the corpse's hair? Are the fingernails and toenails of the dear departed clipped one final time? Is it true that the dead are encoffined sans shoes? Who dresses them for their final star turn in the mortuary viewing room? How is a bullet hole plugged and concealed? How are strangulation bruises hidden?

The answers to all those questions are available, but they are not common knowledge. And if you try to make the answers part of your store of knowledge, people are going to think you a bit peculiar. I know: in the process of researching a forthcoming novel about a father who tries to bring his son back from the dead, I collected a stack of funeral literature a foot high—and any number of peculiar glances from folks who wondered why I was reading *The Funeral: Vestige or Value?*

But this is not to say that people don't have a certain occasional interest in what lies behind the locked door in the basement of the mortuary or what may transpire in the local graveyard after the mourners have left . . . or at the dark of the moon. *The Body Snatcher* is not really a tale of the supernatural, nor was it pitched that way to its audience; it was pitched as a film (as was that notorious sixties documentary *Mondo Cane*) that would take us beyond the pale, over that line that marks the edge of taboo ground.

CEMETERIES RAIDED, CHILDREN SLAIN FOR BODIES TO DISSECT! the movie poster drooled. UNTHINKABLE REALITIES AND UNBELIEVABLE <u>FACTS</u> OF THE DARK DAYS OF EARLY SURGICAL RESEARCH <u>EXPOSED</u> IN <u>THE MOST DARING SHRIEK-AND-SHUDDER SHOCK SENSATION EVER BROUGHT TO THE SCREEN!</u> (All of this printed on a leaning tombstone.)

But the poster does not stop there; it goes on specifically to mark out the exact location of the taboo line and to suggest that not everyone may be adventurous enough to transgress that forbidden ground: IF YOU CAN TAKE IT, SEE GRAVES RAIDED! COFFINS ROBBED! CORPSES CARVED! MIDNIGHT MURDER! BODY BLACKMAIL! STALKING GHOULS! MAD REVENGE! MACABRE MYSTERY! AND DON'T SAY WE DIDN'T WARN YOU!

All of it has sort of a pleasant, alliterative ring, doesn't it?

These areas of unease—the political, social-cultural, and those of the more mythic, fairy-tale variety—have a tendency to overlap, of course; a good horror picture will put the pressure on at as many points as it can. *They Came from Within*, for instance, is about sexual promiscuity on one level; on another level, it's asking you how you'd like to have a leech jump out of a letter slot and fasten itself onto your face. These are not the same areas of unease at all.

But since we're off on the subject of death and decay (a very grave matter, heh-heh-heh), we might look at a couple of films in which this particular area of unease has been used well. The prime example, of course, is *Night of the Living Dead*, in which our horror of these final states is exploited to a point where many audiences found the film well-nigh unbearable. Other taboos are also broken by the film: at one point, a little girl kills her mother with a garden trowel . . . and then begins to eat her. How's that for taboo breaking? Yet the film circles around to its starting point again and again, and the key word in the film's title is not "living" but "dead."

At an early point, the film's female lead, who has barely escaped being killed by a zombie in a graveyard where she and her brother have come to put flowers on their dead father's grave (the brother is not so lucky), stumbles into a lonely farmhouse. As she explores, she hears something dripping . . . dripping . . . dripping. She goes upstairs, sees something, screams . . . and the camera zooms in on the rotting, weeks-old head of a corpse. It is a shocking, memorable moment. Later, a government official tells the watching, beleaguered populace that, although they may not like it (i.e., they will have to cross that taboo line to do it), they must burn their dead; simply soak them with gasoline and light them up. Later still, a local sheriff expresses our own uneasy shock at having come so far over the taboo line. He answers a reporter's question by saying, "Ah, they're dead . . . they're all messed up."

The good horror director must have a clear sense of where the taboo line lies, if he is not to lapse into unconscious absurdity, and a gut understanding of what the countryside is like on the far side of it. In *Night of the Living Dead*, George Romero plays a number of instruments, and he plays them like a virtuoso. A lot has been made of this film's graphic violence, but one of the film's most frightening moments comes near the climax, when the heroine's brother makes his reappearance—still wearing his driving gloves and clutching for his sister with the idiotic, implacable single-mindedness of the hungry dead. The film is violent—as is its sequel, *Dawn of the Dead*—but the violence has its own logic, and in the horror genre, logic goes a long way toward proving morality.

The crowning horror in Alfred Hitchcock's *Psycho* comes when Vera Miles touches that chair in the cellar and it spins lazily around to reveal Norman's mother at last—a wizened, shriveled corpse from which hollow eye sockets stare up blankly. She is not only dead; she has been stuffed like one of the birds that decorate Norman's office. Norman's subsequent entrance in dress and makeup is almost an anticlimax.

In AIP's *The Pit and the Pendulum*, we see another facet of the bad death—perhaps the absolute worst. Vincent Price and his cohorts break into a tomb through its brickwork, using pick and shovel. They discover that the lady, his wife, has, indeed, been entombed alive; for just a moment, the camera shows us her tortured face, frozen in a rictus of terror, her bulging eyes, her clawlike fingers, the skin stretched tight and gray. This is, I think, the most important moment in the post-1960 horror film, signaling a return to an all-out effort to terrify the audience . . . and a willingness to use any means at hand to do it.

Fiction is full of *economic* horror stories, though very few of them are supernatural; *The Crash of '79* comes to mind, as well as *The Money Wolves*, *The Big Company Look*, and the wonderful Frank Norris novel

McTeague. I want to discuss only one movie in this context, *The Ami-tyville Horror.* There may be others, but this one example will serve, I think, to illustrate another idea: that the horror genre is extremely limber, extremely adaptable, extremely useful; the author or filmmaker can use it as a crowbar to lever open locked doors . . . or as a small, slim pick to tease the tumblers into giving. The genre can thus be used to open almost any lock on the fears that lie behind the door, and *The Amityville Horror* is a dollars-and-cents case in point.

It is simple and straightforward, as most horror tales are. The Lutzes, a young married couple with two or three kids (Kathleen Lutz's by a previous marriage), buy a house in Amityville. Previous to their tenancy, a young man has murdered his whole family at the direction of "voices." For this reason, the Lutzes get the house cheaply.

But they soon discover that it wouldn't have been cheap at half the price, because it's haunted. Manifestations include black goop that comes bubbling out of the toilets (and before the festivities are over, it comes oozing out of the walls and the stairs as well), a roomful of flies, a rocking chair that rocks by itself, and something in the cellar that causes the dog to dig everlastingly at the wall. A window crashes down on the little boy's fingers. The little girl develops an "invisible friend" who is apparently really there. Eyes glow outside the window at three in the morning. And so on.

Worst of all, from the audience's standpoint, Lutz himself (James Brolin) apparently falls out of love with his wife (Margot Kidder) and begins to develop a meaningful relationship with his ax. Before things are done, we are drawn to the inescapable conclusion that he is tuning up for something more than splitting wood.

Stripped of its distracting elements (a puking nun, Rod Steiger shamelessly overacting as a priest who is just discovering the devil after forty years or so as a man of the cloth, and Margot Kidder doing calisthenics in a pair of bikini panties and one white stocking), *The Amityville Horror* is a perfect example of the tale to be told around the campfire. All the teller really has to do is to keep the catalog of inexplicable events in the correct order, so that unease escalates into outright fear.

All of which brings us around to the real watchspring of *Amityville* and the reason it works as well as it does: the picture's subtext is one of economic unease, and that is a theme that director Stuart Rosenberg plays on constantly. In terms of the times—18 percent inflation, mortgage rates out of sight, gasoline selling at a cool $1.40 a gallon—*The Amityville Horror*, like *The Exorcist*, could not have come along at a more opportune moment.

This breaks through most clearly in a scene that is the film's only moment of true and honest drama, a brief vignette that parts the clouds of hokum like a sunray on a drizzly afternoon. The Lutz family is preparing to go to the wedding of Kathleen Lutz's younger brother (who looks as if he might be all of seventeen). They are, of course, in the Bad House when the scene takes place. The younger brother has lost the $1,500 that is due the caterer and is in an understandable agony of panic and embarrassment.

Brolin says he'll write the caterer a check, which he does, and later he stands off the angry caterer, who has specified cash only in a half-whispered washroom argument while the wedding party whoops it up outside. After the wedding, Lutz turns the living room of the Bad House upside down looking for the lost money, which has now become *his* money, and the only way of backing up the bank paper he has issued the caterer. Brolin's check may not have been 100 percent Goodyear rubber, but in his sunken, purple-pouched eyes, we see a man who doesn't really have the money any more than his hapless brother-in-law does. Here is a man tottering on the brink of his own financial crash.

He finds the only trace under the couch: a bank money band with the numerals $500 stamped on it. The band lies there on the rug, tauntingly empty. "*Where is it?*" Brolin screams, his voice vibrating with anger, frustration, and fear. At that one moment, we hear the ring of Waterford, clear and true—or, if you like, we hear that one quiet phrase of pure music in a film that is otherwise all crash and bash.

Everything that *The Amityville Horror* does well is summed up in that scene. Its implications touch on everything about the house's most obvious and insidious effect—and also the only one that seems empirically undeniable. Little by little, it is ruining the Lutz family financially. The movie might as well have been subtitled *The Horror of the Shrinking Bank Account*. It's the more prosaic fallout of the place where so many haunted-house stories start. "It's on the market for a song," the Realtor says with a big egg-sucking grin. "It's supposed to be haunted."

Well, the house that the Lutzes buy is, indeed, on the market for a song (and there is another good moment—all too short—when Kathleen tells her husband that she will be the first person in her large Catholic family to actually own her own home: "We've always been renters," she says), but it ends up costing them dearly. At the conclusion, the house seems to literally tear itself apart. Windows crash in, black goop comes dribbling out of the walls, the cellar stairs cave in . . . and I found myself wondering not if the Lutz clan would get out alive but if they had adequate homeowner's insurance.

This is a movie for every woman who ever wept over a plugged-up toilet or a spreading water stain on the ceiling from the upstairs shower; for every man who ever did a slow burn when the weight of the snow caused his gutters to give way; for every child who ever jammed his fingers and felt that the door or window that did the jamming was out to get him. As horror goes, *Amityville* is pretty pedestrian. So's beer, but you can get drunk on it.

"Think of the bills," a woman sitting behind me in the theater moaned at one point. I suspect it was her own bills she was thinking about. It was impossible to make a silk purse out of this particular sow's ear, but Rosenberg at least manages to give us Qiana, and the main reason that people went to see it, I think, is that *The Amityville Horror*, beneath its ghost-story exterior, is really a financial demolition derby.

Think of the bills, indeed.

If movies are the dreams of the mass culture—one film critic, in fact, has called watching a movie dreaming with one's eyes open—and if horror movies are the nightmares of the mass culture, then many horror movies of recent times express America's coming to terms with the possibility of nuclear annihilation over political differences.

The contemporary political horror films begin, I think, with *The Thing* (1951), directed by Christian Nyby and produced by Howard Hawks (who also had a hand in the direction, one suspects). It stars Margaret Sheridan, Kenneth Tobey, and James Arness as the blood-drinking human carrot from Planet X.

A polar encampment of soldiers and scientists discovers a strong magnetic field emanating from an area where there has been a recent meteor fall: the field is strong enough to throw all the electronic gadgets and gizmos off whack. Further, a camera designed to start shooting pictures when and if the normal background radiation count suddenly goes up has taken photos of an object that dips, swoops, and turns at high speeds—strange behavior for a meteor.

An expedition is dispatched to the spot, and it discovers a flying saucer buried in the ice. The saucer, superhot on touchdown, melted its way into the ice, which then refroze, leaving only the tail fin sticking out (thus relieving the special effects corps of a potentially big-budget item). The army guys, who demonstrate frostbite of the brain throughout most of the film, promptly destroy the extraterrestrial ship while trying to burn it out of the ice with thermite.

The occupant (Arness) is saved, however, and carted back to the experimental station in a block of ice. He/it is placed in a storage shed, under guard. One of the guards is so freaked out by the thing that he throws a blanket over it. Unlucky man! Quite obviously, all his good stars are in retrograde, his biorhythms low, and his mental magnetic poles temporarily reversed. The blanket he's used is of the electric variety, and it miraculously melts the ice without shorting out. The Thing escapes and the fun begins.

The fun ends about sixty minutes later with the creature being roasted medium rare on an electric sidewalk sort of thing that the scientists have set up. A reporter on the scene sends back the news of humankind's first victory over invaders from space, and the film fades out, not with a THE END but with a question mark.

The Thing is a small movie done on a low budget. Like *Alien*, which would come more than a quarter century later, it achieves its best effects from feelings of claustrophobia and xenophobia. But, as I said before, the best horror movies will try to get at you on many different levels, and *The Thing* is also operating on a political level. It has grim things to say about eggheads (and knee-jerk liberals—in the early fifties, you could have put an equal sign between the two) who would indulge in the crime of appeasement.

The Thing is the first movie of the fifties to offer us the scientist in the role of the Appeaser, that creature who for reasons either craven or misguided would open the gates to the Garden of Eden and let all the evils fly in (as opposed, say, to those Mad Labs proprietors of the thirties, who were more than willing to open Pandora's box and let all the evils fly out—a major distinction, though the results are the same). That scientists should be so constantly vilified in the technohorror films of the fifties—a decade that was apparently dedicated to the idea of turning out a whole marching corps of men and women in white lab coats—is perhaps not so surprising when we remember that it was science that opened those same gates so that the atomic bomb could be brought into Eden: first by itself and then trundled on missiles.

The average Jane or Joe during those spooky eight or nine years that followed the surrender of Japan had extremely schizoid feelings about science and scientists—recognizing the need for them and, at the same time, loathing the things they had let in forever. On the one hand, the average Jane or Joe had found a new pal, that neat little all-around guy, Reddy Kilowatt; on the other hand, before getting into the first reel of *The Thing*, they had to watch newsreel footage as an army mockup of a town *just like theirs* was vaporized in a nuclear furnace.

Robert Cornthwaite plays the appeasing scientist in *The Thing*, and we hear from his lips the first verse of a psalm that any filmgoer who grew up in the fifties and sixties became familiar with very quickly: "We must preserve this creature for science." The second verse goes: "If it comes from a society more advanced than ours, it must come in peace. If we can only establish communications with it, and find out what it wants——"

Twice, near the film's conclusion, Cornthwaite is hauled away by soldiers; at the climax, he breaks free of his guards and faces the creature with his hands open and empty. He begs it to communicate with him and to see that he means it no harm. The creature stares at him for a long, pregnant moment . . . and then bats him casually aside, as you or I might swat a mosquito. The medium rare roasting on the electric sidewalk follows.

Now, I'm only a journeyman writer and I will not presume to teach history here. I will point out that the Americans of that time were perhaps more paranoid about the idea of appeasement than at any other time before or since. The dreadful humiliation of Neville Chamberlain and England's resulting close squeak at the beginning of Hitler's war was still very much with those Americans, and why not? It had all happened only twelve years prior to *The Thing*'s release, and even Americans who were just turning twenty-one in 1951 could remember it all very clearly. The moral was simple—such appeasement doesn't work: you gotta cut 'em if they stand and shoot 'em if they run. Otherwise, they'll take you over a bite at a time (and in the case of the Thing, you could take that literally).

If all this seems much too heavy a cargo for a modest little fright flick like *The Thing* to bear, remember that a man's point of view is shaped by the events he experiences and that his politics is shaped by his point of view. I am only suggesting that, given the political temper of the times and the cataclysmic world events that had occurred only a few years before, the viewpoint of this movie is almost preordained. What do you do with a blood-drinking carrot from outer space? Simple. Cut him if he stands and shoot him if he runs. And if you're an appeasing scientist like Cornthwaite (with a yellow streak up your back as wide as the no-passing line on a highway), you simply get bulldozed under.

By contrast, consider the other end of this telescope. The children of World War II produced *The Thing*; twenty-six years later, a child of Vietnam and the self-proclaimed Love Generation, Steven Spielberg, gives us a fitting balance weight to *The Thing* in *Close Encounters of the Third Kind*. In 1951, the soldier standing sentry duty (the one who has foolishly covered the block of ice with an electric blanket) empties his automatic into the alien when he hears it coming; in 1977, a young guy with a happy, spaced-out smile holds up a sign reading STOP AND BE FRIENDLY. Somewhere between the two, John Foster Dulles evolved into Henry Kissinger and the pugnacious politics of confrontation became détente.

In *The Thing*, Tobey occupies himself with building an electric boardwalk to kill the creature; in *Close Encounters*, Richard Dreyfuss occupies himself with building a mockup of Devils Tower, the creatures' landing place, in his living room. The Thing is a big, hulking brute who grunts; the creatures from the stars in Spielberg's film are small, delicate, childlike. They do not speak, but their mother ship plays lovely harmonic tones—the music of the spheres, we assume. And Dreyfuss, far from wanting to murder these emissaries from space, goes with them.

I'm not saying that Spielberg is or would think of himself as a member of the Love Generation simply because he came to his majority while students were putting daisies in the muzzles of M-1s and Jimi Hendrix and Janis Joplin were playing at Fillmore West. Neither am I saying that Hawks, Nyby, Charles Lederer (who wrote the screenplay for *The Thing*), and John W. Campbell (whose novella *Who Goes There?* formed the basis for the film) fought their way up the beaches of Anzio or helped raise the Stars and Stripes on Iwo Jima. But events determine point of view and point of view determines politics, and *CE3K* seems to me every bit as preordained as *The Thing*. We can understand that the latter's "Let the military handle this" thesis was a perfectly acceptable one in 1951, because the military had handled the Japs and the Nazis perfectly well in Duke Wayne's Big One, and we can also understand that the former's attitude of "Don't let the military handle this" was a perfectly acceptable one in 1977, following the military's less than sterling record in Vietnam, or even in 1980 (when *CE3K* was released with additional footage), the year American military personnel lost the chance to free our hostages in Iran following three hours of mechanical fuckups.

It may be that nothing in the world is so hard to comprehend as a terror whose time has come and gone—which may be why parents can scold their children for their fear of the bogeyman, when as children themselves, they had to cope with exactly the same fears (and the same sympathetic but uncomprehending parents). That may be why one generation's nightmare becomes the next generation's sociology, and even those who have walked through the fire have trouble remembering exactly what those burning coals felt like.

In the fifties, the terror of the bomb and of fallout was real, and it left a scar on those children who wanted to be good, just as the Depression of the thirties had left a scar on their elders. A newer generation—now teenagers, with no memory of either the Cuban Missile Crisis or of the Kennedy assassination in Dallas, raised on the milk of détente—may find it hard to comprehend the terror of these things, but they will undoubtedly have a chance to discover it in the years of tightening belts and heightening tensions that lie ahead . . . and the movies will be there to give their vague fears concrete focusing points in the horror movies yet to come.

I can remember, for instance, that in 1968, when I was twenty-one, the issue of long hair was an extremely nasty, extremely explosive one. That seems as hard to believe now as the idea of people killing each other over whether the sun went around the earth or the earth went around the sun, but that happened, too.

I was thrown out of a bar in Brewer, Maine, by a construction worker back in that happy year of 1968. The guy had muscles on his muscles and told me I could come back and finish my beer "after you get a haircut, you faggot fairy." There were the standard catcalls thrown from passing cars (usually old cars with fins and cancer of the rocker panels): Are you a boy or are you a girl? Do you give head, honey? When was the last time you had a bath?

I can remember such things in an intellectual, even analytical way, as I can remember having a dressing that had actually grown into the tissue yanked from the site of a cyst-removal operation that occurred when I was twelve. I screamed from the pain and then fainted dead away. I can remember the pulling sensation as the gauze tore free of the new, healthy tissue (the dressing removal was performed by a nurse's aide who apparently had no idea what she was doing), I can remember the scream, and I can remember the faint. What I can't remember is the pain itself. It's the same with the hair thing and, in a larger sense, all the other pains associated with coming of age in the decade of napalm and the Nehru jacket.

I've purposely avoided writing a novel with a sixties time setting because all of that seems, like the pulling of that surgical dressing, very distant to me now—almost as if it had happened to another person. But those things did happen: the hate, paranoia, and fear on both sides were all too real. If we doubt it, we need only review that quintessential sixties counterculture horror film, *Easy Rider*, in which Peter Fonda and Dennis Hopper end up being blown away by a couple of rednecks in a pickup truck as Roger McGuinn sings Bob Dylan's "It's Alright, Ma (I'm Only Bleeding)" on the soundtrack.

Similarly, it is difficult to remember in any gut way the fears that came with those boom years of atomic technology twenty-five years ago. The technology itself was strictly Apollonian: as Apollonian as nice guy Larry Talbot, who "said his prayers at night." The atom was not split by a gibbering Colin Clive or Boris Karloff in some eastern European mad lab; it was not done by alchemy and moonlight in the center of a rune-struck circle; it was done by a lot of little guys at Oak Ridge and White Sands who wore tweed jackets and smoked Luckies, guys who worried about dandruff and psoriasis and whether or not they could afford a new car and how to get rid of the goddamn crab grass. Splitting the atom, producing fission, opening that door on a new world that the old scientist speaks of at the end of *Them!*—these things were accomplished on a business-as-usual basis.

People understood this and could live with it (fifties science books extolled the wonderful world the friendly atom would produce, a world fueled by nice safe nuclear reactors, and grammar school kids got free comic books produced by the power companies), but they suspected and feared the hairy, simian face on the other side of the coin as well. They learned that the atom might be, for a number of reasons both technological and political, essentially uncontrollable. These feelings of deep unease came out in movies such as *Beginning of the End*, *Them!*, *Tarantula*, *The Incredible Shrinking Man* (in which radiation combined with a pesticide causes a very personal horror for one man, Scott Carey), *The H-Man*, and *4D Man*. The entire cycle reaches its supreme pinnacle of absurdity with *The Night of the Lepus*, in which the world is menaced by giant bunnies.

All of the foregoing are examples of the horror film with a technological subtext . . . sometimes referred to as the "nature run amuck" sort of horror picture. In all of them, it is mankind and mankind's technology that must bear the blame. "You brought it on yourselves," they all say: a fitting epitaph for the mass grave of mankind, I think, when the big balloon finally goes up and the ICBMs start to fly. It is here, in the technohorror film, that we really strike the mother lode. No more panning for the occasional nugget, as in the case of the economic horror film or the political horror film: pard, we could dig the gold right out of the ground with our bare hands here, if we wanted to. Here is a corner of the old horror film corral where even such an abysmal little wet fart of a picture as *The Horror of Party Beach* will yield a technological aspect upon analysis—you see, all those beach-blanket boppers in their bikinis and ball huggers are being menaced by monsters that were created when drums of radioactive waste leaked. But not to worry; although a few girls get carved up, all comes right in the end in time for one last wiener roast before school starts again.

The concerns of the technohorror films of the sixties and seventies change with the concerns of the people who lived through those times; the big-bug movies give way to pictures such as *The Forbin Project* ("The Software That Conquered the World") and *2001*, which offer us the possibility of the computer as God, or the even nastier idea (ludicrously executed, I'll readily admit) of the computer as satyr that is laboriously produced in *Demon Seed* and *Saturn 3*. In the sixties, horror proceeds from a vision of technology as an octopus—perhaps sentient—burying us alive in red tape and information-retrieval systems that are terrible when they work (*The Forbin Project*) and even more terrible when they don't. In *The Andromeda Strain*, for instance, a small scrap of paper gets caught in the striker of a teletype machine, keeps the bell from ringing, and thereby (in a fashion Rube Goldberg certainly would have approved of) nearly causes the end of the world.

Finally, there are the seventies, culminating in John Frankenheimer's not-very-good but certainly well-meant film *Prophecy*, which is so strikingly similar to those fifties big-bug movies (only the first cause has changed), and *The China Syndrome*, a horror movie that synthesizes all three of these major technological fears: fear of radiation, fear for the ecology, fear of the machinery gone out of control.

Even such a much-loved American institution as the motor vehicle has not entirely escaped the troubled dreams of Hollywood: before being run out of his mortgaged house in Amityville, James Brolin had to face the terrors of *The Car* (1977), a customized something or other that looked like a squatty airport limo from one of hell's used car lots. The movie degenerates into a ho-hum piece of hackwork before the end of the second reel (the sort of movie in which you can safely go out for a popcorn refill at certain intervals because you know the car isn't going to strike again for ten minutes or so), but there is a marvelous opening sequence in which the car chases two bicyclists through Utah's Zion National Park, its horn blatting arrhythmically as it gains on them and finally runs them down. There's something working in that opening that calls up a deep, almost primitive unease about the cars we zip ourselves into, thereby becoming anonymous . . . and perhaps homicidal.

There are a few films that have tried to walk the borderline between horror and social satire: one of those that seems to me to tread this borderline most successfully is *The Stepford Wives*. The film is based on the novel by Ira Levin, and Levin has actually been able to pull this difficult trick off twice, the other case being that of *Rosemary's Baby*. *The Stepford Wives* has some witty things to say about women's liberation and some disquieting things to say about the American male's response to it.

It is as satiric as the best of Stanley Kubrick's work (though a good deal less elegant), and I defy an audience not to laugh when Katharine Ross and Paula Prentiss step into the home of a neighbor (he's the local druggist, and a Walter Mitty type if ever there were one) and hear his wife moaning upstairs, "Oh, Frank, you're the greatest . . . Frank, you're the best . . . you're the champ . . ."

The original Levin story avoided the label "horror novel" (something like the label "pariah dog" in the more exalted circles of literary criticism) because most critics saw it as Levin's sly poke at the women's movement. But the scarier implications of Levin's jape are not directed at women at all: they are aimed unerringly at those men who consider it only their due to leave for the golf course on Saturday morning after breakfast has been served to them and to reappear (loaded, more likely than not) in time for their dinner to be served to them. After some uneasy backing and filling—during which it seems unsure of just what it does want to be—the film does, indeed, become a social horror story.

Katharine Ross and her husband (played by Peter Masterson) move from New York City to Stepford, a Connecticut suburb, because they feel it will be better for the children, and themselves as well. Stepford is a perfect little village where children wait good-humoredly for the school bus, where you can see two or three fellows washing their car on any given day, where (you feel) the yearly United Fund quota is not merely met but exceeded.

Yet there's a strangeness in Stepford. A lot of the wives seem a little, well, spacy. Pretty, always attired in flowing dresses that are almost gowns (a place where the movie slips, I think; as a labeling device, it's pretty crude. These women might as well be wearing stickers pasted to their foreheads that read I AM ONE OF THE <u>WEIRD</u> STEPFORD WIVES), they all drive station wagons, discuss housework with an inordinate degree of enthusiasm, and seem to spend any spare time at the supermarket.

One of the Stepford wives (one of the *weird* ones) cracks her head in a minor parking-lot fender bender; later, we see her at a lawn party, repeating over and over again, "I simply *must* get that recipe . . . I simply *must* get that recipe . . . I simply *must* . . ." The secret of Stepford becomes clear immediately: these women are *robots*. Freud, in a tone that sounded suspiciously like despair, asked, "Woman . . . what does she want?" Bryan Forbes and company ask the opposite question and come up with a stinging answer. Men, the film says, do not want women; they want robots with sex organs.

There are several funny scenes in the movie. My own favorite comes when, at a women's bitch session that Ross and Prentiss have arranged, the Stepford wives begin discussing cleaning products and laundry soaps with a slow and yet earnest intensity: everyone seems to have walked right into one of those commercials Madison Avenue male execs sometimes refer to as "two Cs in a K"—meaning two cunts in a kitchen.

But the movie waltzes slowly out of this brightly lit room of social satire and into a darker chamber by far. We feel the ring closing, first around Prentiss, then around Ross.

Stepford, a bedroom community serving a number of high-technology software companies, is exactly the wrong place for New Women such as Prentiss and Ross to have landed, we find. Instead of playing poker and drinking beer at the local Men's Association, the Stepford husbands are creating counterfeit women; the final sellout in which the real women are replaced with their Malibu Barbie counterparts is left for the viewer to grapple with. The fact that we don't actually know the answers to how some of these things are done, or where the bodies are being buried—if there are, indeed, bodies once the changeover is complete—gives the film a grim, surrealist feel that is almost unique in the annals of modern horror films.

The movie reserves its ultimate horror and its most telling social shot for its closing moments when the "new" Ross walks in on the old one . . . perhaps, we think, to murder her. Under her flowing negligee, which might have come from Frederick's of Hollywood, we see Ross's rather small breasts built up to the size of what men discussing women over beers sometimes refer to as "knockers." And, of course, they are no longer the woman's breasts at all: they now belong solely to her husband. The dummy is not quite complete, however: there are two horrible black pools where the eyes should be. The best social horror movies achieve their effect by implication, and *The Stepford Wives*, by showing us only the surface of things and never troubling to explain exactly how these things are done, implies plenty.

Another film that relies on the unease generated by changing mores is William Friedkin's *The Exorcist*, and I'll not bore you by rehashing the plot. I'll simply assume that if your interest in the genre has been sufficient to sustain you this far, you've probably seen it.

If the late fifties and early sixties were the curtain raiser on the generation gap, the seven years from 1966 to 1972 were the play itself. Little Richard, who had horrified parents in the fifties when he leaped atop his piano and began boogying on it in his lizardskin loafers, looked tame next to John Lennon, who proclaimed that the Beatles were more popular than Jesus—a statement that set off a rash of fundamentalist record burnings.

It was more than a generation gap. The two generations seemed, like the San Andreas Fault, to be moving along opposing plates of social and cultural conscience, commitment, and definitions of civilized behavior itself. And with all of this young vs. old nuttiness as a backdrop, Friedkin's film appeared and became a social phenomenon in itself. Lines stretched around the block in every major city where it played, and even in towns that normally rolled up their sidewalks promptly at 7:30 p.m., midnight shows were scheduled. Church groups picketed; sociologists pontificated; newscasters did back-of-the-book segments for their programs on slow nights. The country, in fact, went on a two-month possession jag.

The movie (and the novel) is nominally about the attempts of two priests to cast a demon out of young Regan MacNeil, of course, a pretty little subteen played by Linda Blair (who later went on to a *High Noon* showdown with a bathroom plunger in the infamous NBC movie *Born Innocent*). Substantively, however, it is a film about explosive social change, a finely honed focusing point for that entire youth explosion that occurred in the late sixties and early seventies. It was a movie for all those parents who felt, in a kind of agony and terror, that they were losing their children and could not understand why or how it was happening. It's the face of the Werewolf, a Jekyll-and-Hyde tale in which sweet, lovely, and loving Regan turns into a foul-talking monster strapped into her bed and croaking (in the voice of Mercedes McCambridge) such charming homilies as "You're going to let Jesus fuck you, fuck you, fuck you." Religious trappings aside, every adult in America understood what the film's powerful subtext was saying: they understood that the demon in Regan would have responded enthusiastically to the Fish Cheer at Woodstock.

A Warner Bros. executive told me recently that movie surveys show the average filmgoer to be fifteen years of age, which may be the biggest reason the movies so often seem afflicted with a terminal case of arrested development: for every film like *Julia* or *The Turning Point*, there are a dozen like *Roller Boogie* and *If You Don't Stop It, You'll Go Blind*. But it is worth noting that when the infrequent blockbusters that every film producer hopes for finally come along—pictures like *Star Wars, Jaws, American Graffiti, The Godfather, Gone with the Wind*, and, of course, *The Exorcist*—they always break the demographic hammerlock that is the enemy of intelligent filmmaking. It is comparatively rare for horror movies to do this, but *The Exorcist* is a case in point (and we have already spoken of *The Amityville Horror*, another film that has enjoyed a surprisingly old audience).

A film that appealed directly to the fifteen-year-olds who provide the spike point for moviegoing audiences—and one with a subtext tailored to match—was the Brian De Palma adaptation of my novel *Carrie*. While I believe that both the book and the film depend on largely the same social situations to provide a text and a subtext of horror, there's enough difference to make interesting observations on De Palma's film version.

Both novel and movie have a pleasant *High School Confidential* feel, and while there are some superficial changes from the book in the film (Carrie's mother, for instance, seems to be presented in the film as a kind of weird renegade Roman Catholic), the basic story skeleton is pretty much the same. The story deals with a girl named Carrie White, the browbeaten daughter of a religious fanatic. Because of her strange clothes and shy mannerisms, Carrie is the butt of every class joke, the social outsider in every situation. She also has a mild telekinetic ability that intensifies after her first menstrual period, and she finally uses that power to "bring down the house" following a terrible social disaster at her high school prom.

De Palma's approach to the material is lighter and more deft than my own—and a good deal more artistic; the book tries to deal with the loneliness of one girl, her desperate effort to become a part of the peer society in which she must exist, and how her effort fails. If this deliberate updating of *High School Confidential* has any thesis to offer, it is that high school is a place of almost bottomless conservatism and bigotry, a place where adolescents are no more allowed to rise above their station than a Hindu would be allowed to rise above his caste.

But there's a little more subtext to the book than that—at least, I hope so. If *The Stepford Wives* concerns itself with what men want from women, then *Carrie* is largely about how women find their own channels of power and what men fear about women and women's sexuality—which is only to say that, writing the book in 1973 and out of college only three years, I was fully aware of what women's liberation implied for me and others of my sex. The book is, in its more adult implications, an uneasy masculine shrinking from a future of female equality. For me, Carrie is a sadly misused teenager, an example of the sort of person whose spirit is so often broken for good in that pit of man- and woman-eaters that is your normal suburban high school. But she's also Woman, feeling her powers for the first time and, like Samson, pulling down the temple on everyone in sight at the end of the book.

Heavy, turgid stuff—but in the novel, it's there only if you want to take it. If you don't, that's OK with me. A subtext works well only if it's unobtrusive (in that, I perhaps succeeded too well; in her review of De Palma's film, Pauline Kael dismissed my novel as "an unassuming potboiler"—as depressing a description as one could imagine but not completely inaccurate).

De Palma's film is up to more ambitious things. As in *The Stepford Wives*, humor and horror exist side by side in *Carrie*, playing off each other, and it is only as the film nears its conclusion that horror takes over completely. We see Billy Nolan (well played by John Travolta) giving the cops a big aw-shucks grin as he hides a beer against his crotch early on; it is a moment reminiscent of *American Graffiti*. Not long after, however, we see him swinging a sledgehammer at the head of a pig in a stockyard—the aw-shucks grin has crossed the line into madness, somehow, and that line crossing is what the film as a whole is about.

We see three boys (one of them the film's nominal hero, played by William Katt) trying on tuxedos for the prom in a kind of Gas House Kids routine that includes Donald Duck talk and speeded-up action.

We see the girls who have humiliated Carrie in the shower room by throwing tampons and sanitary napkins at her, doing penance on the exercise field to tootling, lumbering music that is reminiscent of "Baby Elephant Walk." And yet beyond all these sophomoric and mildly amusing high school cutups, we sense a vacuous, almost unfocused hate, the almost unplanned revenge upon a girl who is trying to rise above her station. Much of De Palma's film is surprisingly jolly, but we sense that his jocoseness is dangerous: behind it lurks the aw-shucks grin becoming a frozen rictus, and the girls laboring over their calisthenics are the same girls who shouted "Plug it up, plug it up, plug it up!" at Carrie not long before. Most of all, there is that bucket of pig's blood poised on the beam above the place where Carrie and Tommy will eventually be crowned . . . only waiting its time.

The film came along at a time when movie critics were bewailing the fact that there were no movies being made with good, meaty roles for women in them . . . but none of those critics seems to have noticed that in its film incarnation, *Carrie* belongs almost entirely to the ladies. Billy Nolan, a major—and frightening—character in the book, has been reduced to a semi-supporting role in the movie. Tommy, the boy who takes Carrie to the prom, is presented in the novel as a boy who is honestly trying to do something manly—in his own way, he is trying to opt out of the caste system. In the film, however, he becomes little more than his girlfriend's cat's-paw, her tool of atonement for her part in the shower-room scene.

"I don't go around with anyone I don't want to," Tommy says patiently. "I'm asking because I want to ask you." Ultimately, he knew this to be the truth.

In the film, however, when Carrie asks Tommy why he is favoring her with an invitation to the prom, he offers her a dizzy sun 'n' surf grin and says, "Because you liked my poem." Which, by the way, his girlfriend had written.

The novel views high school in a fairly common way: as that pit of man- and woman-eaters already mentioned. De Palma's social stance is more original: he sees this suburban white kids' high school as a kind of matriarchy. No matter where you look, there are girls behind the scenes, pulling invisible wires, rigging elections, using their boyfriends as stalking horses. Against such a backdrop, Carrie becomes doubly pitiful, because she is unable to do any of those things—she can only wait to be saved or damned by the actions of others. Her only power is her telekinetic ability, and both book and movie eventually arrive at the same point: Carrie uses her "wild talent" to pull down the whole rotten society. And one reason for the success of the story in both print and film, I think, lies in this: Carrie's revenge is something that any student who ever had his gym shorts pulled down in phys ed or his glasses thumb-rubbed in study hall could approve of. In Carrie's destruction of the gym (and her destructive walk back home in the book, a sequence left out of the movie because of tight budgeting), we see a dream revolution of the socially downtrodden.

The movies I have been discussing are those that try to link real (if sometimes free-floating) anxieties to the nightmare fears of the horror film. But now, let me put out even this dim light of rationality and discuss a few of those films whose effects go considerably deeper, past the rational and into those fears that seem universal.

Here is where we cross into the taboo lands for sure, and it's best to be frank up front. I think that we're all mentally ill; those of us outside the asylums only hide it a little better—and maybe not all that much better, after all. We've all known people who talk to themselves, people who sometimes squinch their faces into horrible grimaces when they believe no one is watching, people who have some hysterical fear—of snakes, the dark, the tight place, the long drop . . . and, of course, those final worms and grubs that are waiting so patiently underground.

When we pay our four or five bucks and seat ourselves at tenth-row center in a theater showing a horror movie, we are daring the nightmare.

Why? Some of the reasons are simple and obvious. To show that we can, that we are not afraid, that we can ride this roller coaster. Which is not to say that a really good horror movie may not surprise a scream out of us at some point, the way we may scream when the roller coaster twists through a complete 360 or plows through a lake at the bottom of the drop. And horror movies, like roller coasters, have always been the special province of the young: by the time one turns forty or fifty, one's appetite for double twists or 360-degree loops may be considerably depleted.

We also go to reestablish our feelings of essential normality; the horror movie is innately conservative, even reactionary. Freda Jackson as the horrible melting woman in *Die, Monster, Die!* confirms for us that no matter how far we may be removed from the beauty of a Robert Redford or a Diana Ross, we are still light years from true ugliness.

And we go to have fun.

Ah, but this is where the ground starts to slope away, isn't it? Because this is a very peculiar sort of fun, indeed. The fun comes from seeing others menaced—sometimes killed. One critic has suggested that if pro football has become the voyeur's version of combat, then the horror film has become the modern version of the public lynching.

It is true that the mythic, "fairy-tale" horror film intends to take away the shades of gray (which is one reason *When a Stranger Calls* doesn't work; the psycho, well and honestly played by Tony Beckley, is a poor schmuck beset by the miseries of his own psychosis; our unwilling sympathy for him dilutes the film's success as surely as water dilutes Scotch): it urges us to put away our more civilized and adult penchant for analysis and to become children again, seeing things in pure blacks and whites. It may be that horror movies provide psychic relief on this level because this invitation to lapse into simplicity, irrationality, and even outright madness is extended so rarely. We are told we may allow our emotions a free rein . . . or no rein at all.

If we are all insane, then sanity becomes a matter of degree. If your insanity leads you to carve up women like Jack the Ripper or the Cleveland Torso Murderer, we clap you away in the funny farm (but neither of those two amateur-night surgeons was ever caught, heh-heh-heh); if, on the other hand, your insanity leads you only to talk to yourself when you're under stress or to pick your nose on your morning bus, then you are left alone to go about your business . . . though it is doubtful that you will ever be invited to the best parties.

The potential lyncher is in almost all of us (excluding saints, past and present; but then, most saints have been crazy in their own ways), and every now and then, he has to be let loose to scream and roll around in the grass. Our emotions and our fears form their own body, and we recognize that it demands its own exercise to maintain proper muscle tone. Certain of these emotional muscles are accepted—even exalted—in civilized society; they are, of course, the emotions that tend to maintain the status quo of civilization itself. Love, friendship, loyalty, kindness—these are all the emotions that we applaud, emotions that have been immortalized in the couplets of Hallmark cards and in the verses (I don't dare call it poetry) of Leonard Nimoy.

When we exhibit these emotions, society showers us with positive reinforcement; we learn this even before we get out of diapers. When, as children, we hug our rotten little puke of a sister and give her a kiss, all the aunts and uncles smile and twit and cry, "Isn't he the sweetest little thing?" Such coveted treats as chocolate-covered graham crackers often follow. But if we deliberately slam the rotten little puke of a sister's fingers in the door, sanctions follow—angry remonstrance from parents, aunts, and uncles; instead of a chocolate-covered graham cracker, a spanking.

But anticivilization emotions don't go away, and they demand periodic exercise. We have such "sick" jokes as, "What's the difference between a truckload of bowling balls and a truckload of dead babies?" (You can't unload a truckload of bowling balls with a pitchfork . . . a joke, by the way, that I heard originally from a ten-year-old.) Such a joke may surprise a laugh or a grin out of us even as we recoil, a possibility that confirms the thesis: if we share a brotherhood of man, then we also share an insanity of man. None of which is intended as a defense of either the sick joke or insanity but merely as an explanation of why the best horror films, like the best fairy tales, manage to be reactionary, anarchistic, and revolutionary all at the same time.

The mythic horror movie, like the sick joke, has a dirty job to do. It deliberately appeals to all that is worst in us. It is morbidity unchained, our most base instincts let free, our nastiest fantasies realized . . . and it all happens, fittingly enough, in the dark. For those reasons, good liberals often shy away from horror films. For myself, I like to see the most aggressive of them—*Dawn of the Dead*, for instance—as lifting a trapdoor in the civilized forebrain and throwing a basket of raw meat to the hungry alligators swimming around in that subterranean river beneath.

Why bother? Because it keeps them from getting out, man. It keeps them down there and me up here. It was Lennon and McCartney who said that all you need is love, and I would agree with that.

As long as you keep the gators fed.

Matinée

Robert Coover

Weary of the tedium of her days, her lonely life going nowhere, she skips work and steps inside a half-empty old movie house showing a scratched and grainy romantic film from her youth; she takes her favorite seat in the middle of the seventh row, hoping to experience once again the consoling power of sudden uncomplicated love, even if not one's own, love that has no trajectory attached to it but is a pure and immediate enrichment of the soul and delight of the body. In the film, two strangers separately board a train back in a time when trains had compartments with sliding doors and windows that could be pulled down for lingering, handkerchief-waving farewells. The woman waves goodbye to her husband, if that's who he is, the man to a woman who may be his fiancée, or perhaps his sister. There are shouts from the stationmaster, whistles, the slamming of heavy doors, slow wheezy movement, wisps of steam curling past as though to erase one reality in anticipation of another. He raises the window, then they turn and nod politely to each other, settling in for the journey. "Going far?" he asks. She looks up with a smile. The smile fades. Something seems to happen between them. The train is chugging along just as trains used to do, and for a magical moment they seem to be all alone, rocking through space, their hearts beating to the rhythm of the train, though in fact the compartment is full and they are being closely watched over newspapers and knitting. They lean toward each other to speak earnestly about the weather and the vexations of travel, their hearts visibly melting, and receive from a severe old lady sitting near the compartment door a particularly withering glance, but there is a telltale tear in her eye, as if she might once long ago have been similarly struck—just as there is a tear in her own eye, as she sits there in the musty old movie house. All of these people in the film are, of course, dead, which reminds her, as if she needed reminding, of the irreversible passing of time, adding therewith to her sadness, for, sooner or later, she, like they, will also be dead, but without ever having had a man gaze into her eyes that way, a moment so human, so iconic, so unspeakably beautiful—essential, really, to a well-lived life—but one never granted her or to be granted. As the dead actor and the dead actress fall into an immortal clinch, the film breaks and rattles in the projector and the lights come up while repairs are made. She knows how it all turns out, and knows that it will only deepen her melancholy, so she rises to leave, pulling her coat on, just as a man four rows in front of her rises and gathers up his own coat and hat, glancing at her fleetingly. As she steps out into the aisle and he steps out into the aisle, they will accidentally bump into each other, or maybe it won't be an accident but something, well, something ordained.

Alone at home, he watches this old film, imagining that it is he who rises from the third row as the movie-house lights come up and, as he lifts his hat and coat from the adjoining seat, catches a glimpse of the sorrowful woman four rows back, who seems to be tearfully staring at him. A sourceless music rises, throbbing, as though from out of their shared gaze. As the man in the film pulls his coat on and starts up the aisle toward where he and the woman will jostle each other, intentionally or accidentally or as if both compelled to so collide, it's purposefully ambiguous, he also dons his coat—he knows how the movie turns out—and heads off for a drink at the neighborhood bar, called there by what he feels to be his vocation to rescue sad maidens. Of whom, no shortage, he has only to choose or wait to be chosen. Meanwhile, drink in hand, he watches the old movie that is playing silently on the TV above the bar, one he remembers well. It once had the power to excite him inordinately, and it excites him now: A man, out hiking, meets a young woman on the trail. She looks up, pauses, her smile fading, holds his gaze for a timeless moment, and then, as if deflected by the stunning power of it, veers off the trail and into the wilderness. The man continues on his path, but he, too, is somewhat stunned, and after a few steps he changes his mind and leaves the trail to follow her. The wilderness is thick, confusing, no sign of her, easy to get lost, he decides to go no farther—but then he sees her, standing knee-deep, nude, her back to him, in a softly lit pond. Film nudity was rare in those days, never more than a teasing glimpse, but in this restored version using recovered footage the camera remains fixed on the woman, approaching her from behind as the hero of the movie, spellbound (as he, too, perched at the bar, is spellbound, before an ancient mystery being spectacularly revealed), approaches her. After pausing to gaze tenderly a moment upon this vision (she knows he is watching her, he knows she knows), the man strips down and steps out in front of the camera and into the pond, their paired bodies bathed in a strange unearthly light. "Their backsides are beautiful," a woman sitting on the next barstool says. Absorbed in the film, he hadn't noticed her climb up beside him, and he's not sure he's pleased by the interruption. This is the best part. "But what always gets me," she says, "is that first moment when they look into each other's eyes." He nods in agreement, unable to take his own eyes off the film until both actors have entered the water up to their shoulders and turned toward each other. "That's when it all happens," he says, turning at last, as the actors have turned, to gaze deeply into her gazing eyes. "The rest is just mechanics." "Like a spark to fire," she replies throatily. "Which, sadly, always goes out," he adds with a wistful smile. "But before it does . . ."

She doesn't object to leaving the bar; she went there hoping for something like this, this spark-to-fire lady. Nor does she regret missing the rest of the movie—she knows how it turns out: the two strangers will make love in the water, but will never see each other again, she walking away into the wilderness, he, momentarily sated, smiling as he watches her go, but later overtaken by a terrible longing that sends him all over the world in a futile search for her. A fairy tale of sorts. Not so the present encounter. They have somehow got to the sadness of such affairs without experiencing the ecstasy that is supposed to come first. To break the awkward silence that has fallen, they pull their underwear back on and turn on the TV to see what movies are showing. "Ah, I like this one," he says. She knows it. It's about a blind flower girl from whom, every afternoon at the same hour, a gentleman buys a fresh bouquet. For his fiancée or his wife, the flower girl assumes, and she always wishes the recipient well, though it is clear that she is falling helplessly in love with the man's kind, mellifluous voice, and she waits every day, listening for him with transparent longing. It reminds her, curled up there on the sofa in her underpants, her shirt draped over her shoulders, of another film she likes much more, also ultimately about a blind person, in which a winsome governess falls in love with the master of the house and he, after only a moment's hesitation (either it happens like that or it doesn't), with her. The mistress of the house, his wife, is a cruel, vindictive woman, and the movie takes a tragic turn—it's the master who ends up blind—but before that there are about ten magical minutes as beautiful as anything in the history of the movies. Now, on the TV, the soothing voice is saying in a soft whisper perhaps not meant to be overheard that the flower girl is very beautiful, and she turns her face toward the whisper with abject adoration burning in her blind eyes. We see him now. He is a hideously disfigured war veteran, but the flower girl, of course, doesn't see this—she sees only the noble soul within, as a disembodied voice seems to say. In the other movie, the one she prefers, the master is not yet blind when his wife coldly dismisses the governess, mainly because of the ten good minutes that have gone before, and at the door, before the poor governess steps out and disappears into a winter storm, there is a final shared glance between her and the master that tears at the heart. The expressions on their faces, as best she remembers them, are much like those of the scarred veteran and the flower girl now, the old soldier stunned by the worshipful way the girl *looks* at him, even if unseeing—he could not have believed that something like this would ever happen to him again. Unfortunately, he is also guiltily aware that he has been misleading the poor child, for the flowers he buys are indeed for his wife, who is lying in the hospital in a coma brought on by the shock of his return, a coma from which she is not expected to emerge. Consequently, though it wrenches his heart, he forgoes any further contact with the flower girl, who waits and waits in gathering dismay, listening in vain for that voice she loves. In the other movie, the one she remembers, the master suffers a similar agony. His sight gone, his wife institutionalized, he spends his fortune sending emissaries around the world in search of the governess. Most of these emissaries are merely taking advantage of his anguish, accepting his money without even trying to find her. One invents a rumor that she is dead or dying, others that she is believed to have married a desert sheikh or entered a nunnery under an assumed name. In utter despair, his fortune exhausted, his false friends departed, the master leaves his house and, following the sound of the breaking waves, feels his way with his white cane to the edge of the cliff. He is about to take his final fatal step when he hears a beloved voice calling his name. He turns, staggers backward toward the edge, dropping his cane, but the governess rushes forward and pulls him to safety, and they fall into a tearfully ecstatic embrace. Not so lucky the flower girl. The disfigured veteran waits until the first anniversary of his wife's burial before returning to the flower stall, only to see the blind girl, having abandoned all hope, step out, unseeing eyes to the heavens, into the onrushing traffic. Brakes squeal, people scream, there is the sound of crunching metal. He rushes to her side. She lies crushed on the pavement, a confusion of wrecked vehicles all around her, blood leaking from her lips. "My love!" he gasps. Her eyes flutter open and seem to see him and, with a faint ethereal smile, she dies. The rescuer of sad maidens and the spark-to-fire lady are both weeping. They take their underwear off again.

If only the wife had died sooner, there could have been a happy ending. That's what a young woman in a love hotel room rented by the hour believes—"She just ruined the story hanging on like that!"—and the fellow she's with laughs and says, "There are no happy endings, kid. Just these moments." "But she never really had her moment." "Sure she did. Right there in the street." "But all that blood! It was coming out her ears!" "Yeah. Glorious." This is her first time in such a place. When she understood what it was, she was too shy to say no. She's so susceptible to that little flutter of the heart—one long, deep kiss will carry her right away—and he seemed like such a nice boy. If he's really a boy. He looks older now, with his clothes off. As soon as they got to the room, he turned on an adult channel and insisted that they had to do everything that happened on the screen, no matter how gross. "Here are your real brief encounters," he said with a crooked grin, making fun of her romantic ways. Encounters, yes, though more like collisions, really, and certainly brief, but without the maddening joy, the dissolving of the self into something more than the self, the anguished longing afterward. He doesn't understand a thing. So when he'd finally exhausted himself she switched to the nostalgia channel, where the end of the blind-flower-girl film was playing. Now, after the credits and ads (hawking the very lubricant the hotel provides), a new film starts up called *Matinée*. She remembers walking out of this one years ago, because she didn't really understand it. It's not exactly a romantic film, but it's also not exactly not one. It's about a bored suburban housewife who, on an afternoon shopping trip into the city, steps into a rundown old cinema to lose herself in the more adventurous lives of others. The film being shown there is about a young woman on a holiday in an exotic foreign city, who meets a handsome, pipe-smoking gentleman on a sightseeing riverboat and embarks on a sudden but ill-fated romance with him. The film fills the housewife with such longing that when the man sitting beside her in the darkened movie house takes her hand to lead her away to a nearby hotel she just can't seem to resist. ("There we go, kid!" the guy she's with says, laughing and giving her a slap on the bum as she leans forward on her hands and knees to turn up the volume.) Or maybe this is why the housewife in the film went to that old cinema in the first place, though she'd never done anything like that before. When the man gives her some money, she accepts it without saying anything, and this becomes the pattern of her afternoons, sneaking away from her domestic family life to pick up men in the old movie house—she sees the beginnings of lots of matinées—and otherwise carrying on exactly as before. Sometimes she uses the money the men give her to buy toys for her children or something nice for her husband; other times she just forgets about it. The movie also has another story line, about an unmarried lady of the streets, a sort of brief-encounters careerist, who dreams of becoming a happy suburban housewife. When her clients ask her questions about herself, she starts to invent such a life and, like a wish coming true, that life begins to happen, unless it's just her imagination. These are completely separate stories, about completely different people, but the confusing thing is that the same actress plays both parts, and eventually everything gets mixed up, their lives weaving in and out of each other, until neither the housewife nor the prostitute knows for sure who she is or where she is. To make it even more complicated, the client for the housewife and/or prostitute is always the same person, though she never recognizes him, while the husband and the children are different people every time they're seen, and neither the housewife nor the prostitute seems surprised by this. Both of them appear ready to fix breakfast for anybody and to put any child to bed at night. She'd like to ask the guy she's with what he thinks is going on, but the brute, his fingers like talons on her thighs, has jerked her back to sit on his face, so he's not even watching.

But it *is* confusing. She's a working girl, she doesn't go to the movies, no time for that—she does her marketing on the street and provides her services in a room she rents—and yet here she is in an old movie house, watching a romantic musical about a happy suburban family, and some guy takes her hand and she thinks, I've never done this before! Or she is working the streets when a man stops his car and picks her up and he turns out to be her husband. The kids in the car give her a hug and call her Mommy. She reaches into her bag to see if she has any candy for them, but all she finds are lubricants and condoms. Her husband winks. Or, in her sad little rented room, she gets herself tricked out for the evening in a tight miniskirt, black net stockings, and stilettos, and opens the door to step out onto the street: it's morning and she's at home. "What are you dressed up like that for, dear?" her husband asks, looking up from the television, pipe in hand. Though she doesn't recognize him, the family photos on the walls and on tabletops suggest that they've been married for decades. "I—I'm going shopping," she says, which is not really an explanation. "I have to go in to the office later," he says with a loving smile. "I'll pick you up outside the department store at five." So on this day, which already seems like several, she skips the matinée (not her sort of movie anyway, a serial-killer thing called *The Love Hotel Murders*) and waits for him outside the store at five. He pulls up, she gets in the car, and he takes her to a convenience hotel, so he's probably not her husband. She arrives home late from this encounter (he wanted to do everything), worried about the children (she has children!), and finds a man who must be her long-suffering husband preparing breakfast for them. "Why are you carrying all that money?" he asks. Indeed, she is clutching a fistful of it. "It's for you," she says in her bewilderment, dropping it on the table, and she goes to her room to look at herself in the mirror. She knows she should recognize the person she sees there, but the best she can say is that she's vaguely familiar, like someone she has passed on the street or in a grocery-store aisle.

Or like that man on the department-store escalator today. She had picked up a new ruffled blouse and a silk kerchief and was taking the escalator up a floor to look for a winter scarf for her husband. A man taking the escalator down to street level was wearing a very handsome one and she wondered, as he passed, if it would suit her husband. But then their eyes met and both she and he turned in stunned amazement to watch the other descend/ascend, though she found herself wondering, even as her love-struck heart beat wildly, if perhaps he *was* her husband. She took the down escalator in the hope of seeing him again, but he had vanished. Perhaps he had taken the up escalator, looking for her. Perhaps he never was: What can the lonely heart not imagine? The intensity of her emotions frightened her. To calm herself, she decided to go to a matinée showing of a grainy old movie about two people on a busy train platform who say goodbye to the people they love—his wife, her fiancé—then turn and, as the platform empties out, see each other standing there by the tracks under the high domed roof in the dissipating steam, sad and alone. They introduce themselves, and, to console each other, they go off to have tea together in a cozy little hotel nearby, end up in bed, and, while sharing a cigarette (this is an old movie, they don't show the part in between), talk about the strangeness of the moment. Though they have discovered a sudden undying love for each other, they have not told each other their names, nor will they. "Sometimes I feel like my whole life is just a movie I'm in," she says, somewhat tearfully, "and I don't even have the best part." "Or two movies," he says, "or more. All happening"—"I adore you," she whispers, kissing his speaking lips—"at the same time, like some kind of montage." "Yes, fraught moments like these are like that," she replies in her deepening melancholy, "but"—"I feel like I've always loved you," he murmurs, nibbling her earlobe—"it's an illusion. Real life is more like a train that never stops to let you off. The days come and go, you get older, and then you die." "But sometimes something happens. You bump into somebody in the aisle while leaving a movie and your life changes." "Or it doesn't. If you're married, you have to choose. Are you married to that woman on the train you were waving goodbye to?" "Yes. That's how we met—leaving the cinema. It was a sad movie about a despairing blind man who was standing at the edge of a cliff when the woman he loved turned up and cried out his name, and he was so startled that he dropped his cane and staggered backward off the cliff. There was a smile on his face, though, from hearing the voice of his beloved, and he reached out his arms toward her as he fell, so you might say he died happy. Not that it's easy, of course, to be happy when falling off a cliff." "No." "We were both bawling and we fell into a hug right there in the aisle, though we didn't even know each other, and we left the movie house and got married." "Are you sorry? That you got married, I mean?" "No, it's all right. I miss the freedom I had before, but I don't miss the anxiety or the loneliness. I'm more comfortable when I can, as you might say, move with the plot." "I know that's the right thing to say," she says, beginning to weep, "but it means you're uncomfortable now and it makes me feel evil and unwanted." He is also weeping. "What can I say?" he says. "It's all so very sad." They are making love again. It's even better than before. Both are wondering if they can bear to part.

They can and do, though it wrenches their hearts. Years later, in the city, he is having lunch in a popular restaurant, his wife having joined him before her usual afternoon shopping trip, when he spies a woman sitting at a table by the window with a man in a business suit, and he wonders if it is the same woman he met on that steamy train platform so long ago. He remembers suddenly and vividly the room they shared in the little hotel, the yellow flowered wallpaper, the pink bedspread and matching curtains, the chipped amber ashtray sitting on a white crocheted doily stained at one edge with tea or coffee. Why does he recall all this? If asked, he could barely describe his bedroom at home. At the time, he felt as if he'd been in that room forever and would be there for all time (there was no such thing as time), but then it all vanished in an instant as he stepped out the door, only to return now like a haunting. His wife rises to get on with her shopping, or perhaps to take in a movie matinée, as is her wont of late; she leans over and kisses his forehead in farewell just as the man at the other table rises and, fedora in hand, leans over to peck the woman's cheek, leaving them both alone at their tables, staring across the room at each other. She stands, holding his gaze, crosses the room, takes the chair vacated by his wife. "Didn't we meet many years ago?" she asks breathily, as though in awe of the moment. "Yes, on a train platform." "No, on a sightseeing boat in a large city." He doesn't remember this, but seeing her sitting there before him in the soft restaurant light, so familiar, so beautiful, he wonders if perhaps he is mistaken. He glances at her blouse, seeing in his mind still the stained doily and the chipped ashtray, things also now in doubt. "You had a mustache then and smoked a pipe." He desires this to be true, so in a sense it is true. He strokes his upper lip thoughtfully and gazes, spellbound, into her adoring gaze. "You were wearing a white dress with puff sleeves and a red silk kerchief," he says softly. "Was I?" They are leaning, somewhat desperately, toward each other. A kiss is imminent, yet impossible. "What will we do?" "I don't know," she says. "I am lost." "Maybe we could go to a movie? Down the street they're showing *The Rescuer of Sad Maidens*. Have you seen it?" "Is that the one that takes place aboard a doomed cruise ship?" "No, it's a stories-within-stories kind of thing." "I don't think I'd like it. I'm more straightforward than that." "Well, all right. A hotel room, then?"

She has been sitting in the old half-empty cinema with tears in her eyes, watching this poignant movie about the reunited lovers and thinking about life, how sad it is, when the man sitting next to her puts his hand over hers. When he leads her out (the movie is not over, but she knows what happens next), she somehow cannot resist, though he is not her husband. He takes her to a room in a small hotel. She seems to recognize it, though she has never been there, nor indeed has she ever done anything like this before. The windows, under the slanting ceiling, look out on rooftops and chimney pots. Next to one of the windows a porcelain washbasin sits on a table draped with a faded yellow cloth, a used bar of brown soap in a tin dish and a pitcher of water beside it. She knows without looking that there is a frayed green towel on the chrome bar screwed into the side of the table, a white one on the floor to stand on, and a blue drinking glass beside the basin, catching the late-afternoon light. She has never been here, so how does she know all this? Perhaps she has seen too many movies. The priest's barren cell in that film she saw recently about the passionate but impossible romance between a priest and a nun, for example, had slanted ceilings and a washstand with a towel bar and a basin that looked much like this one, though everything was white. Earlier, in the garden, in the soft light of a tree's shade, the priest and the nun, utterly love-struck, had drawn together, gazing deeply into each other's eyes—much like the two married people in the restaurant in the movie she was just watching—then had parted in anguish, suffering the shame of their iniquitous desire. Alone afterward, in the cell with the washstand, the priest—though you couldn't actually see this—was committing the sin of onanism when the nun reappeared before him in all her resplendent earthly beauty, dressed only in her wimple, with a golden crucifix dangling from a chain between her exquisite breasts. Was she real or only his crazed and hapless fantasy? It was unclear, but she was played by a living actress—living then, anyway—and so she seemed real, and what happened between them also seemed real. Did they use the washbasin afterward? Maybe they did, since she remembers it so vividly. Meanwhile, the man she is with now, while removing his tie, is telling her a strange story about his obsession with a woodland nymph, whom he met briefly one afternoon while out hiking and for whom, whether she actually exists or not, he has been ceaselessly searching ever since. "I thought for a moment you might be she," he says sorrowfully, as she kicks off her pumps and peels down her stockings. "How do you know that I'm not?" "Because I cannot forget her, though I often wish that I could. I see her features even when I look at myself in the mirror." He unbuttons his shirt, setting the cufflinks thoughtfully beside the blue glass. "It took me forever to find my way back to the trail, and you could say I've not found it yet." He lowers his pants. "You are chasing phantoms," she says, lifting her dress over her head. "Though the past may once have existed, it does not now exist. Something has taken its place." She feels certain that she has said this before. Or heard it said. She wants to explain what the something is, but it's too late—even as she steps out of her underwear the film is breaking and rattling in the projector.

The Last Movie

Rachel Hadas

In memory of Charles Barber

Saturday, April 5. Welles's *Othello*:
black and white grid of rage,

steam of sheer fury spewing from the vent
of violence that followed where they went.

Wind howled on the battlements, but sun
gilded glum canals. The lovers floated

beneath black bridges, coupled in stone rooms.
The unrepentant villain (at the start

so all the rest was flashback)
dangled from a cage

squinting inscrutably at the funeral
procession winding through the town below.

The air was full of wailing.
Knives of sunlight glittered on the sea.

We lurched out onto Fifty-Seventh Street.
You said "I think I'm dying."

Next week your eyes went out.
Shining under the lamp,

your blue gaze, now opaque,
your face drawn sharper but still beautiful:

from this extremity you can attempt
to rise to rage and grief. Or you can yield

to the cozy quicksand of the bed.
You wave your hand at walls of books:

"What do I do? Do I throw these away?"
Their anecdotes, their comforts—now black glass.

Some Months After My Father's Death

Sheryl St. Germain

I am watching the movie *Twelve Angry Men*
because there is a character in it
who reminds me of him.

He is the one who wants to go to the baseball game
instead of decide on a man's life,
he is the weak one, the one afraid to reveal
what he really feels, the one for whom everything
is a joke. He is not Henry Fonda,
the tight-lipped moral one.

The man is despicable, his weaknesses obvious
to all, as obvious as Henry Fonda's goodness.
I watch the movie again and again, loving
the black and white of it, soothed
by the sound of my father's voice,
the careless pronunciation, the easy
shrugging of the shoulders at every crucial question.

I sink lower into the dark arms of the sofa.
Strange how comfortable the familiar is,
how we can even prefer it,
however terrifying.

COMMENTING

COMMENTING

Film has long attracted commentary and analysis in the vein of critical works on literature and fine art. Film criticism ranges from the theoretical to the intensely personal, but as the pieces included here show, a central tenet is often to grapple with the big ideas found throughout movies.

The selection from *The Birds* (1998) by **Camille Paglia** dissects how director Alfred Hitchcock builds suspense scene by scene and how the composition of frames contributes to the film's construction of gender and power.

In "Your Childhood Entertainment Is Not Sacred" (2015), **Nathan Rabin** considers the fierce partiality audiences often feel toward the films of their childhood. His analysis of how audiences mythologize their own early cinematic experiences prompts intriguing questions about cinema as a dynamic and changing form.

Angelica Jade Bastién asks how gender and technology intersect in science fiction in "Pygmalion's Ghost: Female AI and Technological Dream Girls" (2017). Drawing from classical and twentieth-century progenitors, she explores how the silenced female is portrayed in contemporary cinema.

In "The Solace of Preparing Fried Foods and Other Quaint Remembrances from 1960s Mississippi: Thoughts on *The Help*" (2014), **Roxane Gay** eviscerates the 2011 Oscar-winning movie, decrying what she sees as its casual racism and patronizing treatment of race and gender.

A. O. Scott, in this excerpt from *Better Living Through Criticism: How to Think About Art, Pleasure, Beauty, and Truth* (2016), takes an unusual approach, using the form of a dialogue—he "interviews" himself—to defend the role of the critic and the value critics can bring to public discourse.

The Birds
(selection)

Camille Paglia

The transition to the long, last section of the film [*The Birds*] is the sound of hammering, prelude to a crucifixion. The camera pans the facade of the shuttered Brenner house, whose windows have been unevenly boarded up with jagged, weathered planks. Architecture is devolving: Mitch has evidently torn apart a barn to turn the house into a blind bunker. It's back to caveman days. High on a ladder, Mitch in his green-khaki safari pants is nailing up the attic windows, while Melanie, as if carrying her own cross, hands up a big piece of timber: she has a predestined appointment on that very floor. Mitch as prudent householder is preparing for an avian missile crisis: when *The Birds* was made, Americans were just emerging from the Cold War, in which bomb shelters, or at least ample emergency provisions of food and water (with which my father stocked our cellar), were advised for private homes. The couple glance uneasily at Bodega Bay: birds rise from the marsh, while black smoke hangs over the distant town, as if it were Berlin or Sodom. Have the birds taken vengeance for Mitch's bonfire holocaust?

"The phone's dead," Melanie says, for the first time unable to reach her all-protecting father. So it's the end of the line for the phone theme, whose climax was Melanie's entrapment with a pay phone that she was too frantic and purseless to use. Lydia summons them to listen to San Francisco news on the radio, their last link with the outside world (a du Maurier detail), which is reporting the problems in Bodega Bay: a "seriously injured" girl—presumably the one with lacerated face whom Melanie pulled into the station wagon—has been taken to the hospital in Santa Rosa. Explicitly worried about the attic windows, Lydia wants to leave, but Mitch thinks it's unsafe. At this point Lydia goes berserk—"If only your father were here!"—and a weeping Cathy rushes to separate them, showing the habitual, demasculinizing forces at work in the Brenner home that too rarely surface in the script. Before sealing themselves in for the night, Mitch and Melanie go out for firewood and pause on the porch to watch a giant formation of gulls flying overhead and heading inland, presumably toward sitting-duck Santa Rosa (whose dopey police classified Dan Fawcett's death as "felony murder" during burglary). As they leave the house, in fact, the president can be heard obliviously speaking of other matters on the radio from Washington, suggesting the ineffectualness of political power when dealing with angry nature.

Attack night begins with Lydia stationed, like a priestess at the shrine, in a chair next to the piano beneath her husband's photograph. Annie's schoolroom was also overseen by a dead father figure, George Washington, the "Father of His Country." With Lydia so withdrawn, Cathy is sheltering with Melanie on the sofa, while faithful dog Mitch patrols the interior perimeter, latching, checking, and reinforcing. (He has even, as we shall see, cleverly blocked the glass doors with huge barn doors.) It's a night watch or rather a wake. The lovebirds, with what Mrs. Bundy called their "small brain pans," have been exiled by a hostile Lydia to the kitchen with the rest of the pots. Resting next to the stove where so many of their brethren have been cooked, they peer amiably at the anxious Mitch as he passes by and seem as comically delightful as Hitchcock's brace of dogs in the first scene. In a rare Hitchcock continuity error, the birds in close-up are decorously perched, while their cavorting, clambering shadow was just glimpsed against the kitchen door.

Dumbly reorienting herself by familiar domestic ritual, Lydia slowly gathers the cups and coffeepot onto a tray and carries it into the kitchen, flinching for a moment at the off-camera lovebirds inside the door. After she returns, Cathy starts to vomit (Lydia's cooking?), but her apathetic mother doesn't stir to help. It's Melanie who rushes Cathy off to the toilet and, when they return, is pressing a white napkin to the girl's forehead, just as Mitch stanched Melanie's bleeding in the restaurant. (Is it relevant that, as Spoto reports, "from his childhood Hitchcock had a terror of vomiting"?) Photographed at a tense angle, Lydia watches this transaction with chilly fatigue.

There is an arresting, low-angle wide shot of Melanie's slender ankles and legs as she elegantly crosses them, with a lovely flex of the foot, while settling herself again on the sofa. Hitchcock cunningly accentuates the lines of her legs with the barn door's wide, diagonal plank. It's a zoological tableau of legs: muscular Mitch on the piano bench hunches over his widespread thighs with animal readiness; Lydia, in fading, autumnal browns and grays, sits with legs stuck stiffly out like bowling pins, her knees curtained by a tweedy skirt; Cathy's prepubescent stick calves are clad in chaste, woolly, sky-blue knee socks. Melanie, however, with her short, revealing skirt and stylish high heels, gracefully extends her long, smooth legs with the gleaming hose (soon to be pillaged), like the polished artifacts they are. We contemplate, as at the Eleusinian mysteries, the three stages of womanhood, from virginity through sexual maturity to sexual senescence.

Crisscross (the theme of *Strangers on a Train*): literally from the moment Melanie crosses her legs, the bird attack begins. Has Lydia's witchy malice evoked it? Either a warning or welcoming cheep comes from the unseen spectator lovebirds, as a deafening shrieking starts, reverberating like shaken sheet metal. When Lydia shakily stands up, Cathy instantly abandons Melanie, who seems to have lost her nerve, and throws herself into her mother's arms. Mother and daughter, rebonded, run frantically around the room like hunted animals (Hitchcock compared them to "rats scurrying into corners"), eventually sinking down near the built-in shelves of books, which have no answers. Lydia "panics," Hitchcock told Bogdanovich, because "she is not strong, it is a facade": so architecturally, she is crumbling.

Lacking the electronic soundtrack, Hitchcock had a musician do thunderous rolls on a miked side drum for the actors in this scene to have something to react to. Starting to lose her wits, Melanie shrinks back on the couch, drawing her legs up and finally rearing back to crush the lampshade as she nearly swoons. Hitchcock said he chose the angles here "to express the fear of the unknown," and he kept the camera back "to show the nothingness from which she is shrinking." Melanie's movements are so floridly overwrought that she seems like the generic gal-turned-to-jelly of '50s screamer flicks, where women were always being delectably stalked by juvenile delinquents or space aliens. (Hitchcock makes Hedren repeat these gestures in *Marnie*, as she cowers on the sofa of the shipboard honeymoon suite.) Melanie ends up plastered to the mantelpiece like Lydia gone batty in the chimney attack. It's as if the house itself were aggressively haunted, as in a classic horror movie like *The Haunting* (1963).

Mitch, meanwhile, is a masculine whirlwind, getting his arms and hands bitten and gashed by birds, ripping out a lamp cord to bind the shutter, and nearly getting clawed by his own desperate, literally grasping, clutching mother as he firmly props her in an armchair (cf. Mrs. Bates in her rocker). A convenient, hulking umbrella rack, mirrored like the diner cigarette machine, becomes his Dadaesque barrier against the Plywood Modern front door, which is being neatly drilled by gull beaks (actually awls manned by grips), with a shower of sawdust. Raymond Durgnat astutely compares the besieged Brenner house to the "log cabin" of America's fabled past, which is invaded here by the terrible "beak-tomahawks" of bloodthirsty Indians. Do the birds plan to turn the taxidermic tables? Hitchcock said that *Psycho*'s Norman "filled his own mother with sawdust."

When the power suddenly goes off, apparently because the outside wires have been gnawed, the situation becomes grim. But the birds capriciously withdraw. "They're going," says Mitch with wonder, and we see one of the film's most stylized sequences: the heads of the three principals, side-lit in flickering chiaroscuro from the fireplace, are dramatically photographed from below. First, Mitch's face swings out of silhouette across a blank ceiling panel, which weighs down like the lid of a box or cage. Then Melanie's head, with shadows hollowing her cheekbones and contouring her shapely chin, hovers wide-eyed like Carl Dreyer's suffering Joan of Arc. When Lydia's head looms up into empty space, the camera pulls back to take in the three figures at full length, as they stand stock-still, listening, turned to stone like entombed colossi. They are as isolated as Giacometti specters or Kon-Tiki sentinels and as unified in shared fear as the survivors of the Blitz. The scene is as beautifully blocked as in live theatre.

All sense of time has been lost in the subterranean gloom. Nearly everyone is asleep, as the fire burns merrily in the hearth, the sole light and heat left to the cave dwellers. Suddenly, the logs ominously break and collapse. Lydia is sleeping bolt upright on the piano stool, her head fallen forward corpse-like on her chest, looking just like the fierce Red Queen leaning heavily asleep and snoring on Alice. Cathy is curled up under a blanket on the sofa, and Mitch, looking like one of the damned from Michelangelo's *Last Judgment*, is slumped exhausted in a chair, his right hand on his groin and his head resting on his bandaged left hand—now sporting the heraldic white table napkin that has made the rounds from birdcage to infant brow. Only Melanie is awake, and once again she is the canary in the coal mine: hearing a flutter, she starts to call Mitch but decides to spare him. Picking up the torch that Mitch unearthed in the kitchen when the power failed (cf. Hitchcock's reference to Annie as "the school teacher who's carrying a torch for him"), she checks the lovebirds first. But when they prove quiet, she goes to the attic stairs to investigate. She moves as if hypnotically drawn to her quest. Some critics find Melanie's ascent foolhardy and self-destructive, but it seems to me a positive return to her early independence and initiative, when she had a flair for this kind of detective work. She is living up to her name—a Daniels who enters the lions' den.

As she hesitates before yet another unknocked door, Melanie's hand with its glossy crimson nails hovers near the knob, lit by torchlight. In her misty close-ups, Hedren again does the kind of magnetic, visibly apprehensive thinking that distinguished her performance at the jungle gym. As Hitchcock said of her performance in this film: "There is not one redundant expression on Hedren's face. Every expression makes a point." The first thing Melanie sees when she opens the attic door is a ragged hole in the roof, through which shines the radiant blue sky. So it's dawn. A glimpse of light would normally mean deliverance in a science fiction film such as *Journey to the Center of the Earth* (1959), but here it's like a blasted bomb hole or a breakdown in a spaceship's radiation shields, through which evil forces rush from beyond. The blue square reminds me of the smashed brothel window in Picasso's *Les Demoiselles d'Avignon*, which also overlooks a sitting room of carnivorous creatures. The parallel within the film is the smashed window that Lydia first sees in Dan Fawcett's ransacked bedroom. When

Melanie's torchlight scans the room, a horde of birds rises from the bed and rafters, and all hell breaks loose. It's a jungle gym again, but this time Melanie is trapped with the birds in the phone booth. The white canopy bed and children's book on the floor indicate that this is a young virgin's room, which has itself been gang-raped even before the mass assault begins on Melanie. As a sexual principle, bedrooms in *The Birds* are primal scenes of savagery.

The gulls and crows come storming at Melanie like a great wind, in undulations of sound. Hitchcock called for "a menacing wave of vibration." We hear only the percussive flapping of wings, with very few bird cries and no scream whatever from Melanie. Sometimes the camera takes her view, so that birds with surreally gaping, almost unhinged jaws, fly directly in our face. Melanie tries to defend herself with the torch (symbolizing her attempts to comprehend logically), which looks like the torch of the Statue of Liberty in *Saboteur* or the endangered light of freedom in Picasso's war-torn, animal-filled *Guernica*. As her arm goes back and forth like a pendulum, the jumping beam creates a flashing, strobe-like effect in the chaotic room. It's like the failing windshield wipers and oncoming, blinking headlights of Marion's drive in *Psycho*. It also looks forward to the special effects in psychedelic discos, where sensory overload was a sine qua non: Melanie at times seems like one very strung-out partygoer, passing out as the other revelers rage on. And she prefigures another San Francisco newspaper heiress, Patty Hearst, who would be kidnapped and locked in a closet by her own pack of predators (the Symbionese Liberation Army) in 1974.

Arms raised (like the Christ images of *I Confess*), Melanie seems scourged and crucified simultaneously, her clothing shredded and her silky skin ripped by beaks. As it's punctured and pulled, her hosiery looks like a second skin being flayed. Calling out to Mitch too weakly to be heard (her last thought is for Cathy's safety), Melanie is slammed against the half-open door, which does wake the others. But as she sinks to the floor, in a wonderfully choreographed cross-legged drop that completes the sequence from her sofa leg-cross, she blocks the door with her body, impeding her rescue. It's as if the room is underwater, and she is a swimmer swarmed by piranha or baby sharks. Wood sees "voluptuous surrender and prostration" in her gestures, "a despairing desire for annihilation."

By the time Mitch drags her out like a sack of potatoes (cf. *Frenzy*) or like Marion plastic-wrapped in *Psycho*, Melanie is being ravaged by birds jabbing at her breasts and furiously chewing on her lacquered fingertips. Comically disappearing last from view are her high heels: it's the last dance for the wily witch of the West. "Oh, poor thing!" says Lydia (a phrase applied to birds by Annie and Mrs. Bundy), who has courageously stood in the doorway batting back birds. Lying on the sofa downstairs, Melanie seems to have suffered a psychotic break. Eyes wide, she sees us and flails wildly at the camera, which jumps back to give her space: Hitchcock and we are yet more hungry birds. She's hallucinating, like a hippie chick on a bad trip. Like Annie, Mitch gives her brandy now, not peroxide, a bottle of which appears anyway in Lydia's hands as she sponges Melanie's wounds and binds her brow with bandages—the Oedipal wrap of blindman's buff. The socialite turned hobo has melted completely into birthday-girl Cathy.

Melanie's injuries, requiring medical aid, become a reason to flee Bodega Bay. Mitch steals out of the house with excruciating care past the burbling masses of birds lining fences, roofs, and tree limbs. It's like a lynch mob forming outside the palace. Different species are indeed flocking together, as Mrs. Bundy warned they never do. For this scene, Hitchcock said he wanted "an electronic silence, a sort of monotonous low hum" to suggest the distant sea as well as "the language of the birds." Like all the film's electronic effects, it was produced by the Trautonium, an atonal keyboard designed by Remi Gassmann and Oskar Sala, with whom Hitchcock consulted for a month in West Berlin. Mitch fetches Melanie's car from the garage, which is oddly furnished with a skylight (a feature the birds-as-architects-unlicensed imposed on the bedroom). Lydia's metal-enclosed truck is not "fast" enough (like its aging owner). Where's Mitch's hardtop car?—which would be a lot safer. Either it's at the diner, where it may have been incinerated in the parking lot, or at the Fawcett farm, from which Mitch may have got a quick police-car lift to the diner when Melanie called with news of the schoolhouse attack. In a Hitchcock film, such minor plot details are always deftly worked out.

On the car radio, Mitch hears that Bodega Bay is the epicenter of the disaster, that most people have gotten out, and that "the military" may have to go in. There have been other attacks on Santa Rosa and

Sebastopol: the "attacks come in waves," says the announcer, evoking images of civilization sinking backward into the primal ocean. Some critics complain the sports car makes no noise as it emerges from the garage and pushes past the chattering birds: I do hear Mitch start the engine and give the accelerator a single burst, which gets the car moving but allows it to coast in neutral into the driveway.

Sitting mournfully in her fur coat like a moppet doll of Little Orphan Annie, her head wrapped in bandages like the newest look in scarf-tied turbans (with the chin strap of a dowager's overnight double-chin reducer), the catatonic Melanie often evokes laughter from an audience—which mortified scriptwriter Hunter when he first heard it. But this is Hitchcock's characteristic black humor, extorting from the audience an admission of our guilty pleasure in seeing the mighty fallen. Not even recognizing her own car, which gleams in the pearly light like a fleet chariot of the sun god, Melanie panics at first sight of the bird yard and must be half carried out, where she sinks into the tender arms of an apparently all-forgiving Lydia in the jump seat. The scene recalls the end of *Notorious*, where the half-conscious heroine is also rescued from captivity in an upstairs bedroom and helped to a car under the suspicious gaze of Nazis in tuxedoes—here a row of crows on a porch rail! Cathy's desire to bring the lovebirds along ("They haven't harmed anyone") is generally interpreted as a sign of hope for humanity's recovery, endorsed by early morning's rainbow beams. *The Birds* ends like *Psycho* with a shot of a car being extricated from Mother Nature's black morass. So will the hostile audience of watchful birds turn doves of peace? But as the car roars away, their cries start up and rise to a sustained screech.

The psychological dynamics of the finale can be read in two ways. "Lydia has become the mother Melanie never had," Wood says, but he asks whether Lydia's "cradling" is "a gesture of acceptance . . . or a new maternal possessiveness" and whether the moment marks Melanie's "development into true womanhood, or a final relapse into infantile dependence." Hedren declared to me about Lydia, "I thought she accepted the daughter, and they lived happily ever after!" And Hedren firmly believed that Melanie would rebound: "Melanie Daniels is a *strong woman*—absolutely!"

But I think Hitchcock has left the ending ambiguous: the two women's intimately intertwined hand and wrist (we see, from Lydia's point of view, Melanie's once-perfect nails now chipped like the [film's] titles) remind me of Mother's overlapping, wrist-clasping bronzed hands in the bedroom of *Psycho*, which ends with Mother in charge and her son in the loony bin. At the end of *The Birds*, who wields the claw? I agree with Margaret M. Horwitz's view that Lydia certainly appears "victorious" and that she and the birds have "achieved dominance." Melanie is now damaged goods, which Madonna Lydia prefers for her pietà. It's like the Pompeiian wall panels of the Villa of the Mysteries, where the exhausted, flagellated acolyte buries her face in the receptive maternal lap: rogue vixen Melanie has been whipped back to her biological place in the pecking order. Horwitz sees Melanie's eclipse in the film's treatment of her car: first, it gives her the "power to come to Bodega Bay," then Mitch "ends up driving it," and finally she's "banished to the back seat"—becoming one of two children to Lydia as mother and Mitch as father (and Oedipal son). Oddly, when Mitch slips into the driver's seat, it's he who now seems the intruder, as his spidery hand startles Lydia from her dreamy communing with Melanie.

Hitchcock wanted the film to be literally open-ended, without "THE END" indicated onscreen, so as to leave the audience wondering. But the studio found this too confusing to preview audiences and ordered the rubric added.

Your Childhood Entertainment Is Not Sacred

Nathan Rabin

I t seems like whenever someone remakes a movie, television show, cartoon, board game, or series of shape-shifting action figures, an outcry erupts on the internet that the usurper is retroactively ruining (or worse, "raping") people's childhoods. Sometimes this criticism is made in jest, with an implicit acknowledgment that it's ridiculous for grown-ups to get apoplectic over the notion of someone rebooting a series about martial-arts-adept mutant amphibians. But there's often a real sense of hurt and injury, even betrayal, to these criticisms as well. Sure enough, the announcement that Paul Feig will reboot the *Ghostbusters* franchise with an all-female cast led by Kristen Wiig and Melissa McCarthy prompted the usual deluge of complaints that Feig and company were ruining people's childhoods and tainting something sacred.

With the case of *Ghostbusters* at least, these criticisms are aimed at defending, or protecting, something genuinely good. Too often, the "you monsters are ruining our childhoods" brigade direct their anger toward contemporary versions of entertainment like *The Smurfs*, *Teenage Mutant Ninja Turtles*, *Scooby-Doo*, or *Yogi Bear*—stuff that was never any good in the first place. When someone makes a terrible movie out of *The Smurfs*, they're not desecrating it so much as honoring the franchise's legacy of lazy submediocrity. But nostalgia is a powerful force, particularly when connected to adults defending the entertainment they worshiped during a precritical phase of their thinking. Nostalgia can cloud judgment in ways that romanticize an often-crappy past while damning a future that radiates a lot more promise than the nostalgic are willing to allow.

Myopic nostalgia assumes that the new will inherently be worse than the old out of a combination of misplaced romanticization of the past and knee-jerk cynicism about the future. Some were enraged by the notion of Chris Pratt as a new Indiana Jones, but which would you rather see, a charming, fresh-faced new star in his thirties tackling an iconic role, or cranky, dispirited old Harrison Ford lugging his aged bones around in a follow-up to the widely reviled *Indiana Jones and the Kingdom of the Crystal Skull*? Perhaps because I was not a *Star Trek* fan growing up, I found J. J. Abrams's reboot of the franchise exciting, dynamic, and fun. Who's to say that talented people like Feig, Wiig, and McCarthy won't find ways to make *Ghostbusters* their own? Would audiences really prefer the thinking behind *Ghostbusters 2* (the same as before, but worse) over a radical reinvention of the series from people who grew up revering *Ghostbusters*?

There's an unmistakable element of generational chauvinism to these complaints as well. I want my son, who is now just under four months old, to watch and love *Ghostbusters* the way I did when I was eight years old. But I'm also excited about him growing up with a *Ghostbusters* franchise where women are front and center in heroic, central roles, rather than limited to supporting roles as secretaries and love interests inhabited by demons at key moments. Old isn't necessarily good, just as new isn't necessarily bad.

I want my son to be a cinephile with a deep sense of history, but I would also understand if he wanted to watch *Star Wars*, *Star Trek*, or *Ghostbusters* movies with technology, fashion, and a sensibility he can relate to immediately, rather than trying to force him to love movies and shows that he'll likely see as period pieces made long ago, in a land far away. I would not mind at all if my son skipped over the Jar Jar years of the *Star Wars* franchise movies to the ones directed by the dependable, fresh likes of Rian Johnson and J. J. Abrams. And I'm not invested enough in the supremacy of the original *Star Wars* trilogy to demand that my generation's version of it be the conclusive, unbeatable version. Nor am I pessimistic enough to assume that the upcoming slate of sequels won't live up to the originals. Besides, isn't it better to have a bold new generation of filmmakers and storytellers charting new paths and directions for *Star Wars*? After the culturewide shrugs of disappointment that greeted *Crystal Skull* and *The Phantom Menace,* doesn't it make sense to give someone else a crack at telling these stories?

If Chris Pratt stars in an *Indiana Jones* reboot, the Harrison Ford movies will not magically disappear. They'll continue to exist and to delight new generations who'll understand that characters and roles can be played by different people of different races and genders in different ways in different movies. Otherwise, their fragile young psyches will explode from the never-ending spate of reboots, reimaginings, and sequels that will dominate the second half of this decade.

As a kid, I understood that Sean Connery and Roger Moore could *both* be James Bond. And truth be told, I liked the Moore Bond movies as much as the Connery versions because they were closer to my sensibility both in terms of the age in which they were made and in appealing somewhat nakedly to kids rather than adults. As an adult, I can now objectively see that Connery's films were superior in almost every way, but as a kid, I didn't find Moore's campy, tongue-in-cheek take on Bond to be inferior: it was just different. And we all better stop being terrified of difference if we're ever going to evolve as a culture.

So let's all try to calm down. The entertainment of your childhood is not sacred. Adults, our childhoods are over, and waxing apoplectic over Michael Bay's *Transformers* or *Teenage Mutant Ninja Turtles* movies won't do anything but broadcast our inability to move beyond the silly, entertaining ephemera of our youth or understand how it might appeal to a younger generation with a different set of ideas about how entertainment works. And for those rending their garments and weeping openly in the streets at the idea that new people are going to come along and change *Star Wars* and *Ghostbusters* and *Indiana Jones* in ways that deviate radically from the ones we cherished in our childhoods, let's at least allow the possibility, radical as it may seem, that these new versions of old favorites might be just as good as the movies we loved as kids. Maybe even better, even if they *are* suddenly full of cooties-carrying girl actors guilty of not being Bill Murray.

Pygmalion's Ghost: Female AI and Technological Dream Girls

Angelica Jade Bastién

n Ovid's retelling of the Pygmalion myth, there is no mention of what Pygmalion's beloved is thinking as she is transformed from a statue carved of ivory into a flesh-and-blood woman. During the transformation from an inanimate object of desire into a real person, did she ponder what life could hold beyond becoming Pygmalion's wife? Did she have desires of her own? Did she struggle with coming into consciousness? Throughout the centuries, as other writers have retold the myth, the story has taken on new contours, but in these retellings Pygmalion's creation has gained neither interiority nor much of an identity. Essentially, she remains a dream girl with no dreams of her own.

In film and television, science fiction has made a meal of the horror bubbling beneath the surface of this story, particularly in the many narratives of female androids grappling with artificial intelligence. From Fritz Lang's 1927 epic, *Metropolis*, to the HBO phenomenon *Westworld*, science fiction has tapped into the Pygmalion myth, drawing from its central story an exploration of identity, female autonomy, and the power that beauty holds. No recent films more deeply interrogate the intricacies and contradictions of the myth than the 2015 releases *Ex Machina* (written and directed by Alex Garland) and *Advantageous* (co-written and directed by Jennifer Phang). Neither *Advantageous* nor *Ex Machina* is a direct adaptation of the Pygmalion myth, but the ghostly echo of Pygmalion's creation underpins both.

Advantageous does something still all too rare in science fiction films: it places a woman of color at its center. In this case it's the middle-aged Asian American Gwen Koh (Jacqueline Kim). Some time in the near future, Gwen is let go from her job as spokesperson for the Center for Advanced Health and Living. Soon her life spins in a terrifying direction as she worries about her ability to ensure her daughter, Jules (Samantha Kim), a good future. Then a higher-up at the Center (Isa Cryer, played with chilly indifference by Jennifer Ehle) encourages an experiment: Gwen can undergo a cosmetic procedure the Center offers to transfer her consciousness into a new body and so regain her job, rather than continue to struggle with little hope of ever finding work. Lurking beneath the surface of Isa's plan is an insult: Gwen doesn't have the "broad appeal" necessary to act as a spokesperson, but the procedure could give her that. It's a way of saying that Gwen is too old, too Asian, and too "niche." *Advantageous* isn't afraid to use its science fiction trappings to critique how white women, like Isa, manipulate women of color for profit in a society where beauty is a currency in and of itself.

While *Advantageous* finds its power in complicating the emotional landscape of its characters, *Ex Machina* builds suspense by keeping the interiority of its most pivotal characters at a perpetual distance. The film follows Caleb (Domnhall Gleeson), a kind-hearted programmer who gets more than he bargained for when he wins a weeklong stay at the isolated, immaculate home of Nathan (Oscar Isaac), an ultra-rich, hypermasculine tech genius. Nathan tasks Caleb with determining whether the beautiful robot he created, Ava (Alicia Vikander), has true consciousness. As their sessions gain a more flirtatious edge, it's clear that Caleb is falling for Ava and struggling with the moral complexity of leaving her in what amounts to a prison. Does she share his attraction, or is it all a ploy to gain freedom from her creator?

Both *Ex Machina* and *Advantageous* demonstrate the inherent horror of the Pygmalion myth—how the narratives of bodies can be rewritten by technology. While *Ex Machina* is a propulsive chamber piece that turns into an outright thriller, *Advantageous* is a slow burn more interested in emotional tragedy than plot twists. But despite their differences, each film is powered by the same questions. When it comes to female power, who gets it, how is it wielded, and what are the ways it is culturally reckoned with? *Advantageous* proves to be radical and fresh in ways *Ex Machina* only pretends to be. The film brings to light the dangers of taking the Pygmalion myth at face value, particularly for women of color, who must deal with thorny beauty politics. Phang's movie expresses a healthy skepticism toward the idea that technology can free humanity from the shackles of entrenched ideologies, such as racism and sexism, and it argues that women lose far too much in the quest for perfection. *Ex Machina* is diametrically opposed to this position, choosing instead to present a world where youth and beauty are instrumental, even necessary, for women to gain autonomy. Don't get me wrong, *Ex Machina* is an easy film to love. It's exceedingly beautiful, with fluid camera work and dazzling production design. The performances of its three leads are wholly engaging and nuanced. Its suspense is piercing. The many philosophical conversations between Nathan and Caleb gesture toward a radical conception of gender and flirt with ideas of female power. But the way in which Ava and other female characters are framed dances around more complex renderings of these ideas.

When Donna Haraway published "A Cyborg Manifesto" in 1985, she presented the possibility that technology could be used to garner radical, boundary-breaking identities for women. To Haraway, technology could be a feminist tool freeing women from the kind of shackles that bind characters like the exasperated Gwen Koh and the quicksilver Ava. "Cyborg imagery can suggest a way out of the maze of dualisms in which we have explained our bodies and our tools to ourselves," Haraway writes. There is something liberating about this theory. Cyborgs, androids, and other technologically altered figures can rewrite and even destroy the strictures placed upon women's bodies, Haraway posits. She describes her vision as "a dream not of a common language. . . . It is an imagination of a feminist speaking in tongues to strike fear into the circuits of the supersavers of the new right. It means both building and destroying machines, identities, categories, relationships, spaces, stories. Though both are bound in the spiral dance, I would rather be a cyborg than a goddess." Haraway's words are revelatory. But films like *Ex Machina* and *Advantageous* demonstrate how technology can be used to engender further oppression rather than enable revolution for the very people who need it most.

The first meeting of Caleb and Ava sets the tone for the rest of *Ex Machina*. When Caleb first enters the glass box that separates him from Ava, he is nothing if not curious. His hand tentatively traces a sharp crack in the glass, which is later revealed to be the aftermath of another of Nathan's creations trying futilely to escape. Then Caleb sees Ava. She's in the distance, but it's clear she's not human. Only her face, hands, and feet are covered by skin. The rest of her makes her origin apparent—she has wires, chrome, and soft lights where her entrails should be. She turns to him, but her expression is too mired in shadow to be readable. But his is clear—a mix of puzzlement, awe, and the whisper of attraction. Each session between Caleb and Ava is watched by Nathan, a fact that can't be forgotten; her performance is as much for Nathan as it is for Caleb. Is that all Ava amounts to—a performance she has carefully calibrated to ensure her escape? Even in the bloody conclusion, when she is able to find freedom, kill Nathan, and leave Caleb trapped in the home to starve to death, Ava's true self remains unknowable. From the moment she's onscreen to the very end (save for one important moment I'll discuss later), the film remains rooted in Caleb's perspective. We do not learn who Ava really is or how she sees the world; rather, we learn the ways men like Caleb and Nathan interpret her. The film takes the large-scale machinations of the patriarchy and whittles them down to a story between three people.

The clearest difference between the women at the center of *Advantageous* and *Ex Machina* is a matter of perspective. *Ex Machina* does not interrogate how Ava thinks, feels, or acts on her own; the film is interested in how she's interpreted and caged. Director Jennifer Phang, however, takes a different approach in *Advantageous*, tilling the anxieties surrounding technology and identity by continuously using close-ups of Gwen in critical moments, such as when she meets with a cabal of high-powered mothers whose children are currently getting the great education she wants for Jules. While Alicia Vikander's performance as Ava is predicated upon a startling gracefulness and touches of innocence, Jacqueline Kim makes apparent the strain and sorrow that Gwen contends with. In this manner, Ava is (at least on the surface) the ultimate dream girl—desirable and vulnerable while needing to be saved. Gwen is "just" a normal woman with the unattractive status of a single mother trying to make ends meet. *Ex Machina* primarily cares about what Ava represents to the men who are interested in either saving or imprisoning her. *Advantageous* is instead concerned with who Gwen really is, while navigating the ways her body informs this identity.

The gleaming surfaces of *Ex Machina* hide an ugly truth—this film couldn't care less about the women its camera lovingly frames. They remain merely symbols. Take, for example, this exchange from a 2015 interview that Vulture critic Kyle Buchanan conducted with writer/director Alex Garland during the press tour for the film:

> "The patriarchy—which is a buzzword at the moment, for all sorts of completely good reasons—does not interest me," he replied, "because I'm not interested in things that, to me, feel self-evident. Yes, I get that it exists. It's like the objectification of girls in their early 20s: Yes, I get it, it happens."
>
> "Isn't that casual dismissal of the patriarchy an easy stance for a straight man to take, though?" I asked.
>
> "No, it's just a statement of fact," said Garland.

Garland seems uninterested in the real-life gender politics that make Ava's storyline so trenchant. That's curious, considering that the dynamics of patriarchal culture are clearly at play in *Ex Machina,* since Ava knows how to use them to her advantage. When she pours herself into a demure dress and dons a short-cropped wig, she's of course gauging Caleb's reaction. "Are you attracted to me?" Ava asks after noticing Caleb's discomfort and refusal to express excitement when she tells him she would wear this same outfit on the date she imagines they'd go on, if only she were free. "Do you think about me when we aren't together? Sometimes at night I'm wondering if you are watching me on the cameras. And I hope you are," she continues. The answer to her questions is clearly yes. But what's most important in this scene isn't Ava's clever manipulation of Caleb's attraction, it's what she's wearing. Ava doesn't put on a slinky number or a long, luxurious wig. The hair she wears looks like it was cut in a lawnmower, and the dress is an ill-fitting, rather ugly babydoll. This outfit makes Ava look young, vulnerable, yearning. She's angling for Caleb not only to desire her, but to want to save her. It also is no coincidence that Ava continues to wear this outfit for their next few sessions. It's a tactic to ensure that Caleb will humanize her even further.

This narrative in *Ex Machina* has the potential to explore the political weight of gender expression and presentation. But coupled with the tropes of a rote femme fatale–focused thriller, it is troubling. By remaining emotionally distant from the characters—save for Caleb, whose emotional landscape is established early on and continuously explored—the film can dip into suspense and horror. The final act is predicated upon keeping Ava's true motives in shadow. Yes, *Ex Machina* ponders the nature of gender identity itself. It even posits the question, does Ava identify as a woman or is this an identity thrust upon her? Unfortunately, she never answers this question. But Caleb and Nathan have heady debates about the ways sexuality and gender affect Ava's conception of her own identity. The film's emotional remove is exemplified in the construction of Ava and how this construction prevents ideas about gender from coming together in a way that challenges viewers. Instead, the film reaffirms age-old biases about ambitious women.

As *Ex Machina* continues, it's evident that Nathan purposefully created Ava in a way that Caleb would find attractive. Caleb's winning this trip wasn't a coincidence at all. "An AI doesn't need a gender, she could have been a gray box," Caleb says. Nathan counters, "Can you give an example of consciousness on any level, human or animal, that exists without a sexual dimension? . . . In answer to your real question, you bet she can fuck." He continues by detailing the construction of Ava that allows her to have sex and a "pleasure response." As Charlie Jane Anders writes for io9,

> So in one sense, *Ex Machina* has no female characters—it features two men, whose attitudes to women are illuminated through their interactions with Ava, who uses her feminine appearance to try and get what she wants but otherwise seems to have no particular attachment to her gender. Looked at that way, *Ex Machina* is entirely about masculinity and the different ways the men try to exert control, not so much about women's experiences. Ava is merely the lens through which male attitudes are refracted.

The problem with this reading, which can be found elsewhere in publications such as *New York Magazine* and *Wired*, is that for this analysis to be accurate we would need to know what Ava thinks about her own identity. Does presenting and acting as a traditionally feminine woman affirm that Ava sees herself as such? She never tells us.

At the very end of the film, Ava's actions upon finally gaining her own freedom prove instructive. As she opens the closets, she finds the remains of previous androids. Their inanimate forms hold muted, lifeless expressions. She takes parts from their bodies—replacing her broken arm, adding fake skin to cover her electronic parts, donning beautiful long brown hair—until she stands fully naked, looking like a human woman. Garland's camera lovingly traces her nude figure in the warm light. Ava gazes at herself from different angles in the mirror, her hand tracing over her naked form. When she finally puts on clothes, she chooses a well-tailored white dress and towering high heels—the picture of acceptable femininity. And yet she doesn't need to perform for anyone any longer, so why this outfit? Why not go to Nathan's closet and take something of his that is more gender neutral? In dressing this way at the very end of the film, Ava reveals her own view of herself, however briefly. She has tapped into the power that comes with being beautiful and she's never letting go. The more challenging narrative thread that questions gender itself comes undone, as the film reaffirms in prosaic fashion that Ava's femininity and women's quest for autonomy are inherently dangerous for patriarchal systems. The latter point is true, but the way the writing, score, and cinematography frame that fact disrupts a feminist reading. This isn't so much a woman's fable of coming into her own, as a man's nightmare.

If *Advantageous* had been released longer after *Ex Machina*, I would consider Phang's film an active critique of Garland's. While *Advantageous* does not focus on questioning the nature of gender, it does turn its gaze to patriarchal systems and how they can be replicated by white women. Films retelling the Pygmalion myth typically focus on how men seek to control the women they create or to reshape women in an image they find more pleasing. In critiquing how white women also internalize the lessons of the patriarchy and use their own power against women of color, *Advantageous* explores the ideological and psychological realities for women of color in a society that seeks to keep them powerless. Isa Cryer does not create Gwen in the same way that Nathan builds his androids, but she does manipulate Gwen's life. Isa is instrumental in firing Gwen and then in making sure she's unable to get a job elsewhere. This forces Gwen to consider the terrifying idea of inhabiting a new body so that she and her daughter don't fall into abject poverty. An early scene in *Advantageous* addresses something *Ex Machina* isn't bold enough to ponder: how racism and sexism coexist and the ways white women can use their own standing for gain.

Isa needles Gwen with questions shortly after she loses her job: "The question we have to answer in this current job market, with shifting desirability targets, is can they get ahead looking like you? And at your age?" Isa continues to ask cutting questions with an empty smile marking her face. She touches on how artificial intelligence is the future and real human beings are "being left behind" in that job market. The only way for human beings to compete is to alter themselves with the technology available. When Isa asks Gwen about her daughter, she's planting a seed of fear. Gwen eventually signs away her rights, agreeing to adopt a new body of the Center's choosing that is "a touch more universal." In doing so she hopes to give her daughter the same sort of freedom that Ava manipulated her way toward in *Ex Machina*.

That the body of Gwen 2.0 is that of a young, white woman is unsurprising. (However, she doesn't read as Midwestern, but as what fashion magazines might consider a touch "exotic.") *Advantageous* makes clear that technology doesn't free us from patriarchal systems, but reaffirms them. Technology isn't neutral. It is given value and purpose by those who wield it. In the hands of tech virtuosos like Nathan and calculating corporate capitalists like Isa, technology becomes another tool of oppression. *Ex Machina* suggests that it is Ava's identity as an android—her physical strength, presentation, and other abilities—that allows her to break from the shackles of an imprisonment which represents the patriarchy in microcosm. What twists *Ex Machina* from a fascinating, albeit frustrating, drama into an unnerving one is how Garland positions women of color (in the form of other androids) within Ava's quest for autonomy.

While combing through Nathan's computer, Caleb finds security footage of other androids he created. Take, for example, "Jade," an Asian robot who was trapped in the same room Ava now finds herself in. Sitting naked in a chair, Jade asks Nathan again and again why he won't let her go. In a fit of fury she beats the wall of her prison until her forearms break down, leaving a halo of metal at her feet. Then there is the black robot coded as "Jasmine." Unlike the others, she is completely lifeless. Nathan manipulates her limbs until he grows bored with her, leaving her crumpled in the corner of the room. To make the horror of this even more gut-wrenching, she doesn't even have a face. The interiority of these women is not explored; they're merely symbols and collateral damage, not actual characters given any development. They are convenient props to be used or discarded at a moment's notice.

From a certain angle the interplay between characters scans as a criticism of the patriarchal system, but the fate of Kyoko (Sonoya Mizuno), Nathan's beautiful Asian servant, who literally has no voice to speak with, contradicts this reading. *Ex Machina* doesn't interrogate what it means for Kyoko to be revealed as an android who neatly embodies the toxic stereotype of the subservient Asian woman. When Kyoko helps Ava plan her escape, she is punished for moving beyond the bounds of this stereotype. Kyoko's death is the distraction necessary for Ava to break free of Nathan's control. It is alarming that in a film so concerned with subversion Kyoko is revealed to be an android incapable of speech only to die soon after because she gets in Nathan's way.

Garland is aware of the territory his film occupies, as his 2015 interview with *New Statesman* makes clear. In the interview, when asked about the lack of male nudity in *Ex Machina* while every female character in the film is shown in states of undress, he responded, "If you are in part doing something about the objectification of women, you undermine it by—in a reflexive or nervous way—doing a bit of equalising objectification of men." *Ex Machina* is undeniably an alluring, tense concoction. At times, it reaches toward a thorny understanding of identity, with androids and their ilk serving as useful vehicles to question long-held assumptions. My issue with *Ex Machina* in many ways comes down to how completely it glides over the intersections of race and gender that mark Nathan's androids. This evasion makes the film's critique of patriarchal systems seem incomplete, even emotionally dishonest, and it makes watching *Ex Machina* and *Advantageous* side by side a curious experience.

Since the early 2010s, conversation about how popular culture often reaffirms troubling racial notions and other forms of bigotry has reached a fever pitch. This is especially true when it comes to discussions of whitewashing in narratives that use various Asian countries and aesthetics as a backdrop, while treating actual Asian and Asian American characters as inconsequential. Most recently, this debate has swirled around such films as *Ghost in the Shell* (2017) and *Doctor Strange* (2016), and the Netflix series *Iron Fist* (2017). A comment by film critic Justin Chang, in a debate on the subject for the *LA Times*, provides a useful framework for interpreting *Advantageous* and *Ex Machina*. In conversation with film reporter Jen Yamato, Chang remarked that

> the dystopian world that [*Ghost in the Shell* director Rupert] Sanders depicts—and on a sheer craft level, depicts rather beautifully—is for all intents and purposes a post-racial society, where individual identity doesn't appear to be constructed predominantly along racial lines. That's (almost) a lovely idea. But every film of course must bridge the gap between the world it depicts and the world we've got.

Ex Machina does not bridge this gap. While it isn't an egregious example of racism through whitewashing, it does, like far too much science fiction, present a curiously post-racial universe in which gender discrimination continues but racial prejudice is an afterthought. *Advantageous* is a much more powerful exploration of the Pygmalion myth, because it circumvents such a naive approach and comments directly on how whitewashing and bigotry become possible.

Reinterpretations of the Pygmalion myth often explore how the body holds its own currency in the world. Cyborgs, androids, and technologically altered dream girls are stronger, faster, and—most crucially—more beautiful than seems possible. They fit ideals in ways no flesh-and-blood woman could fulfill, especially a woman of color like Gwen. Near the end of *Advantageous* there is a heart-wrenching sequence of scenes where Gwen learns from a friend at the company, Dave Fisher (James Urbaniak), that this new body she's already uneasy about assuming isn't exactly what it seems. The process that's been marketed to her will not fully transfer her consciousness. This new body will have her memories, tastes, and ideas, but it won't truly be her. It will be a clone, and aspects of her identity will likely be lost in translation. She'll essentially die. "This is still Jules's only chance, isn't it?" Gwen asks, even as Dave pleads with Gwen not to go through with the procedure. She commits to it for the sake of her daughter. Embodying the perfect creation in *Advantageous* isn't a boon, but a death sentence. Here the ideas of re-creation, beauty, and power typical of science fiction retellings of the Pygmalion myth become a cautionary tale. When Isa asks Gwen 2.0 if her prior feelings for Jules have been carried forward, she responds, "No, that part is lost." Gwen 2.0's face during this moment is oddly vacant, as if she's searching for emotions that no longer exist within her. In Isa's office she's surrounded by the glowing holographic representations of people going through the consciousness-transferring procedure. They have no idea what will be lost in the process.

In *Ex Machina*, Ava finds freedom by using her beauty as a weapon and Kyoko as a shield. In effect, the film puts a new gloss on the old story of a scheming femme fatale who uses her wit and sexual wiles to destroy the men in her way. Such a character can be fascinating and can even have a feminist edge, if the narrative shows her owning a sense of identity rather than merely embodying male neuroses. For Gwen in *Advantageous*, however, there is no triumphant climax, no blissful purchase of her own autonomy, and no hopeful future.

In these two variations on the Pygmalion myth, the body—whether of the creator or the creation—is either a prison or a weapon. I am left with several tantalizing questions about the ongoing fates of Ava and Gwen 2.0. After becoming dream girls and wrestling with the boundaries of this distinction, what do they dream about themselves? Can a lithe android and a lab-created humanoid with the cloned memories of a dead woman ever dream? How do they conceive of their own bodies and the currency they hold?

In "A Cyborg Manifesto," Haraway conceives of a bristling, bright future in which women's bodies become a canvas for them to reassert and play with their own identities. *Ex Machina* and *Advantageous*, for all their differences, suggest the impossibility of such a future, since they show racism, sexism, and capitalist control of human life only being reaffirmed by technology. Yes, Ava finds freedom, but that freedom is predicated on the destruction of women of color like Kyoko. Yes, Gwen is able to ensure her daughter's future and financial safety, but this achievement comes at the cost of her own life. Both films highlight the horror of the Pygmalion myth and the ways in which technology is often a means to further limit women's autonomy. In studying *Ex Machina* and *Advantageous,* a painful truth that women of color learn early and often is made clear: the temporary power that youth and beauty bring, and that Pygmalion and those of his ilk prize, is only possible when society recognizes one's humanity in the first place.

The Solace of Preparing Fried Foods and Other Quaint Remembrances from 1960s Mississippi: Thoughts on *The Help*

Roxane Gay

When my brothers and I have a particularly frustrating day with white people, we'll call one another and say, "Today is a *Rosewood* day." Nothing more needs to be said. *Rosewood* is set in 1923 and tells the story of Rosewood, a deeply segregated, primarily black town in Florida. A married white woman in nearby Sumner is beaten by her lover. With no other way to explain the marks on her body to her husband, she cries rape, and when the townsmen ask her who has done this terrible thing, the white woman, predictably, shrieks, "It was a nigger."

The white men proceed to lose their minds, surrender to a mob mentality, and create a lot of havoc, lynching an innocent black man and tormenting the townsfolk of Rosewood. The angry mob destroys nearly every home and other structure in the town. There are some heartbreaking subplots, but mostly the story hinges on a little white lie, so to speak. It's all very distressing, and the injustice of what happened in Rosewood is, at times, unbearable because it is based on a true story. The first time I saw *Rosewood*, I turned to my friend and said, "I don't want to see a white person for three days." She said, "That's not fair," but she was white so that was to be expected. Fortunately, it was a Friday, so I locked myself in my apartment, and by Monday I was mostly ready to reengage with the world.

If *Rosewood* demands a three-day window of voluntary segregation, *The Help* demands three weeks, maybe longer.

Watching historical movies about the black experience (or white interpretations of the black experience) has become nearly impossible for the same reason I hope I never read another slave narrative. It's too much. It's too painful. Too frustrating and infuriating. The history is too recent and too close. I watch movies like *Rosewood* or *The Help* and realize that if I had been born to different parents, at a different time, I too could have been picking cotton or raising a white woman's babies for less than minimum wage or enduring any number of intolerable circumstances far beyond my control. More than that, though, I am troubled by how little has changed. I am troubled by how complacently we are willing to consume these often revisionist stories of this country's complex and painful racial history. History is important, but sometimes the past renders me hopeless and helpless.

When I first saw the trailer for *The Help*, I was not familiar with the book. The moment I saw the first maid's uniform grace the screen, I knew I was going to be upset. By the end of the trailer, which contained all the familiar, reductive elements of a movie about the segregated South, I had worked myself into a nice, frothy rage. In the following months, I continued to see the trailer, only now it was plastered all over the internet and on television, and the reprinted tie-in book version was heavily hyped, even climbing back to the top of the Amazon bestseller list because this is one of those books nearly everyone seems to love. After seeing the movie, I borrowed the book from a friend, read it, and raged more.

The Help is billed as inspirational, charming, and heartwarming. That's all true if your heart is warmed by narrow, condescending, mostly racist depictions of black people in 1960s Mississippi; overly sympathetic depictions of the white women who employed *the help*; the excessive, inaccurate use of dialect; and the glaring omissions with regards to the stirring civil rights movement in which, as Martha Southgate points out in *Entertainment Weekly*, "white people were the help": "the architects, visionaries, prime movers, and most of the on-the-ground laborers of the civil rights movement were African-American." *The Help*, I have decided, is science fiction, creating an alternate universe.

Hollywood has long been enamored with the magical negro—the insertion of a black character into a narrative who bestows upon the protagonist the wisdom he or she needs to move forward in some way, or, as Matthew Hughey defines the phenomenon in a 2009 article in *Social Problems*,

> The [magical negro] has become a stock character that often appears as a lower class, uneducated black person who possesses supernatural or magical powers. These powers are used to save and transform disheveled, uncultured, lost, or broken whites (almost exclusively white men) into competent, successful, and content people within the context of the American myth of redemption and salvation.

(See: *Ghost*; *The Legend of Bagger Vance*; *Unbreakable*; *Robin Hood: Prince of Thieves*; *The Secret Life of Bees*; *Sex and the City: The Movie*; *The Green Mile*; *Corrina, Corrina,* etc.)

In *The Help*, there are not one but twelve or thirteen magical negroes who use their mystical powers to make the world a better place by sharing their stories of servitude and helping Eugenia "Skeeter" Phelan grow out of her awkwardness and insecurity into a confident, racially aware, independent career woman. It's an embarrassment of riches for fans of the magical negro trope.

The theater was crowded for the screening of *The Help* I attended. Women came in groups of three or four or more, many of them clutching their well-worn copies of the book. As we waited for the movie to start, and a long wait it would be because the projector was malfunctioning (a sign perhaps), I listened to the women around me, certainly well meaning, many of them of the *Golden Girls* demographic, chattering about how much they loved the book and how excited they were and how long they had been waiting for this movie to open. I wondered if they were reminiscing about the *good old days*, then decided that was unfair of me. Still, they were quite enthusiastic. My fellow movie-goers applauded when the movie began, and they applauded when the movie ended. They applauded during inspiring moments and gasped or groaned or clucked their tongues during the uncomfortable or painful moments. Their animated response to the movie was not mild. My faith in humanity was tested. I was the only black person in the theater, though to be fair, that mostly speaks to where I live. As I walked to my car, I came to the bitter realization that *The Help* would make a whole lot of money and be really well received by many.

If you go to the theater without your brain (leave it in the glove compartment), *The Help* is a good movie. The production is competent. The cast is uniformly excellent and includes the immensely talented supporting cast of Cicely Tyson, Allison Janney, and Sissy Spacek. Both Viola Davis and Octavia Spencer received Oscar nominations because they do excellent work in the movie, and Hollywood loves to reward black women for playing magical negroes. Spencer would go on to win, and deservedly, the Oscar for best supporting actress. While I wondered how so many talented people signed on to this movie, the cast is not the problem here. As others have noted, *The Help* is endemic of a much bigger problem, one where even today, a prime role for a two-time Tony Award winner and one-time Oscar nominee like Viola Davis is that of a maid.

Davis, who is always sublime, brings intelligence, gravitas, and heart to the role of Aibileen Clark, an older maid who has just lost her only son to a mill accident and has worked her whole life as a maid and nanny, raising seventeen white children. When we meet her, Aibileen is mourning her son and working as the maid for Elizabeth Leefolt and her daughter, Mae Mobley, a chubby, homely girl who is often neglected by her mother. Aibileen's magical power is making young white children feel good about *theyselves*. Whenever Mae Mobley is feeling down, Aibileen chants, "You is kind. You is smart. You is important." She showers the child with love and affection even while having to listen to young white women discuss black people as a subhuman species, dealing with the indignity of using a bathroom outside of the main house, and coping with her grief. Magic, magic, magic. At the end of the movie, Aibileen offers her inspirational incantation to young Mae Mobley even after she is fired for an infraction she did not commit because that's what the magical negro does—she uses her magic for her white charge and rarely for herself.

Spencer is also formidable as Minny Jackson, the "sassy" maid (where "sassy" is code for "uppity"), who works, at the beginning of the movie, for the petty, vindictive, and socially powerful Hilly Holbrook (Bryce Dallas Howard), president of the Junior League. Hilly Holbrook's claim to fame is, among other cruelties, proposing an initiative ordering all white homes to provide separate bathrooms for the "colored" help. After Minny is fired from her job where she uses her negro magic to look after Hilly's elderly mother, she goes to work for Celia Foote. The women of the Junior League in Jackson ostracize Celia because she was pregnant when she married, is considered white trash, and has committed other petty social sins. Minny uses her mystical negritude to help Celia cope with several miscarriages and learn how to cook, and at the end of the movie, the narrative leads you to believe that Celia indirectly empowers Minny to leave her abusive husband, as if a woman of Minny's strength and character couldn't do that on her own. Then Celia cooks a whole spread for Minny and allows the help to sit at her dining room table just like white folk, aww shucks. Minny asks, "I'm not losing my job?" and Celia's husband says, "You have a job here for the rest of your life." Minny, of course, beams gratefully because a lifetime of servitude to a white family, doing backbreaking work for terrible pay, is like winning the lottery and the best a black woman could hope for in the alternate science fiction universe of The Help.

Emma Stone plays Skeeter, who has just returned to Jackson after graduating from Ole Miss. She gets a job as an advice columnist for the local paper, but she has bigger aspirations and a whole lot of gumption. We know this because she sasses her mother and doesn't make finding a man her first priority. Her first priority is to give grown black women a voice. Being back in Jackson forces Skeeter to confront many of the social norms she has taken for granted for most of her life. While her friends baldly treat "the help" terribly, Skeeter sits silently, rarely protests, but often frowns. Her frown lets us know that racism is very, very bad and that good southern girls should be nice to their mammies.

Skeeter gets the bright idea to tell the stories of the maids who spend their lives cleaning white people's houses, raising white people's babies. Stone is charming and believable even if the character she plays is willfully ignorant. The charm, though, grates because it is fairly obscene to imagine that this wet-behind-the-ears lass would somehow guide the magical negroes to salvation through the spiritual cleansing of occupational confession. When Aibileen reminds Skeeter they shouldn't be seen together, Skeeter briefly educates herself on Jim Crow laws and then ignores whatever she learned, imposing herself on Aibileen's bewildering goodwill, urging her to share her story about what it's *really like* to be a maid in Jackson, Mississippi, as if the truth were not plainly obvious. At the end of *The Help*, Skeeter offers to turn down her dream job in New York City so she can stay and "protect" Aibileen and Minny. We're supposed to see this as a heartwarming gesture, but it only brings the movie's overall condescension into bitter relief.

The Help is, in the absence of thinking, a good movie, but it is also an unfairly emotionally manipulative movie. There are any number of times during the interminable two hours and seventeen minutes of running time when I felt like my soul would shrivel up and die. I was devastated by all of it. Everyone around me cried openly throughout most of the movie. My eyes were not dry. I am certain we were often crying for different reasons. Every transgression, injustice, and tragedy was exploited so that by the end of the movie it was like the director had ripped into my chest, torn my heart out, and jumped up and down on it until it became a flattened piece of worn-out muscle—cardiac jerky, if you will.

The movie is emotionally manipulative but in a highly controlled way. *The Help* provides us with a deeply sanitized view of the segregated South in the early 1960s. There are many unpalatable moments, but they are tempered by a great deal of easy humor and contrived, touching emotional moments. The movie gives the impression that life was difficult in Mississippi in the 1960s for women, white and black, but still somewhat bearable because that's just how things were.

The implausibilities in the science fiction universe of *The Help* are many and wild. Certainly, that happens in most movies, especially these days. What makes these implausibilities offensive in *The Help* is that most of us know better. We know our history. There is not enough height in the atmosphere for us to suspend our disbelief.

If you do bring your brain to *The Help,* the movie is worse than you might imagine. Seeing *The Help* through a critical lens is excruciating. At one point, while teaching Celia Foote to make fried chicken, Minny says, "Frying chicken tend to make me feel better about life." That a line about the solace found in the preparation of fried foods made it into a book *and* movie produced in this decade says a great deal about where we are in acting right about race. We are nowhere. That line was one of many that made me cringe, cry, roll my eyes, or hide my face in my hands. To say I was uncomfortable is an understatement.

Little things also grate. The overexaggerated dialect spoken by the maids evokes cowed black folk shuffling through their miserable lives, singing negro spirituals. In Aibileen's home, for example, there are pictures of her recently deceased son and a portrait of white Jesus. After Medgar Evers is shot and JFK attends his funeral, the camera pans to the wall where a picture of JFK joins the other two, not, say, a picture of Medgar Evers himself or another civil rights leader. In another subplot, of which there are many, Skeeter's childhood nanny, Constantine (Cicely Tyson), is so devastated after being fired by the white family for whom she worked for more than twenty-seven years, she dies of a broken heart. The gross implication is that her will to live came from wiping the asses and scrubbing the toilets of white folks. This white wish fulfillment makes the movie rather frustrating.

Men, black and white, are largely absent from the movie. White men are apparently absolved from any responsibility for race relations in 1960s Mississippi. The movie is devoid of any mention of the realities of the sexual misconduct, assault, and harassment black women faced working for white men. We see nary an unwelcome ass grab. I don't think lynching was brought up once. We don't know how Aibileen came to have a son, so we're left to assume, because she is magical, that her child's conception was immaculate. Minny's husband, whom we never see, is abusive. We hear her being abused during a phone call, and toward the end of the movie, we see Minny's bruised face, but we never see Leroy, the man who has committed these acts of violence. There is also the bizarre subtext that the woman with sass is the one who has to be kept in line through brutality. As in most popular portrayals, black men are dealt with in depressing, reductive ways when they are addressed at all. This movie shamelessly indulges in the myth of the absent black man. The actual consequences of black men consorting with a young white girl are glossed over as merely inconvenient instead of mortal. The white women are portrayed as domestically tyrannical while living highly constrained lives as desperate southern housewives, so we can sympathize with *their* plight.

Race is regularly handled ineffectually in movies and fiction. I have become accustomed to this reality. And yet. I have struggled with writing about *The Help* because there is something more to my anger and frustration.

At first I thought I resented the fact that a deeply flawed book has sold more than three million copies, spent more than a hundred weeks on the bestseller list, and is a major motion picture. But books I don't like do well all the time. I don't lose sleep over it. I also cannot deny that the book and movie have their moments. There were times when I laughed or was moved, though certainly, those instances were few and far between.

I think of myself as progressive and open-minded, but I have biases, and in reading and watching *The Help*, I have become painfully aware of just how biased I can be. My real problem is that *The Help* is written by a white woman. The screenplay is written by a white man. The movie is directed by that same white man. I know it's wrong but I think, *How dare they?*

Writing difference is complicated. There is ample evidence that it is quite difficult to get difference *right*, to avoid cultural appropriation, reinscribing stereotypes, revising or minimizing history, or demeaning and trivializing difference or otherness. As writers we are always asking ourselves, *How do I get it right?* That question becomes even more critical when we try to get race right, when we try to find authentic ways of imagining and reimagining the lives of people with different cultural backgrounds and experiences. Writing difference requires a delicate balance, and I don't know how we strike that balance.

I write across race, gender, and sexuality all the time. I would never want to be told I can't write a story where the protagonist is a white man or a Latina lesbian or anyone who doesn't resemble me. The joy of fiction is that, in the right hands, anything is possible. I firmly believe our responsibility as writers is to challenge ourselves to write beyond what we know. When it comes to white writers working through racial difference, though, I am conflicted and far less tolerant than I should be. If I take nothing else from the book and movie in question, it's that I know I have work to do.

I don't expect writers to always get difference right, but I do expect writers to make a credible effort. *The Help* demonstrates that some writers shouldn't try to write across race and difference. Kathryn Stockett tries to write black women, but she doesn't try hard enough. Her depictions of race are almost fetishistic unless they are downright insulting. At one point in the book, Aibileen compares her skin color to that of a cockroach—you know, the most hated insect you can think of. Aibileen says, staring at a cockroach, "He big, inch, inch an a half. He black. Blacker than me." That's simply bad writing, but it's an even worse way of writing difference. If white writers can't do better than to compare a cockroach to black skin, perhaps they should leave the writing of difference in more capable hands. In *The Help*, Stockett doesn't write black women. She caricatures black women, finding pieces of truth and genuine experience and distorting them to repulsive effect. She makes a very strong case for writers strictly writing what they know, not what they think they know but actually know nothing about.

Better Living Through Criticism
How to Think About Art, Pleasure, Beauty, and Truth
(selection)

A. O. Scott

WHAT IS CRITICISM?
(A PRELIMINARY DIALOGUE)

Q: *What's the point of criticism? What are critics good for?*

A: Those are the big questions! The obvious questions, anyway. But they're not exactly the same question.

Q: *But isn't criticism just whatever critics do?*

A: Sure. And everybody who criticizes is a critic. You see the problem. We've barely gotten started and already we're running in circles. When we talk about criticism, are we talking about a job—a kind of writing, a species of journalism or scholarship, an intellectual discipline of some sort—and therefore the people who make their livings at it? Or are we talking about a less specialized undertaking, something like playing cards or cooking or riding a bicycle, something anyone can learn to do? Or maybe even a more elementary, more reflexive activity, like dreaming or breathing or crying?

In this selection, the critic A. O. Scott interviews himself.

Q: *I thought the arrangement was that I would be asking the questions here.*

A: Sorry.

Q: *So let's start again, and start with you. You are a professional critic, and also someone who thinks a lot about what criticism is and what it's for.*

A: Though not necessarily in that order. And not exclusively, of course.

Q: *Okay. But what I'm asking is—*

A: What good am I? What's the point of what I do?

Q: *If you want to put it that way. I might not have been quite so hostile.*

A: No worries. Opposition is true friendship, as William Blake said. Every critic grows accustomed to dealing with skepticism and suspicion and, sometimes, outright contempt. *How dare you! What gives you the right? Why should anyone listen to you?* We get this all the time. Provoking people to question our competence, our intelligence, our very right to exist—that seems to be a big part of what it is to be a critic.

Q: *And now you've decided to fight back. You're feeling defensive. Would it be accurate to say that you wrote this whole book to settle a score with Samuel L. Jackson?*

A: Not exactly. But I'm glad you brought that up. A bit of background: In May 2012, on the day *The Avengers*—you saw it, right? Everyone did—was released on 3,500 screens across North America, I published a review in which I praised some aspects of the movie—the cleverness of its dialogue, the sharpness of the performances—while complaining about others, in particular its sacrifice of originality on the altar of blockbuster conformity. If you'll allow me to quote myself: "The secret of *The Avengers* is that it is a snappy little dialogue comedy dressed up as something else, that something else being a giant ATM for Marvel and its new studio overlords, the Walt Disney Company." That assessment stands up pretty well, if I say so myself. By the time *Avengers: Age of Ultron* came along a few years later everyone else seemed to be saying more or less the same thing: that its charms and thrills were overwhelmed by soulless corporate spectacle. There is some satisfaction in having been in the vanguard of pointing out the obvious.

At the time, though, I was part of a premature backlash. Not long after my review was posted on the *New York Times* website, Jackson, who plays Nick Fury in the movie and in other Marvel Universe franchise installments, posted a Twitter message exhorting "#Avengers fans" that "AO Scott needs a new job! Let's help him find one! One he can ACTUALLY do!" Scores of his followers heeded his call, not by demanding that my editors fire me but, in the best Twitter tradition, by retweeting Jackson's outburst and adding their own vivid suggestions about what I was qualified to do with myself. The more coherent tweets expressed familiar, you might even say canonical, anticritical sentiments: that I had no capacity for joy; that I wanted to ruin everyone else's fun; that I was a hater, a square, and a snob; even—and this was kind of a new one—that the nerdy kid in middle school who everybody picked on because he didn't like comic books had grown up to be me. (In my day, some of the nerdy kids everybody picked on were the ones who did like comic books, but I guess things have changed now that the superheroes and their fanboy followers have taken over everything. I was picked on for reasons that had nothing to do with comic books.)

The *Avengers* incident blew up into one of those absurd and hyperactive internet squalls that are now a fixture of our cultural life. Mace Windu had called me out! I had summoned the righteous wrath of Jules Winnfield! Jackson and I were Photoshopped into action-movie combat poses on entertainment websites. Miniature think pieces sprouted like mushrooms after a rainstorm. Our Twitter beef made the news in Brazil, Germany, and Japan. A few of my colleagues embraced the cause of standing up not only for my own beleaguered self, but also for the integrity and importance of the job I was in Jackson's view unqualified to do.

Q: *Were you scared?*

A: On the contrary. I was grateful. Neither my person nor my livelihood was in any danger, and *The Avengers* went on to become the second-fastest film to date to reach $1 billion at the global box office. I gained a few hundred followers on Twitter and became, for a few minutes, both a hissable villain and a make-believe martyr for a noble and much-maligned cause. It was win-win all around, and then everyone moved on.

But even a tempest in a teapot can have meteorological significance, and I think Jackson raised a valid and vital question. Putting aside the merits or limitations of what I wrote about *The Avengers* or any other movie, it's always worth asking just what the job of the critic is, and how it might ACTUALLY be done.

Q: *So you've set out here to defend the job against the attacks—the criticism—of sensitive movie stars and their fans? Isn't that a little bit hypocritical? It seems like you can dish it out, but you can't take it.*

A: Well, no, actually. I mean, yes, we all get a little sensitive when the people whose work we write about—or for that matter our readers—find fault with what we do. That's only human. What I'm more interested in here is the general tendency—I would really say the universal capacity of our species—to find fault. And also to bestow praise. To judge. That's the bedrock of criticism. How do we know, or think we know, what's good or bad, what's worth attacking or defending or telling our friends about? How do we assess the success or failure of *The Avengers* or anything else? Because whether or not it's our job, we *do* judge. We can't help it.

Q: *And how do we judge? Or maybe the question is "Why do we judge?"*

A: Honestly, when I set out to write this book I thought the answers would come much more easily than they did. That there would in fact be answers of a kind I could state clearly and emphatically. Maybe I'd discover that we know what's beautiful or meaningful or even just fun because of neural switches or hormonal responses that evolved at the dawn of human time in order to help us avoid predators and produce more offspring. Or maybe I'd conclude that we are able to make determinations and discriminations of value because we have access to innate and eternal standards that, though they mutate over the centuries and express themselves differently from place to place, nonetheless keep us on the path of truth and beauty.

You can look at the history of human creativity and find patterns—shapes, sounds, stories—that suggest deep continuity. You can also survey the wild diversity of human making and conclude that no single category or set of criteria could possibly contain it all. Every culture, every class and tribe and coterie, every period in history has developed its own canons of craft and invention. Our modern, cosmopolitan sensibilities graze among the objects they have left behind, sampling and comparing and carrying out the pleasant work of sorting and assimilating what we find. Meanwhile, we are inundated with new stuff, which is also pleasant even if the glut can leave us feeling paralyzed and empty. We marvel at the abundance or worry about the too-muchness of it all. There are so many demands on our attention, so many offers of diversion and enlightenment on the table, that choosing among them can feel like serious work.

Q: *And that work—the winnowing and contrasting, the measuring and interpreting—is what you call criticism.*

A: Yes. But it's also something more basic and more urgent. It's complicated. Let me go back to Samuel L. Jackson. Six months after the *Avengers* episode, he revisited our Twitter quarrel in an interview with the *Huffington Post* and gave voice to a widespread complaint about criticism in general, and about the criticism of popular culture in particular. "Ninety-nine percent of the people in the world look at that movie as what it is," he said. "It's not an intellectual exposition that you have to intellectualize in any way." This is an old and powerful—in some ways an unanswerable—argument against criticism, rooted in the ideas that creative work should be taken on its own terms and that thought is the enemy of experience. And it is indeed precisely the job of the critic to disagree, to refuse to look at anything simply as what it is, to insist on subjecting it to intellectual scrutiny.

"Intellectualize" is a deliberately ugly word, the use of which is an accusation in its own right. But really it's just a synonym for "think," and it's worth asking why it should be necessary to deny so strenuously that *The Avengers* might be both the product and a potential object of thought. The movie is very much an "intellectual exposition" in the general sense of having arisen from the conscious intentions and active intelligence of its creators, including Jackson himself. It also, like many other comic-book entertainments, sets out to explore what fans of the genre and veterans of high school English would be sure to recognize as Big Themes, among them honor, friendship, revenge, and the problem of evil in a lawful universe. And finally (and, from my own perspective, most vexingly), *The Avengers* shows what can happen when a playful storytelling instinct collides with the imperative of global profit that drives so much twenty-first-century Hollywood production.

All of which is to say that *The Avengers* is an extremely interesting and complex artifact, and that its successes and limitations are worth puzzling over. And yet even to contemplate the work of teasing out the good from the bad, finding the context and staking a claim, might be to miss the point. Or, as Jackson put it: "If you say something that's fucked-up about a piece of bullshit pop culture that really is good— *The Avengers* is a fucking great movie; Joss [Whedon] did an awesome job—if you don't get it, then just say, 'I don't get it.'"

But I get it. In particular, I appreciate the double standard that Jackson invokes as he places *The Avengers* simultaneously beneath criticism ("a piece of bullshit pop culture") and beyond it ("a fucking great movie"). He is echoing the reflexive disdain for movies and other low- and middlebrow amusements that came so easily to intellectuals of an earlier era, and at the same time invoking the ancient, superhighbrow idea that a work of art is inviolate and sufficient unto itself. In these circumstances, a critic will be guilty of foolishly taking seriously what was only ever meant as harmless, easy fun, or else of dragging something sublime down to his own ridiculous level. But guilty either way.

Here's the important thing, though: in doing this, a critic will be no different from anyone else who stops to think about the experience of watching *The Avengers* (or reading a novel or beholding a painting or listening to a piece of music). Because that thinking is where criticism begins. We're all guilty of it. Or at least we should be.

Q: *So you've written a book in defense of thinking? Where's the argument? Nobody is really against thinking.*

A: Are you serious? Anti-intellectualism is virtually our civic religion. "Critical thinking" may be a ubiquitous educational slogan—a vaguely defined skill we hope our children pick up on the way to adulthood—but the rewards for not using your intelligence are immediate and abundant.

As consumers of culture, we are lulled into passivity or, at best, prodded toward a state of pseudo-semi-self-awareness, encouraged toward either the defensive group identity of fanhood or a shallow, half-ironic eclecticism. Meanwhile, as citizens of the political commonwealth, we are conscripted into a polarized climate of ideological belligerence in which bluster too often substitutes for argument.

There is no room for doubt and little time for reflection as we find ourselves buffeted by a barrage of sensations and a flood of opinion. We can fantasize about slowing down or opting out, but ultimately we must learn to live in the world as we find it and to see it as clearly as we can. This is no simple task. It is easier to seek out the comforts of groupthink, prejudice, and ignorance. Resisting those temptations requires vigilance, discipline, and curiosity.

Q: *So then what you've written is a manifesto against laziness and stupidity?*

A: You could put it that way. But why cast it in such a negative light? This book is also, I hope, a celebration of art and imagination, an examination of our inborn drive to cultivate delight and of the various ways we refine that impulse.

Q: *And all that is the critic's job?*

A: It's everyone's job, and I believe it's a job we can actually do. I suggest that the effort might begin with the way we address the works that answer our bottomless hunger for meaning and pleasure, and also, simultaneously, with the way we understand our responses to those beautiful, baffling things.

We are far too inclined to regard art as an ornament and to perceive taste as a fixed, narrow track along which each one of us travels, alone or in select, like-minded company. Alternatively, we seek to subordinate the creative, pleasurable aspects of our lives to supposedly more consequential matters, pushing the aesthetic dimensions of existence into the boxes that hold our religious beliefs, political dogmas, or moral assumptions. We trivialize art. We venerate nonsense. We can't see past our own bullshit.

Enough of that! It's the job of art to free our minds, and the task of criticism to figure out what to do with that freedom. That everyone is a critic means, or should mean, that we are each of us capable of thinking against our own prejudices, of balancing skepticism with open-mindedness, of sharpening our dulled and glutted senses and battling the intellectual inertia that surrounds us. We need to put our remarkable minds to use and to pay our own experience the honor of taking it seriously.

Q: *Okay, fine. But how?*

A: Good question!

THE END OF CRITICISM
(A FINAL DIALOGUE)

Q: *You have said a great many things about criticism—that it is an art form in its own right; that it exists to enhance the glory of the other arts; that it is an impossible activity; that it is necessary and vital to human self-understanding; that it can never die; that it is in perpetual danger of extinction—and you have said even more about what criticism is not. It is not mere faultfinding or empty praise. It is not just the expression of personal tastes and judgments. It is not science or philosophy or politics or poetry, though at various times it mimics all of those things. But to be frank I'm still not sure I know what criticism is, unless it is whatever a critic happens to be doing. And in that case what is a critic?*

A: You've put your finger on it! Criticism is both paradoxical and tautological. It's whatever a critic does—a critic being anyone who is, at a given moment, practicing criticism. And it's an impossible undertaking that is at the same time impossible to prevent from happening. You might as well try to stop *thinking*. It can't be done.

Q: *So we're back where we started: criticism is thinking. Is it a particular kind of thinking, or just whatever a given brain gets up to in the presence of a particular stimulus?*

A: Both, naturally. But rather than speaking so abstractly it might be better, in the interests of clarity and our own amusement, to trace the genesis of a particular critical act. Show me what you've been doing there.

Q: *Doing where?*

A: The drawing you've been making on the back page while I've been talking.

Q: *It's just a doodle, I'm not really sure—*

A: So much the better. It issues directly from your unconscious and so is rich with accidental beauty and occult meaning. Let me see it.

Q: *Is that a criterion of value then? Something spontaneous or reflexive— unreflecting, unmotivated—is better than something that required a lot of work and thought? You'd rather look at this offhand sketch than at something I sweated over for hours or days or weeks, something I undertook after years of struggling to master the appropriate techniques? Or are you just arbitrarily looking for an object so you can practice your critical trickery?*

A: Both, naturally. You have nicely identified the foundational act of criticism, which is the selection of an object, the willed decision to look. Your creative intention in this case, whether you thought you were making something worth looking at or just occupying a moment of boredom, is secondary to my intention, which is to scrutinize and judge it.

Q: *So you can just look at anything? Criticize anything? The rug? The window? What's outside it?*

A: Well, yes and no. Anything can be judged, analyzed, investigated, made into a vessel of feeling, meaning, narrative, moral significance, beauty, and so on. But the question is whether the thing in question can bear the scrutiny, which is really to say whether the act of scrutinizing it can be made interesting.

Q: *But then isn't my drawing irrelevant? It would seem that the only interesting thing about it is what you have to say. Doesn't that mean that a critic is just somebody who can say something interesting about anything, and so get in between that thing and the other people who might be interested in it?*

A: Yes and no. Let's say that a critic is a person whose interest can help to activate the interest of others. That's not a bad definition. I should have thought of it before. For that to work, what the critic writes or says has to be interesting in itself. And, of course, it can only really succeed in that way if the critic's own interest is genuine. I may or may not like your drawing, but it's essential that I care about it.

Q: *But might your job also be to tell the world that it isn't worth caring about? Surely there are cases when a critic's duty is deflection and deflation. There is so much hype and hyperventilation in the world—so much breathless selling—that someone needs to draw a calm breath or throw cold water or just say look, it's not that big a deal.*

A: Yes, and we also have a duty to redirect enthusiasm, to call attention to what might otherwise be ignored or undervalued. In either instance, though, whether we're cheerleading or calling bullshit, our assessment has to proceed from a sincere and serious commitment. Otherwise it's empty and reflexive. If I were, let's say, unmoved by any visual art, or hostile to the very notion that your doodle could be beautiful or profound, then the only ethical and honest course of action for me would be to remain silent and leave the discussion to others.

Q: *As if.*

A: I know. That rule is more often honored in the breach than in the observance. It's amazing how often supposedly critical arguments are launched from the logically and morally untenable assumption that the work in question is categorically unfit for criticism. Whole art forms are routinely condemned this way, usually those favored by the young or by other socially marginal groups—the poor, racial and sexual minorities, and so forth. To look at the record of contempt for jazz, hip-hop, disco, rock 'n' roll, video games, comic books, and even television and films is to witness learned and refined people making asses of themselves by embracing their own ignorance. And, of course, you can find a symmetrical, countervailing bias against what is perceived as difficult or highbrow or snobbish, whether it's abstract art or movies with subtitles or classical music. Whatever criticism is, it is surely the opposite of that kind of preformed, unreflecting dismissal.

Q: *So you have said. But doesn't that just reduce criticism to fandom and restrict it to a circle of aficionados, the ones who already "get it" and who speak to one another in the coded language of the initiated? Is there no room for a neutral—or skeptical, or just curious but not necessarily know-ing—perspective, one that comes from outside the inner circle of the already convinced?*

A: In fact, that's *all* there is room for. Now let's see your work.

Q: *Oh, my "work." Really. If you insist. Don't laugh, though.*

A: . . .

Q: *Well?*

A: I—

Q: *Yes?*

A: Is this supposed to be me?

Q: *Well, it's kind of . . .*

A: Do my jowls really sag that much?

Q: *It's more an idea of you, really. I mean, not really you in the literal sense. You were talking, and I just noticed the way your eyes cut sideways when you were looking for the right word, and I just tried to capture that.*

A: Yes, I can see.

Q: *You hate it.*

A: No. The hairline . . .

Q: *Okay, but here's the thing: Let's say it wasn't supposed to be you. And let's say it wasn't drawn by me. Or that you didn't know it was by me, or that you didn't know me. Let's say you saw it in a museum . . .*

A: This? What museum?

Q: *You know what I mean. Suppose you saw it in a different context. Suppose it was attributed to, I don't know, Degas.*

A: Degas.

Q: *It's a silly little cartoon I drew while you were talking. You said you wanted to look at it. And since that's the foundational act or whatever of criticism, I want to know: What are you looking at? How do you make sense of what you see? Do you analyze the formal qualities—the line, the use of negative space, the crosshatching? Do you compare it to other drawings you've seen? Other works by the same artist, in the same genre? Do you try to find out what the artist might have been thinking or what kind of person the artist was, from what kind of background?*

A: Yes, all of that.

Q: *All of that. All of that is going through your head right now? Or all of that is what you will need to consider as you formulate your, ahem, critique . . .*

A: I like it.

Q: *You like it.*

A: It's nice.

Q: *It's nice. That's what the critic has to say?*

A: Well, you have to start somewhere. Of course, it's very complicated.

Q: *Oh, of course. You seem—uncharacteristically, I must say—at a loss for words. And isn't that because you're not really sure who you're talking to? You like to say that the essence of criticism is a conversation—a passionate, rational argument about a shared experience—but I wonder if you really mean it. I think for you it might be more of a performance, a thing you can* *only do if there's an audience. And if it's just me, and I also turn out to be the "artist," then words might fail you. Or put it another way: You have spent many, many pages chasing after the pure aesthetic encounter, the moment of ecstatic contemplation when all context falls away and the beholder and the work find themselves in a state of mutual presence, but isn't that a fantasy? Aren't there always conditions attached? Even when it's just you and me and you're looking at a silly drawing?*

A: Maybe especially then. And maybe—which I think is what you're implying—there's no such thing as private or personal criticism. It has to be a public act, something you're invited to do when something is submitted for your approval (or disdain). Very little happens in the world without some kind of publicity, without it being known, promoted, hyped, whatever. So if criticism can be the corrective to that hype, it might also be true that the hype is the precondition for criticism.

Q: *So if instead of your snatching the doodle out of my hands I had said, "Hey, take a look at this, tell me what you think . . ."*

A: I might have suggested that if the softness of the jaw was meant to convey an indecisive temperament, the effect is undermined by the determined set of the mouth, and that the eyes are weirdly asymmetrical, as if one were turned inward while the other gazed out at the world with puzzlement and hostility. Though it's quite possible that you were not being inconsistent but rather trying to capture the contradictions inherent in your subject, and so turn this tossed-off portrait of a critic into an allegory of criticism itself.

Q: *Now you're just showing off.*

A: Well, yes. And trying to save face, as it were. Have you seen the movie *Ratatouille*?

Q: *We saw it together. You cried the whole time.*

A: I was moved. It's a movie about the symbiosis between artist and critic, the perfect summation of everything I believe, at once "exuberantly democratic and unabashedly elitist, defending good taste and aesthetic accomplishment not as snobbish entitlements but as universal ideals."

Q: *Are you quoting yourself?*

A: Anton Ego, *c'est moi*!

Q: *But isn't Anton Ego kind of the villain?*

A: *Assurément pas!* He is Remy the rat's secret sharer, the only one who truly understands his genius.

Q: *Really, though, doesn't Remy just need the publicity that a good review from Ego will provide? The critic may fancy himself a priest of good taste and a champion of high standards, but isn't he at bottom more of a shill? And doesn't Ego's review of the meal Remy cooks at Gusteau's lay waste to the whole critical enterprise? The part everyone quotes is about how pointless criticism is—how everything a critic does is forgotten, how no one pays attention anyway . . .*

A: "The bitter truth we critics must face is that, in the grand scheme of things, the average piece of junk is probably more meaningful than our criticism designating it so." I know it by heart.

Q: *He also says that the one area where a critic risks something is in "the discovery and defense of the new." "The new needs friends," he says. But that's a fairly limited brief, isn't it? The best you can hope for is to be a carnival barker for novelty, an accomplice in the puffing up of the next big thing. It's pathetic, really. Ego has worked his whole life at something that nobody cares about and that doesn't much matter.*

A: Yes, but there's quite a lot more behind that review, which is hardly the movie's only or final word on criticism. Ego is not pathetic, though he is undoubtedly shrouded in pathos. His is a lonely vocation, exactly as lonely as Remy's, at least at first. And that's because, though one cooks and the other writes restaurant reviews, it is in essence the same vocation. Remy and Ego both devote themselves, for reasons neither one entirely understands but in ways that seem innate and involuntary, to the especially intense appreciation of something everyone else either takes for granted or enjoys in a casual, undisciplined way. Food. This places them at odds with other members of their respective omnivorous species. Remy is driven from his rat family when his culinary ambitions put them in danger. Before that he tries to educate his brother Emile, who like the other rats eats whatever is in front of him, in the higher registers of flavor. Mere nourishment, Remy tries to explain, may be biologically sufficient to keep our bodies going, but there is so much more to our biologically bounded lives than mere survival. Remy, in other words, shows that the artistic impulse can be present even in the meanest, subsistence-driven circumstances—indeed, that it has to be there if it is to exist anywhere. He further shows that the artistic vocation is born in a critical—a comparative, discriminating, novelty-seeking—engagement with the environment. He transforms the given into the special.

If Remy starts at the bottom of the food chain, Ego, when we meet him, dwells at the top. But he is no less lonely and misunderstood. He is fortunate enough to live in Paris, the world capital of gastronomy and also, not coincidentally, of an ideal of culture that fuses intellectual discipline with a devotion to the pursuit of pleasure. But Paris in this movie, as in real life, is harassed by consumerism, threatened by a vulgar, cheapening mode of commerce embodied by Skinner, the bad chef who nearly destroys the legacy of Gusteau. The shallow customers who are happy to eat the branded swill he serves are his coconspirators in culinary corruption. So together, even before their fateful meeting, Ego and Remy are united in a project that the rest of the world can only dimly comprehend but that is nonetheless vital to the world's progress. Remy may think that pleasing Ego will help him realize his professional ambitions, but what he requires more deeply is the recognition of a like-minded soul.

That is precisely what Ego needs from Remy. His love of food has been so frequently and thoroughly disappointed that it has nearly withered into cynicism. This is a moral danger—a danger to morale, and to decency—that many of us face as we age. Nostalgia is part of it: some portion of our formative experience takes on the status either of a lost Eden or a receding utopian ideal. As reality keeps letting us down, a vital source of critical energy is lost.

Q: *By vital source you mean a precritical capacity for simple delight, the ability to be moved without thinking.*

A: Exactly. When Ego tastes Remy's ratatouille he is transported back to that primal scene. For him, the dish evokes a highly specific complex of emotions. They can't be explained, or even narrated, but are rather rendered through the kind of wordless, deeply emotional montage that is something of a Pixar hallmark. Through those images we know the pain of the boy, little Anton, who fell off his bike, and also the maternal solicitude that eased it, in the form of Mme Ego's ratatouille.

Q: *But really, what kind of mother comforts her child with stewed eggplant?*

A: A French one. And also the mother of a future food critic. As Remy well knows, the rustic simplicity of ratatouille belies its technical sophistication. You have probably eaten—or, more likely, politely left uneaten—your share of mediocre, too-sweet, tomatoey sludge sitting alongside a drab piece of chicken or lamb at god knows how many bad restaurants, or eaten the stuff cold from a plastic tub while standing in front of the open refrigerator late at night—

Q: *That was caponata.*

A: Same difference, most of the time. But if you read Julia Child's original ratatouille recipe in *Mastering the Art of French Cooking* you will discover the key procedure that Mme Ego no doubt knew and that most lazy or hasty cooks ignore. It is essential to sauté each vegetable separately, in a prescribed order, in the same olive oil, before layering them for the final simmer. I say essential because the essence of each vegetable—onion, eggplant, tomato, zucchini—is surrendered to the fat, and that sequencing of flavors is the key to the dish. It's not stewed vegetables; it's flavored oil. That oil is the medium and the meaning, the form and the content, the matter and the spirit . . .

Q: *You're losing control of your metaphors.*

A: I am, but let my exaggeration stand for the overwhelming nature of the experience, which our critic Anton Ego must somehow distill into words. Words that may not explicitly give voice to the experience but that will subliminally connect it to the universe of public discourse, so that venturesome palates will want to share in what he has discovered. And, of course, that's just what happens.

Q: *Well, actually, it isn't. When it's discovered that Ego has published a review praising a meal cooked by vermin, he loses his job and his reputation. His greatest act as a critic brings him ruin and disgrace.*

A: Which is exactly what every critic must be willing to risk at any time. The next phase of his career, by the way, makes literal a crucial aspect of the critic's role, which is to function as the artist's silent partner.

Q: *Yes, but he isn't a critic anymore. He's finished. He's returned to the pre- or noncritical state of simple enjoyment. He's a patron in both senses of the word. The last time we see him, he's sipping wine with a smile on his face at Remy's new restaurant, as if he has been freed from all care, granted a new lease on life.*

A: He has attained an ideal state where there is not only no more criticism but no more art. Remember what Gusteau says: not everyone can cook, but a great cook can come from anywhere. I take this to be both an answer to and an elaboration on the insight that anchored Brad Bird's previous Pixar feature, *The Incredibles*. "If everyone is special," that movie insisted, "then no one is." In Gusteau's version, everyone may theoretically have the ability to cook, but only a select few will have the luck or discipline to elevate that skill to the height of art. If Remy is one of those gastro-incredibles, then so too is Mme Ego, whose fame as far as we know is limited to her son's memory. What she and Gusteau represent is a utopian dream, one that Remy and Ego turn into reality: that the boundary between art and life—and therefore the uncomfortably aligned, sometimes antagonistic roles of creator, consumer, and critic—will dissolve, along with the distinction between labor and pleasure.

Q: *That'll be the day. In the meantime, let's have a drink.*

A: If you'll pour. But we're far from done. There is a great deal more to discuss. The horizon of perfection is as far away as it has ever been, and therefore the work of criticism, properly understood, is endless. Nobody has ever figured out where to begin or what to conclude. But in spite of that, a true critic is someone who knows, at long last, when to stop.

Shared Inquiry and Great Ideas in Popular Culture

Great Books Foundation editors chose the readings in *Double Features: Big Ideas in Film* because these selections raise multiple questions and will prompt lively discussion. Suggested questions for each selection are available online at www.greatbooks.org/bigideas.

Some of the suggested questions ask about something very specific in a selection, such as the meaning of a statement or the motivation of an individual. Others ask about more general issues related to the selections; these questions are broader and invite discussion of personal insights and opinions. Addressing both kinds of questions during a discussion, without tipping the balance heavily toward one or the other, will make for a more satisfying experience that not only engages with each author's distinctive voice, but also allows participants in the group to contribute their insights in their own individual way.

A Shared Inquiry™ discussion begins when the leader of the discussion group poses an interpretive question to participants about the meaning of a reading selection. The question is substantial enough that no single answer can resolve it. Instead, several answers—even answers that are in conflict—may be valid.

Participants are free to offer answers and opinions to the group, to request clarification of points, and to raise objections to the remarks of other participants. They also discuss specific passages in the selection that bear on the interpretive question and compare their differing ideas about what these passages mean. The leader, meanwhile, asks additional questions, clarifying and expanding the interpretive question and helping group members to arrive at more cogent answers. All participants don't have to agree with all the answers—each person can decide which answer seems most convincing. This process is called Shared Inquiry.

In Shared Inquiry discussion, three kinds of questions can be raised about a reading selection: factual questions, interpretive questions, and evaluative questions. Interpretation is central to a Shared Inquiry discussion, but factual questions can bring to light evidence in support of interpretations and can clear up misunderstandings. On the other hand, evaluative questions invite participants to compare the experiences and opinions of an author with their own and can introduce a personal dimension into the discussion.

The following guidelines will help keep the conversation focused on the text and ensure all participants a voice:

1. **Read the selection carefully before participating in the discussion.** This ensures that all participants are equally prepared to talk about the ideas in the reading.

2. **Discuss the ideas in the selection, and try to understand them fully.** Reflecting as individuals and as a group on what the author says makes the exploration of both the selection and related issues that will come up in the discussion more rewarding.

3. **Support interpretations of what the author says with evidence from the reading, along with insights from personal experience.** This provides focus for the group on the selection that everyone has read and builds a strong foundation for discussing related issues.

4. **Listen to other participants and respond to them directly.** Shared Inquiry is about the give-and-take of ideas, the willingness to listen to others and talk with them respectfully. Directing your comments and questions to other group members, not always to the leader, will make the discussion livelier and more dynamic.

5. **Expect the leader to mainly ask questions.** Effective leaders help participants develop their own ideas, with everyone gaining a new understanding in the process. When participants hang back and wait for the leader to suggest answers, discussion tends to falter.

Index

Acknowledgments

All possible care has been taken to trace ownership and secure permission for each selection in this anthology. The Great Books Foundation wishes to thank the following authors, publishers, and representatives for permission to reproduce copyrighted material:

Yossarian Is Alive and Well in the Mexican Desert, by Nora Ephron, from the *New York Times*. Copyright © 1969 by Nora Ephron. Reproduced by permission of International Creative Management on behalf of the author.

Countercultural Architecture and Dramatic Structure, from ON DIRECTING FILM, by David Mamet. Copyright © 1991 by David Mamet. Reproduced by permission of Viking Books, an imprint of Penguin Publishing Group, a division of Penguin Random House LLC.

Selection from chapters 1 and 10 in SHOOTING TO KILL, by Christine Vachon. Copyright © 1998, 1999 by Christine Vachon and David Edelstein. Reproduced by permission of HarperCollins Publishers and The Frances Goldin Literary Agency.

Laugh, Cry, Believe: Spielbergization and Its Discontents, by J. Hoberman. Copyright © 2000 by J. Hoberman. Reproduced by permission of SLL/Sterling Lord Literistic, Inc.

Selection from IN THE BLINK OF AN EYE, 2nd ed., by Walter Murch. Copyright © 1995, 2001 by Walter Murch. Reproduced by permission of Silman-James Press.

"One Hang, We All Hang": High Plains Drifter, by Richard Hutson, from CLINT EASTWOOD, ACTOR AND DIRECTOR: NEW PERSPECTIVES, ed. Leonard Engel. Copyright © 2007 by The University of Utah Press. Reproduced by permission of The University of Utah Press.

Selection from LYNCH ON LYNCH, by Chris Rodley. Copyright © 1997 by David Lynch. Commentary and Introduction © 1997 by Chris Rodley. Reproduced by permission of Farrar, Straus and Giroux, and Faber and Faber Ltd.

John Wayne: A Love Song, from SLOUCHING TOWARDS BETHLEHEM, by Joan Didion. Copyright © 1966, 1968, renewed 1996 by Joan Didion. Reproduced by permission of Farrar, Straus and Giroux, and the author.

Nonstop Action: Why Hollywood's Aging Heroes Won't Give Up the Gun, by Adam Mars-Jones, from the *Guardian*. Copyright © 2016 by Guardian News & Media Ltd. Reproduced by permission of Guardian News & Media Ltd.

Acknowledgments

Willing, from BIRDS OF AMERICA: STORIES, by Lorrie Moore. Copyright © 1998 by Lorrie Moore. Reproduced by permission of Alfred A. Knopf, an imprint of the Knopf Doubleday Publishing Group, a division of Penguin Random House LLC, and Faber and Faber Ltd.

Furiosa: The Virago of Mad Max: Fury Road, by Jess Zimmerman. Copyright © 2017 by Jess Zimmerman. Adapted from "A Warrior Woman's Work," by Jess Zimmerman, published on Hazlitt in 2015. Reproduced by permission of the author.

Scary Movies, from WHAT IS THIS THING CALLED LOVE: POEMS, by Kim Addonizio. Copyright © 2004 by Kim Addonizio. Reproduced by permission of W. W. Norton & Company, Inc.

Skyshot, from ZIGZAGGER, by Manuel Muñoz. Copyright © 2003 by Manuel Muñoz. Reproduced by permission of Northwestern University Press.

Edward Hopper's New York Movie, by Joseph Stanton, from *Poetry* magazine. Copyright © 1989 by Joseph Stanton. The poem also appears in *Imaginary Museum: Poems on Art*, by Joseph Stanton. Reproduced by permission of the author.

Why We Crave Horror Movies, by Stephen King. Copyright © 1981 by Stephen King. First published in *Playboy*, 1981. Reproduced by permission of Darhansoff & Verrill, Literary Agents, on behalf of the author.

Matinée, by Robert Coover. Copyright © 2011 by Robert Coover. First published in the *New Yorker* in 2011. Reproduced by permission of Georges Borchardt, Inc., for the author.

The Last Movie, from HALFWAY DOWN THE HALL, by Rachel Hadas. Copyright © 1998 by Rachel Hadas. Reproduced by permission of Wesleyan University Press.

Some Months After My Father's Death, from LET IT BE A DARK ROUX, by Sheryl St. Germain. Copyright © 2007 by Sheryl St. Germain. Reproduced by permission of Autumn House Press.

Selection from THE BIRDS, by Camille Paglia. Copyright © 1998 by Camille Paglia. Reproduced by permission of the author.

Your Childhood Entertainment Is Not Sacred, by Nathan Rabin. Copyright © 2015 by Nathan Rabin. Reproduced by permission of the author.

Pygmalion's Ghost: Female AI and Technological Dream Girls, by Angelica Jade Bastién. Copyright © 2017 by Angelica Jade Bastién. Reproduced by permission of the author.

The Solace of Preparing Fried Foods and Other Quaint Remembrances from 1960s Mississippi: Thoughts on The Help, from BAD FEMINIST, by Roxane Gay. Copyright © 2014 by Roxane Gay. Reproduced by permission of HarperCollins Publishers and Little, Brown Book Group Ltd.

Selection from BETTER LIVING THROUGH CRITICISM: HOW TO THINK ABOUT ART, PLEASURE, BEAUTY, AND TRUTH, by A. O. Scott. Copyright © 2016 by Anthony O. Scott. Reproduced by permission of Penguin Press, an imprint of Penguin Publishing Group, a division of Penguin Random House LLC.